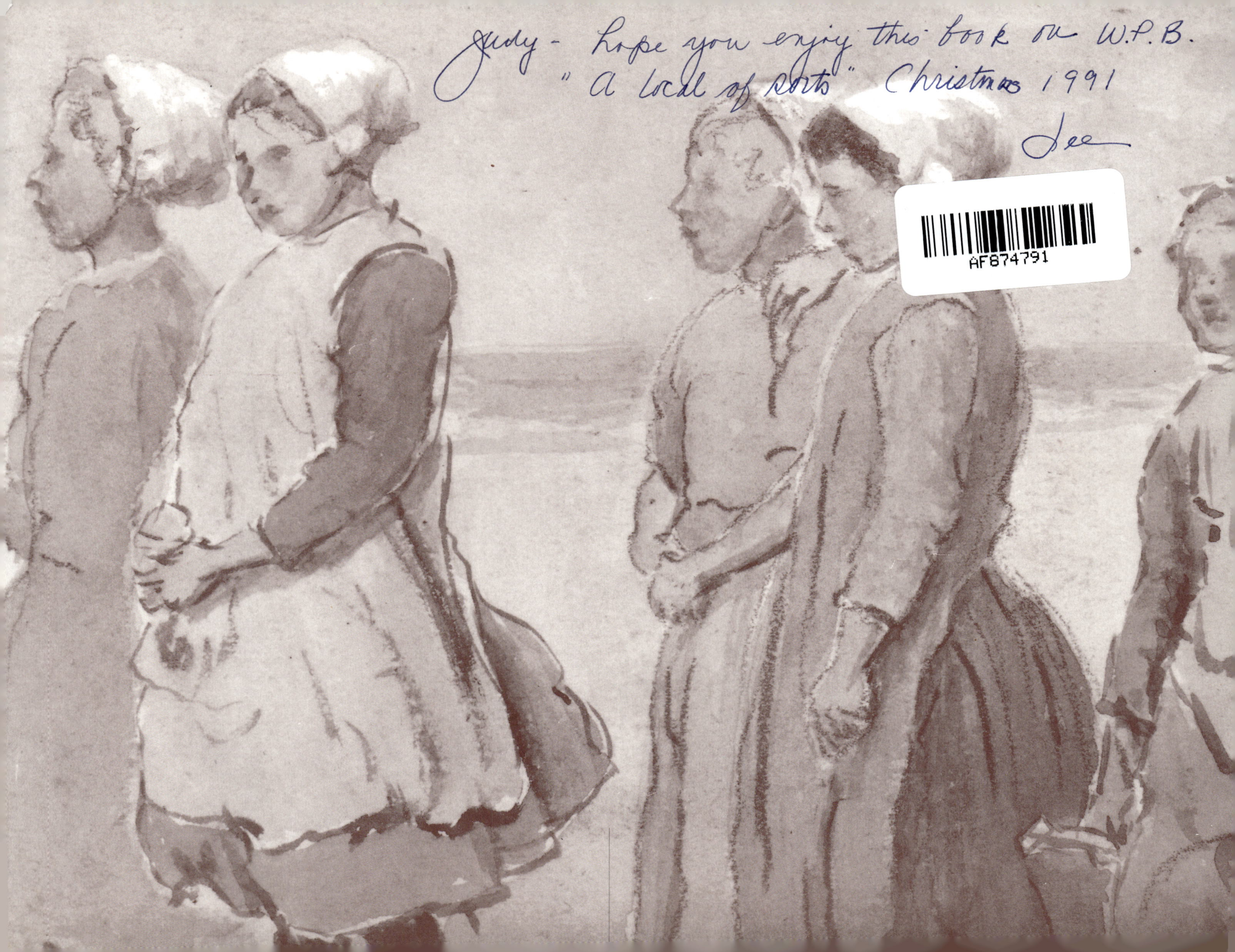

Judy - Hope you enjoy this book on W.P.B.
"A local of sorts" Christmas 1991
Lee

WILLIAM PARTRIDGE BURPEE

American Marine Impressionist

(1846–1940)

by

D. ROGER HOWLETT

foreword by

WILLIAM H. GERDTS

COPLEY SQUARE PRESS • BOSTON

distributed by
Northeastern University Press, Boston

First published in 1991 by

COPLEY SQUARE PRESS • BOSTON
169 Newbury Street
Boston, Massachusetts 02116

Distributed by
Northeastern University Press
Boston, Massachusetts 02115

Library of Congress Catalog Card Number: 90 – 086095

ISBN: 0-9628143-0-X

First Edition
Printed in Hong Kong by South China Printing Company (1988) Ltd.
on acid-free paper

ACKNOWLEDGMENTS

Thanks to:
Jeffrey R. Brown, Anna Brzyski, Laurene Buckley, H. Daniel Butts, III, Richard Candee, Ed Deci, David Dike, Ruth Farrell, Karl Gabosh, Jack Grinold, Dr. John Harbert, Dr. A. Everett James, Jr., Lilly Johnson, Thomas S. Mairs, William B. Osgood, James Saul, Warren A. Seamans, Annette Stott, Cornelius C. Vermeule, Sister Mary Virginia, Alfred J. Walker, John Wilmerding.

Thanks also to the following institutions and their staff:
Archives of American Art, Boston, Robert Brown; Archives of American Art, Washington;
Art Institute of Chicago, Althea H. Huber;
The Boston Globe, Alfred S. Larkin, Jr., and archives; quotations reprinted courtesy of The Globe.
Boston Herald, Kenneth A. Chandler; quotations reprinted with the permission of the Boston Herald.
Boston Public Library, Rare Books, Eugene Zepp, Microfilm, Government Documents, Wiggin Print Room, Sinclair H. Hitchings, Karen Shafts, Allison Cook, Fine Arts Reference, Evelyn Lannon, Kim Tenny, Jane Duggen and especially Janice Chadborne who shared her extensive knowledge on Boston painters and her definitive research on the Boston Art Club;
Brookline Public Library, Ellen Gilmore;
Cape Ann Historical Association, Judith McCulloch;
Cheekwood, Nashville, Kevin Grogan, Beth R. Cunningham;
Corcoran Gallery, D.C., Katherine Kovacs;
Essex Institute, Salem, Massachusetts;
Georgia Museum of Art, Martha Adkins Blakeslee;
Knox County Courthouse, probate office, law library;
Lynn Historical Society, Kenneth Turino, Fay Greenleaf, Diane Shepherd;
Maine State Archives;
Maine State Law Library, Jane Edwards;
Maine State Library, Patty Bouchard, Elaine Stanley;
Maine State Museum, Paul E. Rivard, Steven Miller;
Missouri Historical Society, Beth Rubin;
Museum of American Textile History, North Andover, Mass., Clare Sheridan;
Museum of Fine Arts, Springfield, Mass., Martha Hoppin;
Peabody Museum of Salem, Peter Fetchko, Paul Winfisky, John F. Koza;
Pennsylvania Academy of Fine Arts, Cheryl Liebold;
Portland Museum of Art, Martha R. Severens, Colette Bouchard;
Rockland City Hall, Donna Teague;
Rockland Courier Gazette, Raymond E. Gross, Ivy W. Dodd;
Rockland Public Library, Hazel Frankowski;
Rockland Voter Registration, Ruth Farrell;
The St. Louis Art Museum, Michael Shapiro, Norma Sindelar;
Sawyer Free Public Library, Gloucester, Mass., Judy Clark;
Shore Village Museum, Rockland, Maine, Ken Black, Kenneth N. Black;
University of Lowell;
William A. Farnsworth Library and Art Museum, Rockland, Maine, the staff has been extraordinarily generous with time, talent and information throughout the years that the project has taken. Among others I would like to thank, Christopher B. Crossman, Marius Peledieu, Suzette McAvoy, Edith Murphy, Elizabeth Biddle Jennings, Marilyn Solvay.
Woodstock Historical Society, Vt., Gregory Schwarz.

Mrs. Louis Eaton Shaw for her generous help on Burpee family recollections and lore, and Janet Dickinson.

The extremely patient staff of Childs Gallery, Margaret Bezucha, Inez Chesler, Renee duP. Harrison, Thomas A. Hauck, Angela M. Noel, Judith Ocker, Anne von Schlegell, Elizabeth M. Stahl, Nancy Um, Jane Weinfeld and Catherine Goodrich.

In the preparation of the book, Robert Sennett, Lucy Ferriss and Jennifer Huffman, editors;
William Frohlich and Susan Kuc, Northeastern University Press; Peter Lawrence and Rossana Ong, South China Printing; Carl Andrews for photography;
William H. Gerdts for reading the manuscript and making many helpful suggestions and for his great kindness in providing a foreword for this book. My mother, Dorothy T. Howlett, for reading and proofing several drafts. Richard Bartlett who has again designed an elegant and appropriate format for the publication and, most particularly, thanks to my colleague at Childs Gallery, Cynthia Baule who has executed Bartlett's design under his supervision, arranged permissions, read and made suggestions at each stage of the manuscript, looked after photographers and printers, editors and cataloging in progress as well as her other job running the painting department at Childs Gallery.

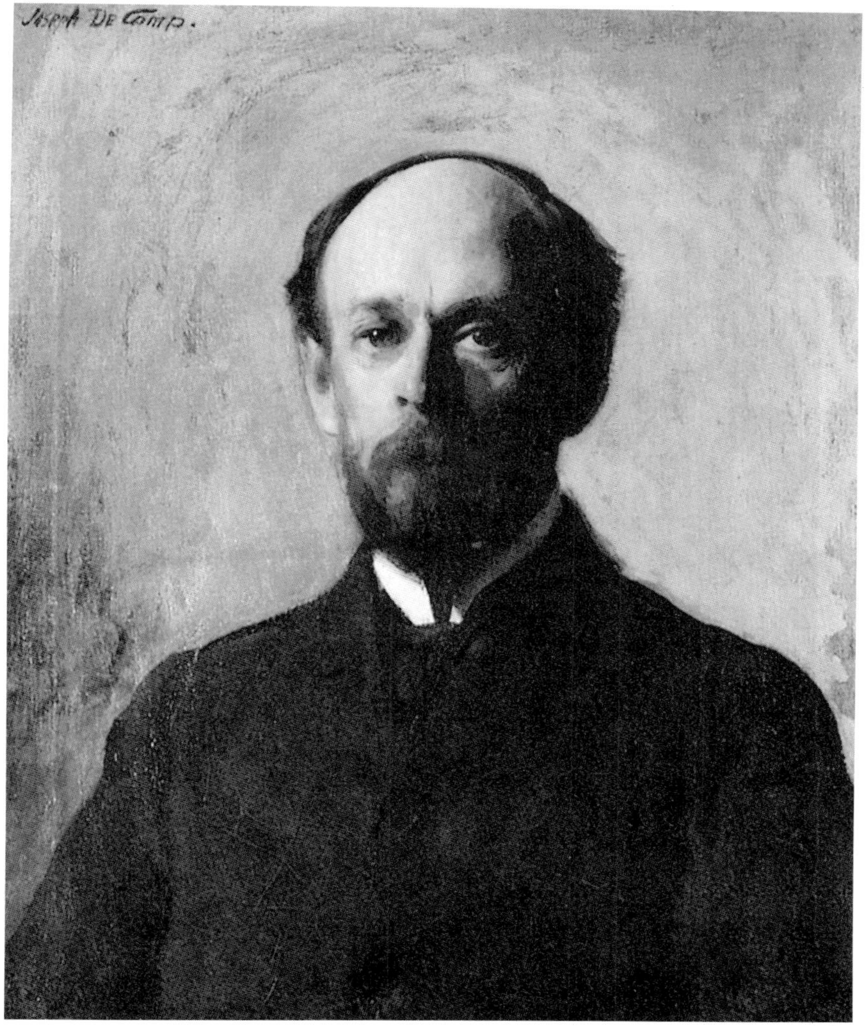

Joseph DeCamp, American (1858 – 1923).

Portrait of William Partridge Burpee, c. 1903.

For Margaret Shaw
and all others who believed in an artist
when the world did not.

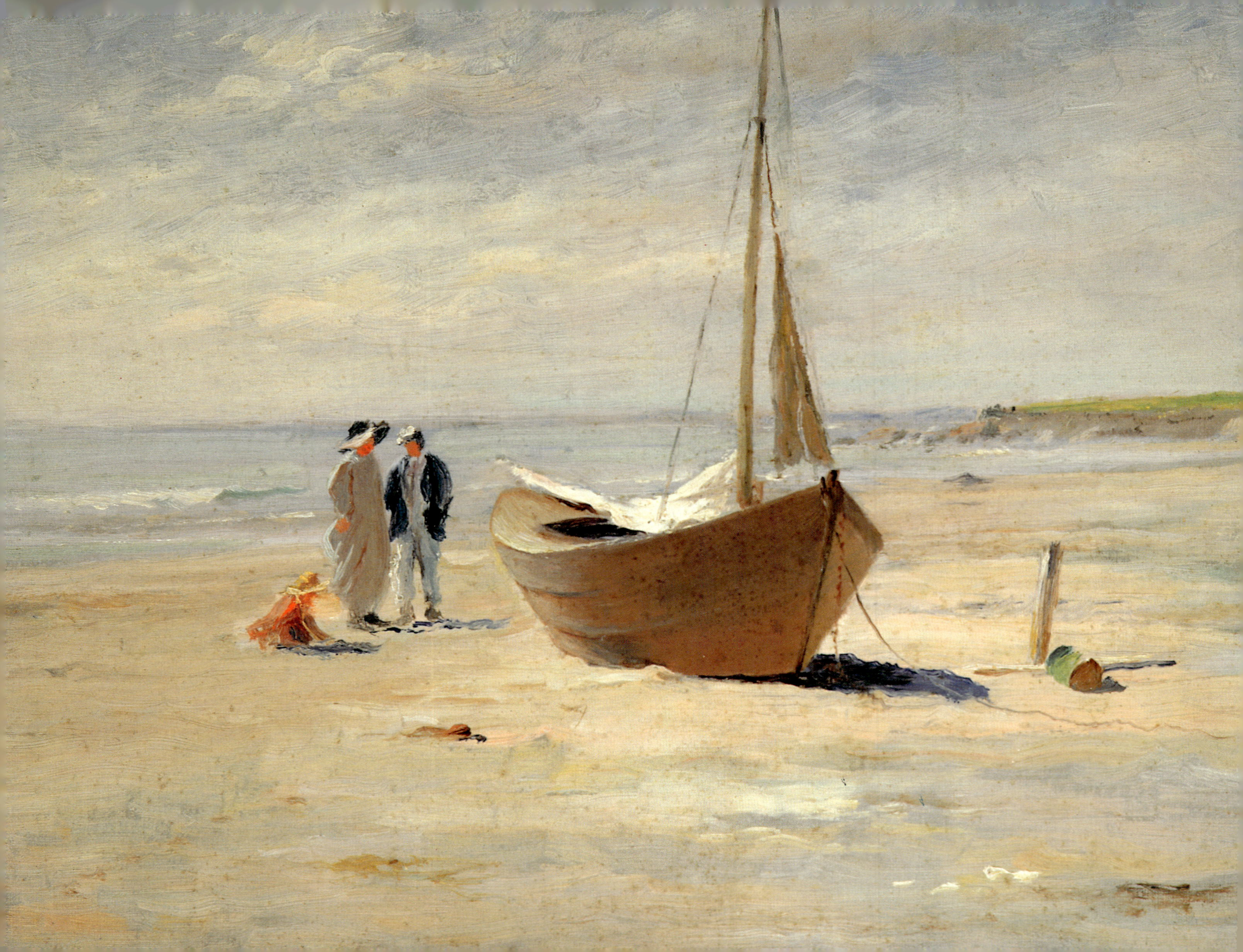

CONTENTS

THE DORYMAN'S FAMILY, c. 1890.
Oil on canvas, 12 x 16 inches.

AUTHOR'S NOTE

William P. Burpee's fortunes and those of his paintings, watercolors, and pastels have paralleled the general interest in his peers and their art, with the added problem, that, following his death in 1940, more than 95 percent of his work was held by his family until the mid-1970s. Perhaps during most of that three and a half decade hiatus, Burpee, like his American Impressionist colleagues, would not have been much noticed, but his oft-mentioned reluctance to sell his work and its consequent unavailability meant that it was not visible even for scholars to consider. The few paintings in private collections that are mentioned by him (the MacMillan and Cornet collections in St. Louis and Mrs. Anson Mills in D.C.) have yet to appear. Sadly, even the public collections in which Burpee placed his paintings during his lifetime (The George Walter Vincent Smith Museum in Springfield, Washington University in St. Louis, The Boston Art Club, The Rockland Public Library and the Rockland High School) no longer have his works. In 1976, the William A. Farnsworth Library and Art Museum mounted the first one-man museum exhibition of Burpee's work, but the catalogue for that show does not contain a single work that can be identified as one of his over 150 exhibition pictures which were shown during his 37 years as a regular exhibitor at major institutions in this country. Nevertheless, the paintings in this book and in the exhibition that coincides with its publication are ample testimony to the real quality of Burpee's art over an astonishingly long painting career.

It is my great regret, and no little surprise, that to date I have not been able to identify a single extant picture as one of Burpee's lifetime exhibition pieces. There are additional events in Burpee's life that I am certain to have missed, he is rumored to have taken a trip to Scotland later in life, learned golf at St. Andrews and returned to Rockland to establish the first golf course there; he certainly took at least one painting trip to Newfoundland, probably after his return to Maine in 1913. The increased interest in his painting over the last several years while I have been engaged on this project has been gratifying, as has the amazing amount of help from scholars, collectors, Burpee family members, museum personnel, librarians, archivists, dealers and my colleagues at Childs Gallery.

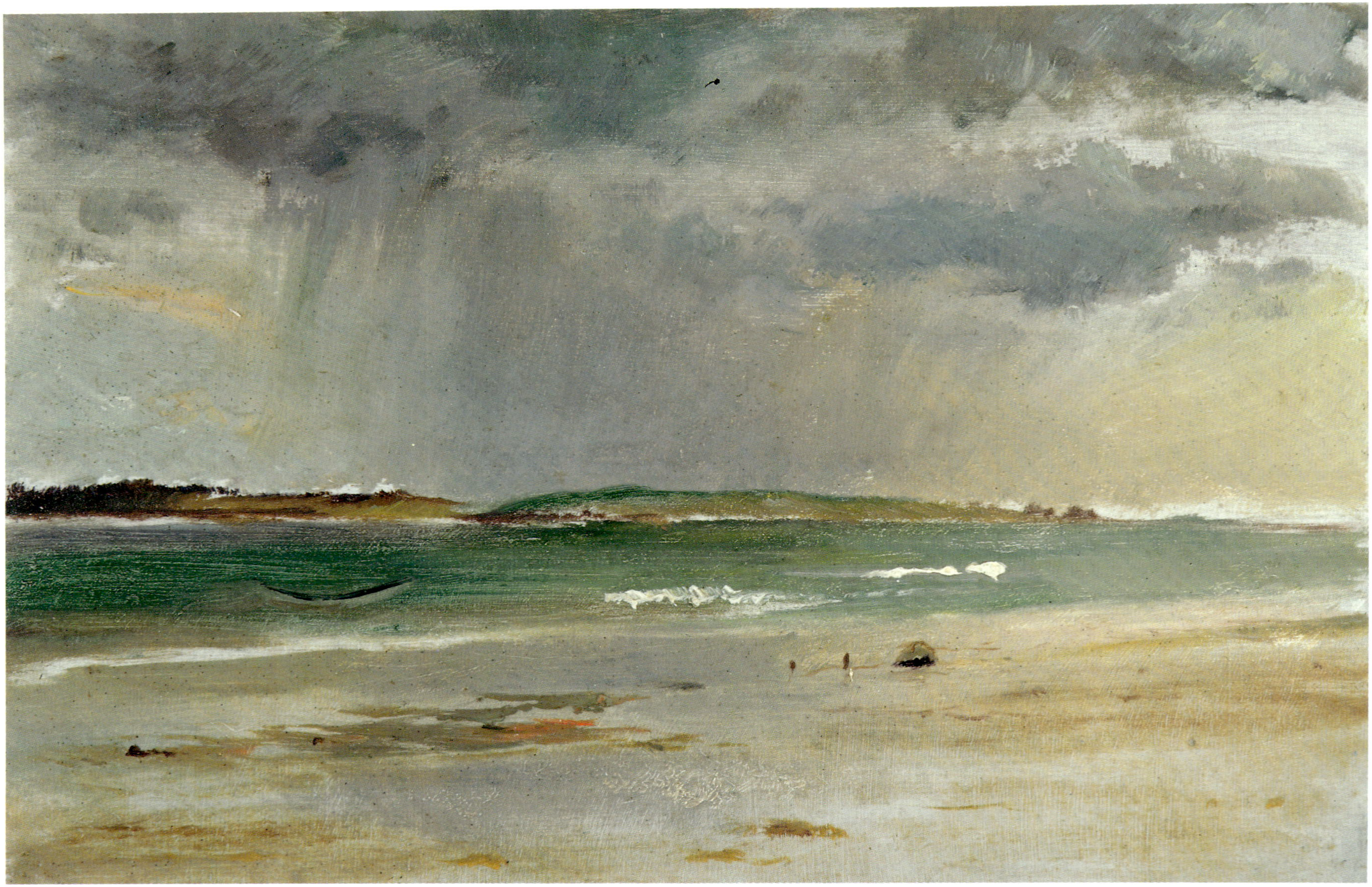

FOREWORD

The long and rich tradition of marine painting in the United States manifested itself especially in northern New England, along the coasts of Massachusetts and Maine, but our present-day recognition of the broad spectrum of artistic response to the sea and to the life and activity of the American fisherfolk in that region has been somewhat circumscribed by our justifiable admiration for the achievements of two successive masters, Fitz Hugh Lane and Winslow Homer. Both these artists had their imitators and emulators, but only in recent years have more independent accomplishments begun to receive their due attention, like that accorded to the marvelous paintings of Charles Woodbury in the exhibition held at the MIT Museum in 1988.

Woodbury's contemporary, William Partridge Burpee, is another master of marine painting who has deserved the recognition now accorded him in this scholarly and entertaining study by D. Roger Howlett; previously, the only attention given to Burpee and his art was the exhibition and accompanying catalogue of Burpee's work held in 1976 at the William A. Farnsworth Library and Art Museum in Burpee's native town of Rockland, Maine.

The names of Lane, Homer, and Woodbury are not randomly invoked. As Howlett demonstrates, Burpee's long career encompassed a stylistic and thematic development which first reflected the early Luminist traditions of Lane and then the more heroic Naturalism of Homer's Prout's Neck paintings; and Woodbury was a significant colleague of Burpee's during the latter's long residence in Boston and in his association with the Boston Art Club. But Burpee was far more than a follower of more celebrated artists. He was one of the more significant American marine painters to investigate the artistic strategies of both the Tonalist and Impressionist movements of the end of the nineteenth century, responding respectively to the impact of the work of James McNeill Whistler and to the strong presence of and interest in both French and American Impressionist paintings in Boston. The earliest Impressionist work by Claude Monet shown in the United States was on view in Boston shortly after Burpee settled there, and among Burpee's colleagues were the American Impressionists Theodore Wendel and Joseph DeCamp, the latter of whom became a close friend and painted an incisive likeness of Burpee. Indeed, Burpee is one of the relatively few late nineteenth century American Impressionists who actually acknowledged the designation at the time.

Howlett's book also offers a fascinating look at a variety of art activities among turn-of-the-century artists, as he chronicles the endeavors of the colony of painters who chose the region around Nahant, Lynn, Marblehead, and Salem for their coastal and marine scenes. One of the most fascinating chapters in this book is a detailed presentation of Burpee's bicycle tour all over Europe in 1897–99, documenting both the art that fascinated the painter and the lifestyle of an American whose Tour was "Grand" not in a luxurious manner of traveling but in the richness of his experiences. And Howlett records more fully than I have previously found both the events and the tragic results of the disastrous Harcourt Studio Building fire of November 11, 1904, in which Burpee was one of the many artists who literally saw much of their lives' achievements go up in smoke.

Burpee enriched the ranks of the Boston art world; with this study, American painting has regained a significant figure in its history.

William H. Gerdts
Graduate School of the City
University of New York

SUMMER SHOWER, c. 1880.

Oil on paper mounted on panel, 7 1/4 x 10 5/8 inches.

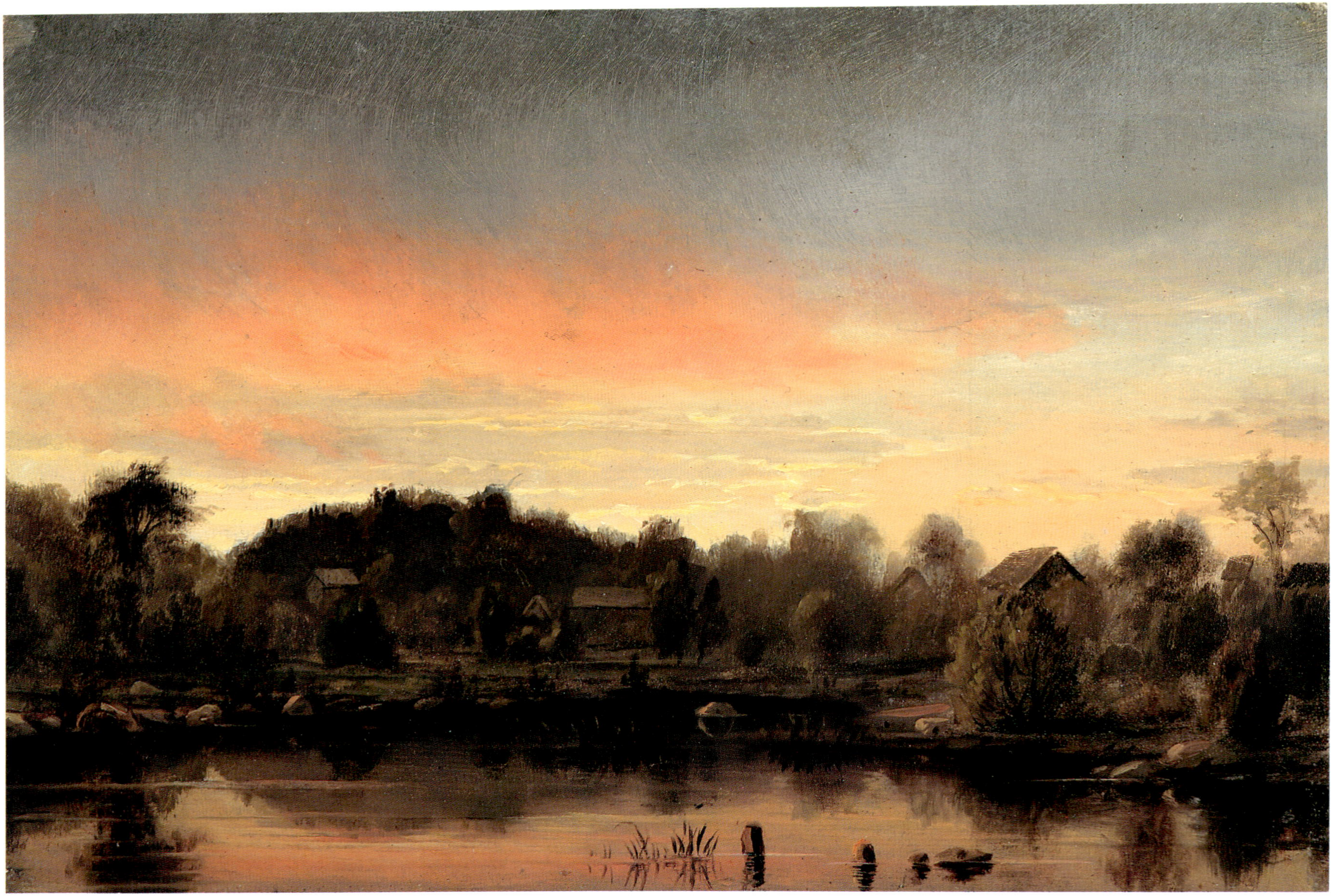

CHAPTER ONE

Early Maine Years (1846 – 1882)

When William Partridge Burpee was born in the town of East Thomaston, Maine, on April 13, 1846, James K. Polk was president of a United States of America not 70 years old. The United States was claiming the Rio Grande as the southern boundary of Texas (which had been annexed to the United States the previous year), and General Zachary Taylor was marching fast toward Chapultepec. When Burpee died on December 15, 1940, Europe was at war, Franklin D. Roosevelt had been elected to his third term as president, and 20 more states had been added to the Union. Burpee had lived during nearly 60 percent of the history of the United States.

He also lived several generations in the development of the arts and painting. When he was born, Thomas Cole was painting and Winslow Homer was 10 years old; at the time of his death, the New York art press was reviewing exhibitions of celluloids for Disney's *Fantasia* and jewelry designs by Alexander Calder. Burpee kept up with many of the stylistic changes as they were absorbed by the art world, and his 80-year artistic evolution from a mid-Victorian to a Post-Impressionist painter provides an insight into several generations of New England painters.

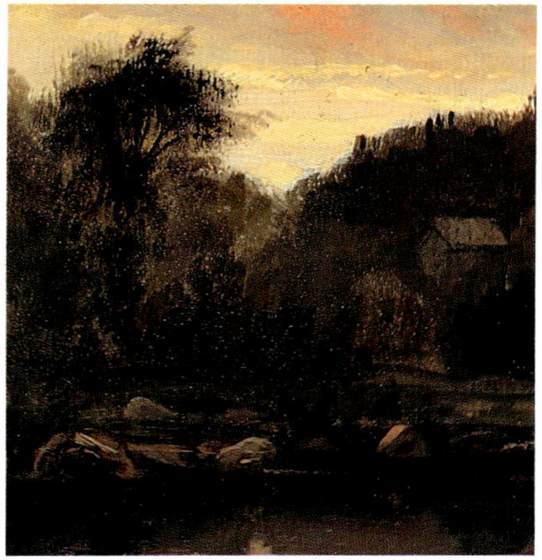

NEW ENGLAND VILLAGE AT SUNSET, late 1870s.

Oil on paper mounted on panel, 5 1/2 x 8 inches.
The play of foreground shadow and silhouette against the effects of light in the sky immediately calls to mind paintings by Frederic Edwin Church at the Bay of Fundy and on the Maine Coast in the 1850s and 1860s.

The Burpees of Rockland

In 1846, East Thomaston, Maine (which would change its name to Rockland in 1850) was a growing port whose economy was based on limeburning and shipbuilding. William Partridge Burpee was born within the sound of the Atlantic Ocean, which would form the subject for the majority of his paintings in the years to follow. Burpee's father, Nathaniel A. Burpee, born in Sterling, Massachusetts, in 1816, had followed his father's trade as a house painter, and had moved with his family to East Thomaston in 1835. When he became of age, he married a local girl, Mary Partridge, whose father, James, was a blacksmith.[1] In 1842 Nathaniel and his brother, Samuel H. Burpee, also a painter, formed a partnership that grew and expanded, eventually making most of its money from the furniture business.[2] N.A. & S.H. Burpee became known as one of Rockland's most successful and stable firms.[3]

Although Nathaniel's father, Herman Burpee, had been an ardent Whig, Nathaniel joined the Republican party at its outset in Maine in 1854. He ran for the Maine House of Representatives and served two terms in Augusta in 1854 and 1855, then was elected to the state senate four times. As senator he served on various committees, including Prisons, Accounts, Mercantile Affairs, Library, Pensions, Fisheries, and Indian Affairs.[4] The tenor of the political times is indicated by the careers of his contemporaries in Maine politics, Hannibal Hamlin and James G. Blaine, who were both ardently antislavery and pro-Republican.[5]

On being elected unanimously by his fellow senators as president of the Maine senate in 1867, directly following the Civil War, Nathaniel A. Burpee addressed them on the crises for the United States during the great debates over Reconstruction.[6] After fulfilling his duty to his state, Nathaniel left the senate and his political career after the 1867 legislative season to return to Rockland and his business career.

By 1868 the partnership had become a corporation, still with Nathaniel's brother Samuel H. Burpee on Main Street in Rockland, and he had achieved recognition from his peers as assistant chief of the fire department.[7] The Rockland City Directory for 1871 noted that the fire department had named one of the companies the "N.A. Burpee, No 4." His great interest in the department may have resulted from his having lost all or most of his business in a great fire on Main Street on January 28, 1856, which destroyed the wooden business block that housed the establishment of N.A. & S.H. Burpee, furniture dealers. He and his brother rebuilt and prospered in the post–Civil War economy; by 1871, they had erected a large brick building at 290 Main Street, known as the Burpee Block, which contained not only the furniture store and warehouse, but a large public hall and a new addition to the business, undertaker's goods. In the same period Nathaniel moved his family into the modest house on Park Street in Rockland that would be the family home until William Partridge Burpee's death.[8]

The arts were clearly in evidence in the Burpee household from the earliest days. Nathaniel Burpee was noted as "prominent in musical circles, and a thoroughly educated musician of the old school."[9] His wife, Mary Partridge, was a noted singer, and both of them played the flute.[10] Later in life Mary "exercised her talents in the direction of drawing and painting in oil and exhibited a pronounced genius in the province of the sculptor. It has often been remarked that the development in her children of the artistic nature, variously displayed, has a natural genesis in the gifted mother."[11] Burpee's older brother, Edgar, played the viola and directed and sang for the Orpheus and Fletcher musical clubs in Rockland; his younger brother Frank played the French horn;[12] and his sister Carrie was a gifted pianist. His uncle, John, painted pictures and took a keen interest in William's progress and artistic success.[13]

William P. Burpee's earliest years were spent in public school in Rockland, but about 1860 he went to Kents Hill Academy to pursue special courses. There is little question that he drew and painted from a very early age. A notebook that dates from before 1860 includes pencil drawings from architectural prints, as well as inventions (*Vessels Rounding a Headland*) that certainly come from the mind of an active boy.

VESSELS ROUNDING A HEADLAND, c.1860.

Pencil on paper, 7 1/16 x 9 15/16 inches.
This drawing is part of a pre–Civil War notebook containing copies of prints and original designs by Burpee.

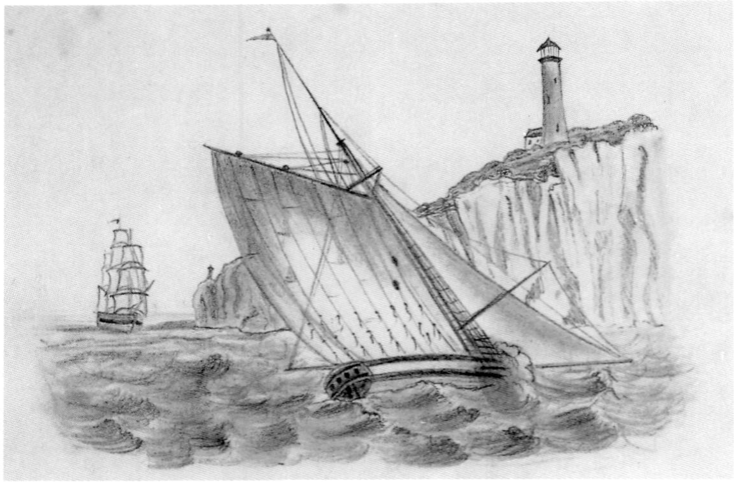

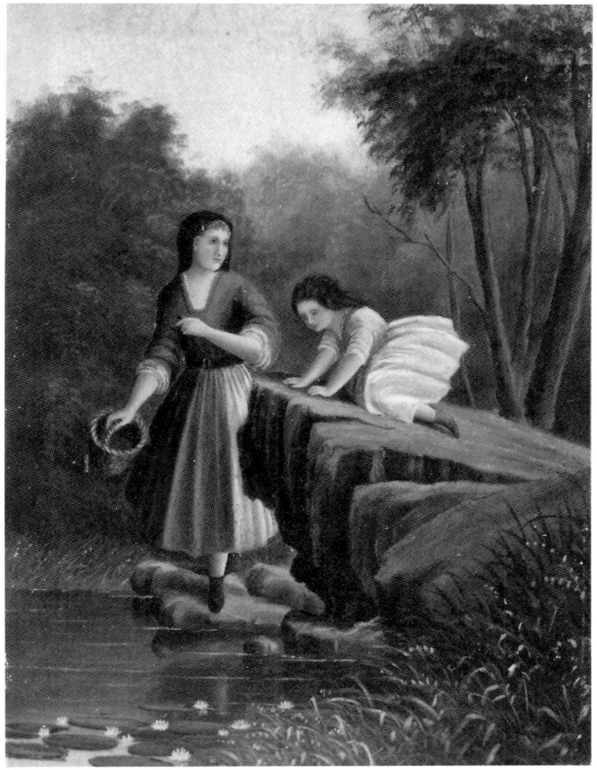

LILY POND, 1868.

Oil on paperboard, 12 1/8 x 9 1/8 inches.
One of three paintings dating from 1868, *Lily Pond* shows that Burpee had not yet had the advantages of training.

Burpee's earliest known signed and dated painting of a young woman and a girl at a pond covered with water lilies shows a mid-Victorian sensibility and sentimentality along with great talent. It also suggests that Burpee had had little opportunity for training by 1868. Family tradition suggested that "with a background of artists and musicians young Burpee naturally became interested in art[14]".

Despite Burpee's evident interest in being an artist, his father apparently had other plans for his son. He seems to have expected him to go into business. William's brother, Edgar had entered the family business and had been able to pursue his interests in the arts without interrupting his duties in trade. The Rockland newspapers gave him full notices for his part in the production of the opera *Pepita* in May of 1876:

> "Pepita" has come and gone, and left in Rockland and every town in its vicinity the largest and most delighted numbers of people who ever attended an entertainment of any description. The operetta was put on in superior style, far eclipsing anything of a like or different nature ever exhibited in this part of the state. The scenery — the most elegant ever seen in our city — was the work of Mr. E. A. Burpee, and the reputation which he wins as a scenic artist will doubtless "stick" to him. Of the merits of "Pepita" as an opera but little can be said in praise. But the old familiar tunes, the pleasant scenes, and above all the clearness of the plot, makes it a "taking" one with average audiences. The characters in the piece were sustained by the best singers in Rockland. Mr. E. A. Burpee as Jose (which is pronounced Hosay) the Gipsey Chief was excellent, having a fine conception of the part. In the scene of the stealing of the child he was particularly good. This scene was introduced and written by Mr. Burpee.[15]

It is likely that Nathaniel believed that his second son, always known in the family as Will, would follow the arts and business with the same considered balance. Thus, Burpee learned the trade of bookkeeper and accountant, and at one point he was employed in this position in Rockland for John Bird and Co. (grocers and lime manufacturers). Later he held many positions in bookkeeping and accounting in Boston, ending with a five-year stint with The Country Club in Brookline, Massachusetts, before he resigned to make his first European trip.

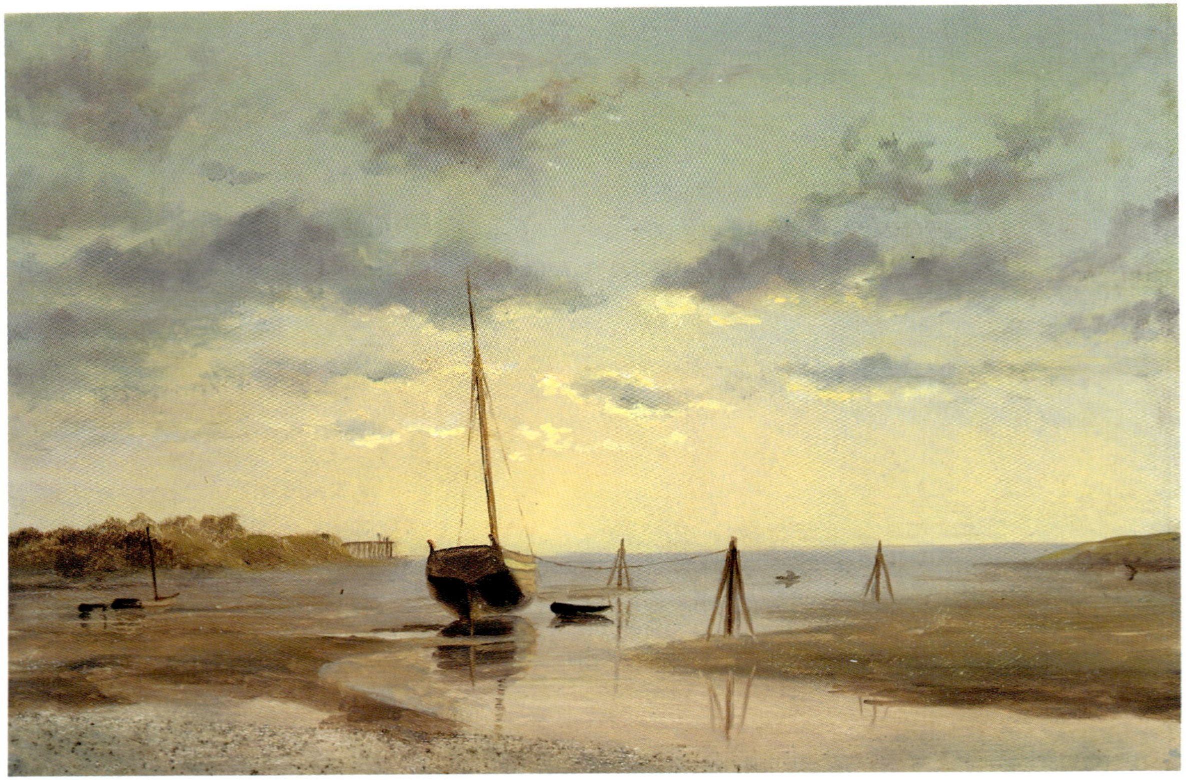

New England Marine Painting Traditions

Presumably the family, which had encouraged painting and music as accomplishments, were pleased at Will's interest in painting; they may even have supported his study with William Bradford. Burpee was introduced to Bradford's work by the Rockland collector David Smith, who owned at least two of Bradford's paintings. Smith asked Burpee "to copy one of them, and make certain changes in color and value. Mr. Burpee's work compared very favorably and in some points excelled that of this master painter. However, at the suggestion of Mr. Smith he became a pupil of the New York artist."[16] Burpee is said to have left Rockland at 18 for Boston and then to have moved on to New York where Smith, who wintered there, could have arranged an introduction with Bradford.[17]

William Bradford (1823 – 1892) was a fortuitous choice as a mentor and teacher for young Burpee. He was the only artist that Burpee cited as having given him formal training, and Burpee's paintings themselves bear witness to Bradford's influence in the 1870s or early 1880s. As mentioned, Burpee had not had the benefit of formal study by 1868; it is equally clear that by his next known dated painting (1885), he had progressed to being an accomplished and even sophisticated academic artist. Bradford was born in Fairhaven, Massachusetts, across the harbor from New Bedford. His father, like Burpee's, was in business and owned a dry goods store where Bradford clerked as a youth.[18] He was marked for a career in business until "one of those financial crises so frequent in this country involved the young merchant in bankruptcy [and] not only justified his decision to renounce thenceforth a pursuit for which he had not the least aptitude or liking, but made it incumbent upon him to seek in art not only the gratification of long baffled aspirations, but the means of subsistence."[19] Bradford's paintings, like Burpee's to follow, depended largely on subjects of the sea. Indeed, one of his first periods after he became a full-time artist in the mid-1850s was spent on the beaches of Lynn and Swampscott, Massachusetts. In 1869 Bradford completed the most extensive of his many trips to Labrador and the neighboring Arctic regions; he was in the process of completing many paintings and a book on the subject when his major sponsor, Le Grand Lockwood, went bankrupt, leaving Bradford in debt. Hoping to recover financially and benefit artistically he sailed in April 1872 for England where he remained nearly two years. During the largest part of the ensuing 1870s he maintained a studio in New York where he painted during the winters, and "during the summers of the seventies he had a studio in New Bedford that afforded a good view of the Acushnet River and part of Buzzard's Bay."[20] Since Bradford spent the first years of the 1880s in San Francisco, it is very likely that Burpee did his studies with Bradford in the 1870s. Burpee's obituary refers to Bradford as a "New York artist," and family tradition suggests that Burpee also lived and worked there, although he is never listed in the New York City directories.

Burpee learned his lessons well. Paintings that must date from his period of study under Bradford (*Boats at Low Tide* and *Evening Tide*) show that the student learned to paint studies from nature that captured the sense of light and calm and even the palette that Bradford preferred (*Sails at Sunset*). John Wilmerding states of Bradford:

> Much of his work at this time [1854] bears unmistakable similarities to the style of Fitz Hugh Lane, the Gloucester artist who had established himself during the preceding decade as the preeminent marine painter of Boston and the northern New England shore. Lane had been in New Bedford in 1845 to draw a lithograph of the town from the Fairhaven side of the harbor, and returned again in 1856 (if not before) to paint the New York Yacht Club regatta, which Bradford also painted, probably at Lane's side. In any case, stylistic evidence alone would suggest that the younger New Bedford painter had seen Lane's work. The paintings of both

opposite

BOATS AT LOW TIDE, mid 1870s.

Oil on paper mounted on panel, 7 3/4 x 11 3/8 inches.
William Bradford's teaching influence shows in the style, mood and palette of this quintessential Luminist painting.

below

EVENING TIDE, mid 1870s.

Oil on canvas, 20 1/4 x 30 inches.
This painting compares directly to William Bradford's New Bedford Harbor pictures of the late 1850s.

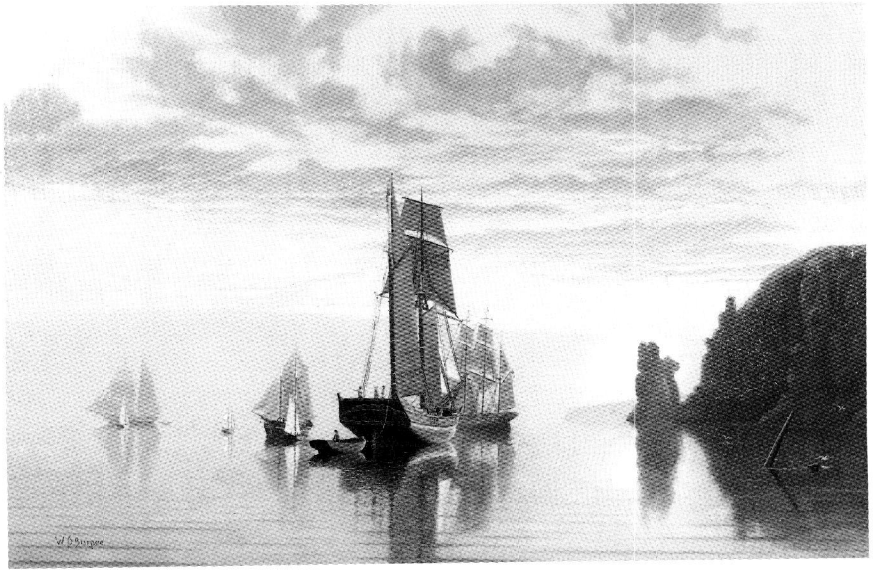

men during the late forties and early fifties possess a common clarity of drawing, interest in narrative detail, cool lighting effects and in some instances a striking similarity of composition.[21]

It would be too much to state that Burpee probably knew Lane. Lane died in Gloucester in 1865, when Burpee was 19, and Burpee may never have visited either Boston or Gloucester up to that point. But Lane had been a constant visitor to Maine to paint the rugged coast and the effects of light, and much of his Maine subject matter centers about Penobscot Bay, of which Rockland forms the southwest corner. His last seasons in Maine produced a final view of *Owl's Head, Penobscot Bay, Maine* in 1862 when Burpee was 16 years old. If he did not meet Lane, then perhaps acquaintances in Rockland (including the collector David Smith) did. In any event, Burpee's *Sunset at Owl's Head* seems to be a direct homage to Lane. Certainly, by the time Burpee lived in Boston the profusion of Lane's Maine coastal scenes owned in that city would have attracted the attention of a young man from Rockland who had studied with Bradford.

Burpee seems to have adopted Bradford's practice of painting rapid oil studies on paper or wood panel. Indeed, Burpee not only carefully selected special papers that were embossed with surfaces that resembled canvas weave or twill, but also seems to have been willing throughout his career to paint or draw on nearly any flat surface that came to hand.

Bradford would have been able to help Burpee pursue a career as an artist and to introduce Burpee to other professional artists. Bradford was a member of the National Academy of Design; he had traveled widely and been acclaimed in London; he knew Albert Bierstadt, his fellow artist from New Bedford (they had both maintained painting rooms in the Tenth Street Studio Building in New York);[22] and he was at ease with clients and artists in Europe and America. He certainly could recommend to Burpee other artists of note, such as Frederic Edwin Church, Martin Johnson Heade,

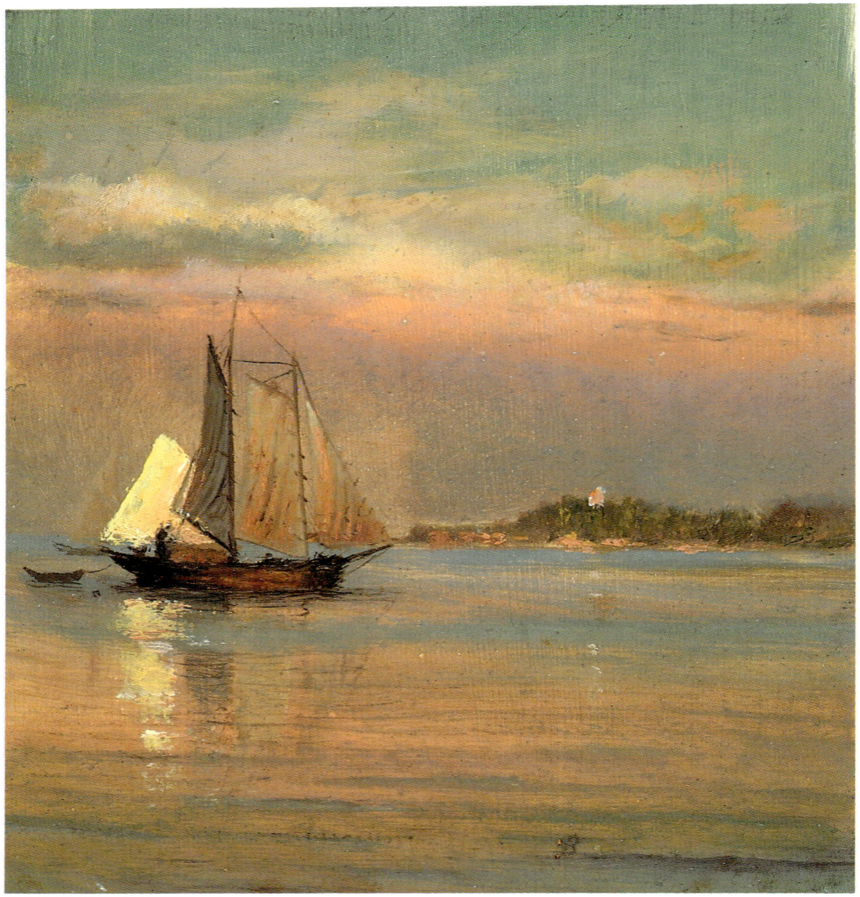

left

SAILS AT SUNSET, c.1880.

Oil on paper mounted on panel, 6 7/8 x 6 7/16 inches.
This picture reflects the preferred palette that Bradford used during much of the 1870s.

opposite, right

SUNSET AT OWL'S HEAD, mid 1870s.

Oil on paper mounted on panel, 5 3/4 x 9 inches.
Burpee seems to make this painting a direct response to F.H. Lane's 1862 *Owl's Head, Penobscot Bay, Maine*.

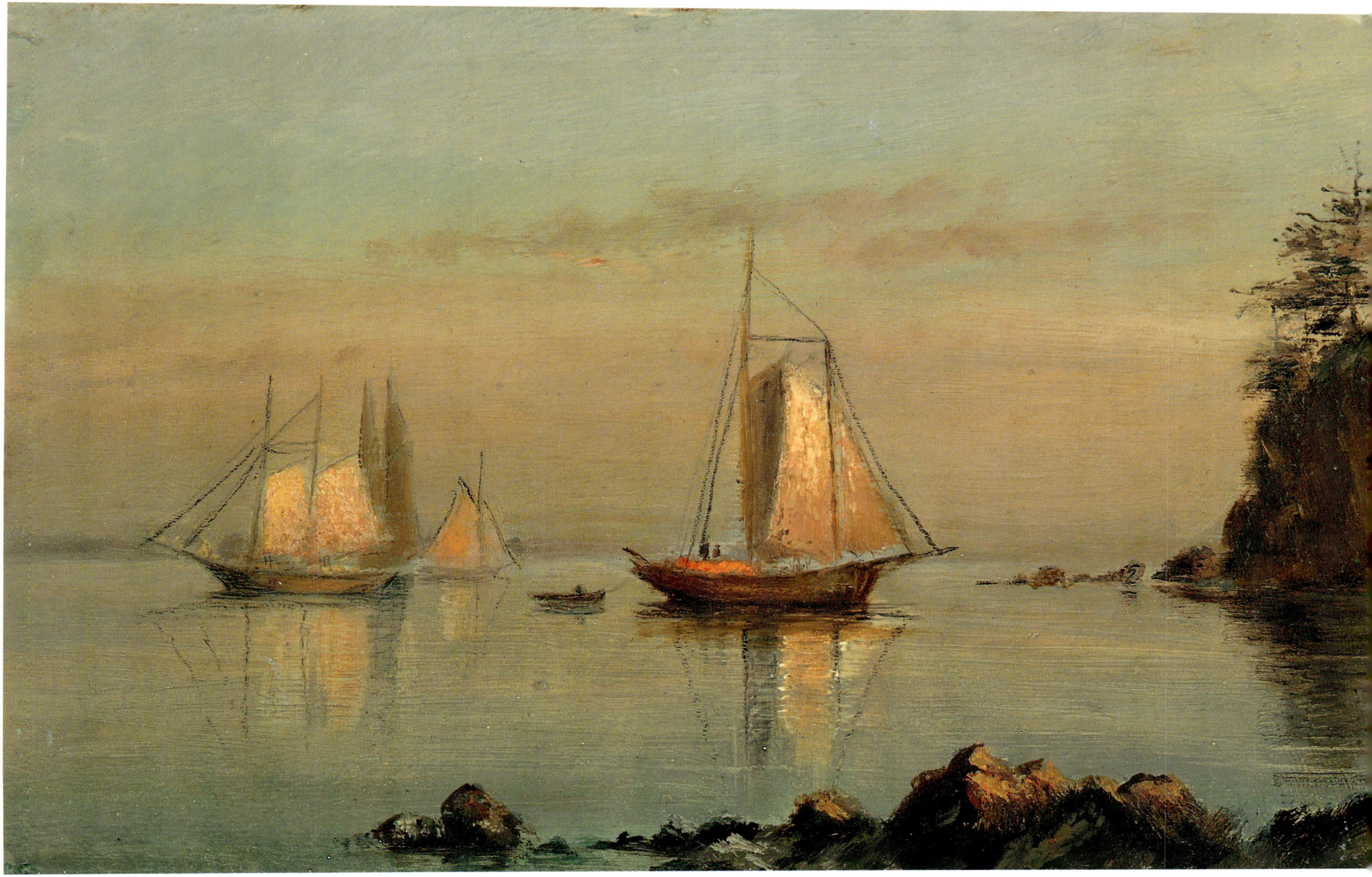

F. A. Silva, and A. T. Bricher, who were interested in marine or coastal subjects in New England. Burpee was also interested in landscape in the late 1870s and early 1880s. He painted a series in this period of small paintings of the hills behind Rockland, including *Maine Hillsides* and *Maine Hills and Pastures*, each in a precise style and with careful observation reminiscent of the New Path painters (or American Pre-Raphaelites) such as Charles Herbert Moore or W. T. Richards. Church is sometimes associated with this movement, which focused on excruciating observation of nature to produce "truth in art."[23]

Luminism

In the middle of the 1960s certain American art historians, searching for a way to unite the obvious visual similarities of the work of a group of mid–nineteenth century American painters, began using the term "Luminism." The most recognizable common bond was painted light effects that seemed more important than the subject, composition, training,

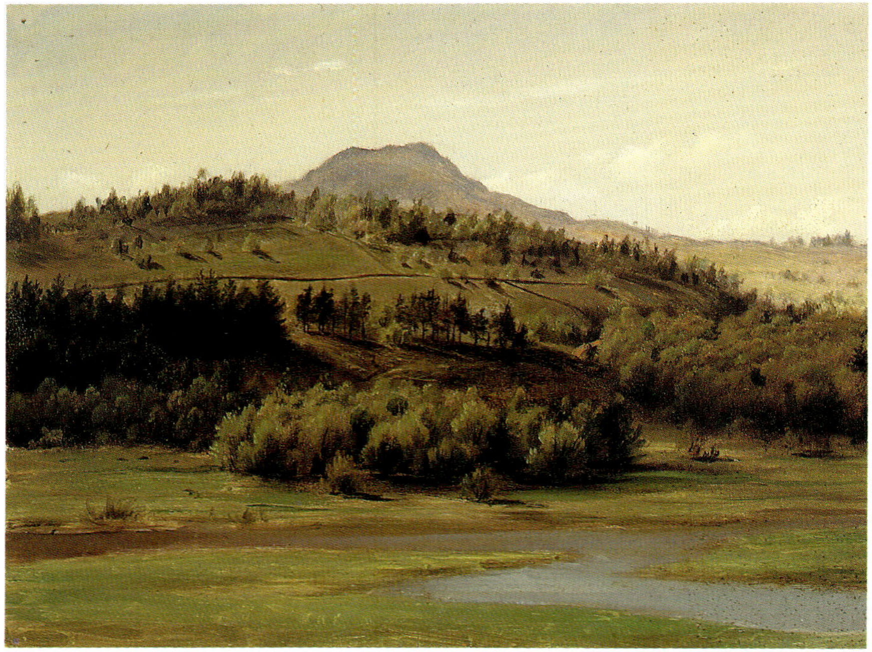

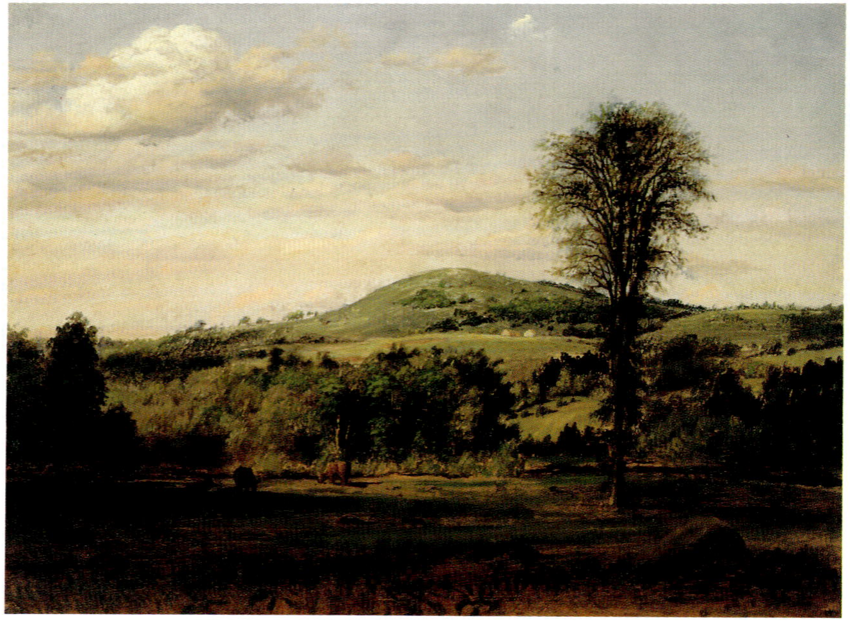

above

MAINE HILLSIDES, late 1870s.

Oil on paper mounted on panel, 10 1/8 x 7 1/2 inches.
The precision of painting and the quality of light relate this to the American Pre-Raphaelites, and especially to the work of Charles H. Moore.

left

MAINE HILLS AND PASTURES, late 1870s.

Oil on paper mounted on panel, 7 3/4 x 10 1/4 inches.
Maine Hills and Pastures shows a "New Path" or American Pre-Raphaelite aesthetic.

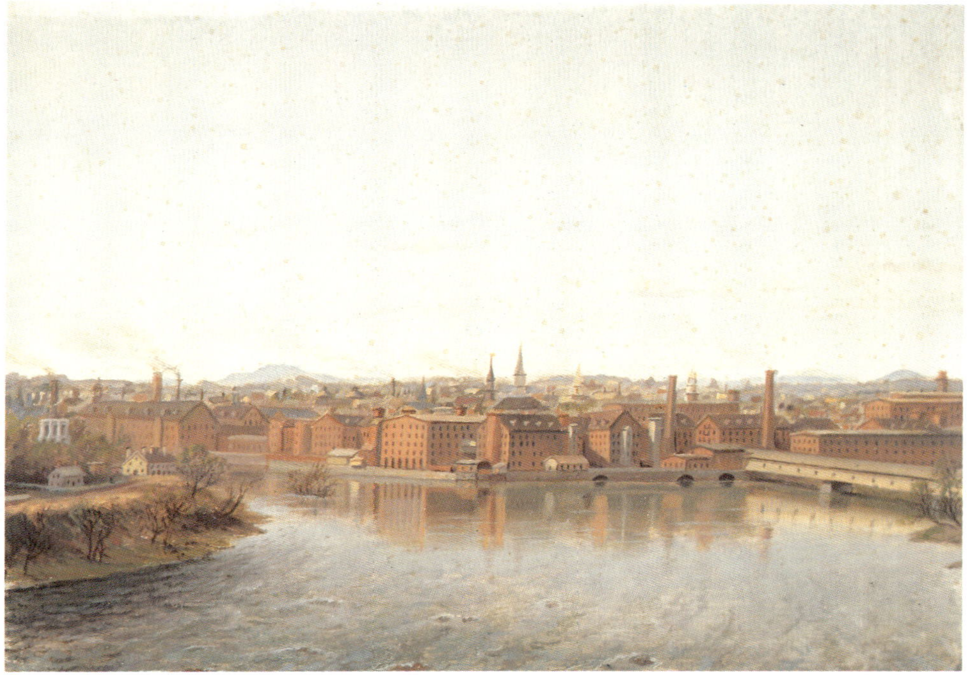

LOWELL, MASSACHUSETTS, mid 1870s.

Oil on paper mounted on panel, 6 3/4 x 9 inches.
From the collection of the William A. Farnsworth Library and Art Museum, Rockland, Maine.

or painting method. Some of these painters were in the mainstream of American painting (Church, Heade, Kensett, Gifford); others, such as the Cape Ann painters (Lane, Mary Mellen, Jerome and Kilby Elwell), were isolated. Bradford perhaps straddled the two groups. They did not know that they were Luminists. The only relationship that they had was a similar visual impact. But Luminism has now been codified, and early work by Burpee, at least through the Lynn Beach paintings, fits the definitions given by Barbara Novak.[24] Light effects, whether in Luminism, Impressionism, or Post-Impressionism, seem to have been one of Burpee's foremost concerns throughout his career.

There is no question that works such as *Boats at Low Tide*, *Sunset at Owl's Head* , and *Sails at Sunset* invite comparison with the Luminist work of Bradford and Lane, and *New England Village at Sunset* with the work of Church and Heade. As he moved into the Lynn Beach paintings, Burpee's Luminism developed to a point of comparison with works by Silva, W. T. Richards, and Bricher.

From a number of Maine paintings that appear to be from the period just after study with Bradford we can suppose that Burpee was spending much of his time in the late 1870s in Maine and that he spent enough time in Lowell, Massachusetts, to create at least two views of that city. Other than

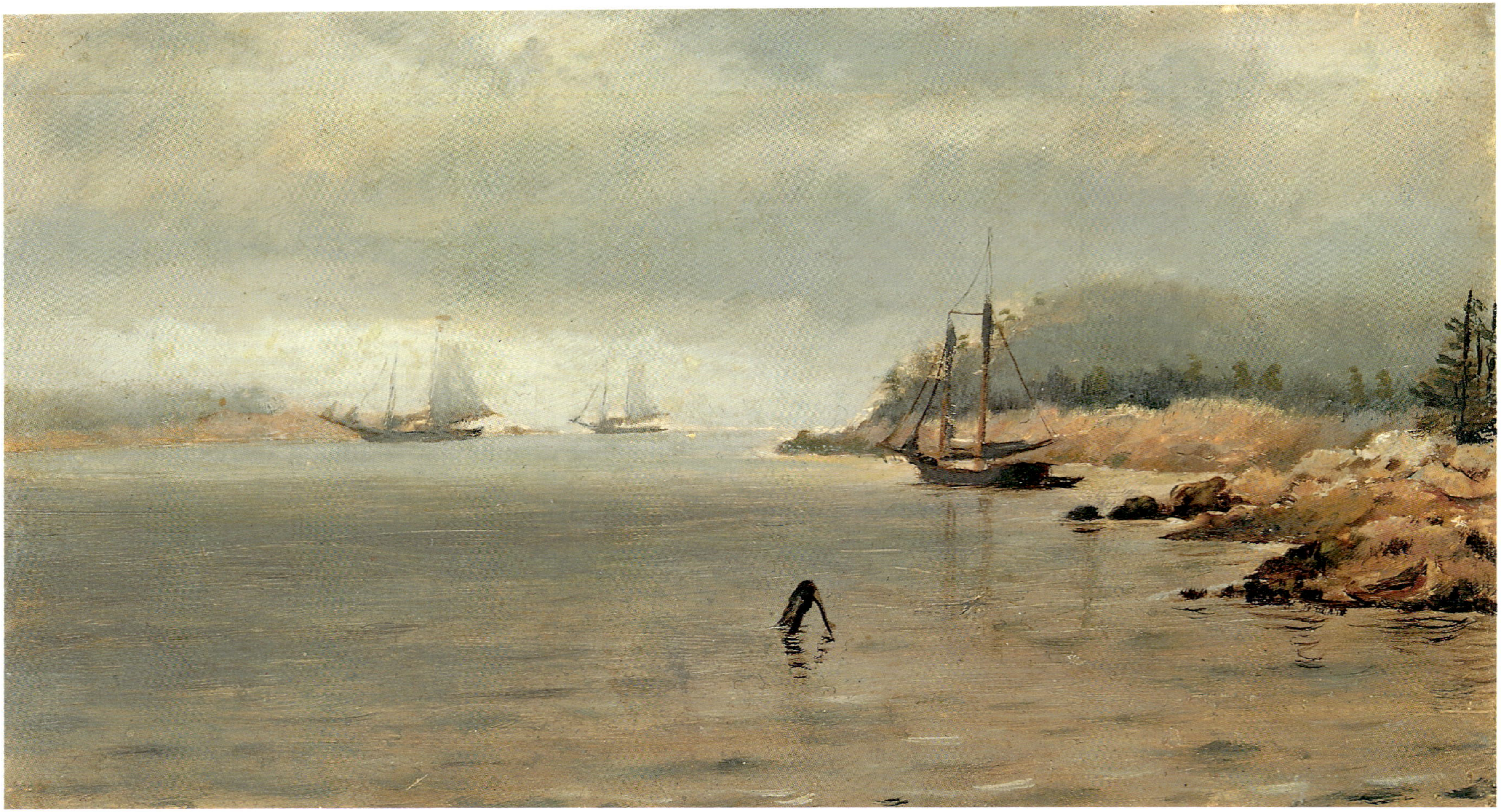

a certainty that Burpee studied with William Bradford and that he was making his way (at least part of the time) in bookkeeping and accounting, we know little of his whereabouts or activities from 1868 to 1882. In 1882, however, he advertised himself as an artist in the Rockland City Directory.[25] Perhaps he discovered the local market was too small for even a local artist. That same year, at age 36, he moved to Boston.

MAINE MISTS, c. 1880.

Oil on paper mounted on panel, 5 6/16 x 9 1/2 inches. Paintings such as this one show Burpee moving beyond Bradford and into new stylistic waters.

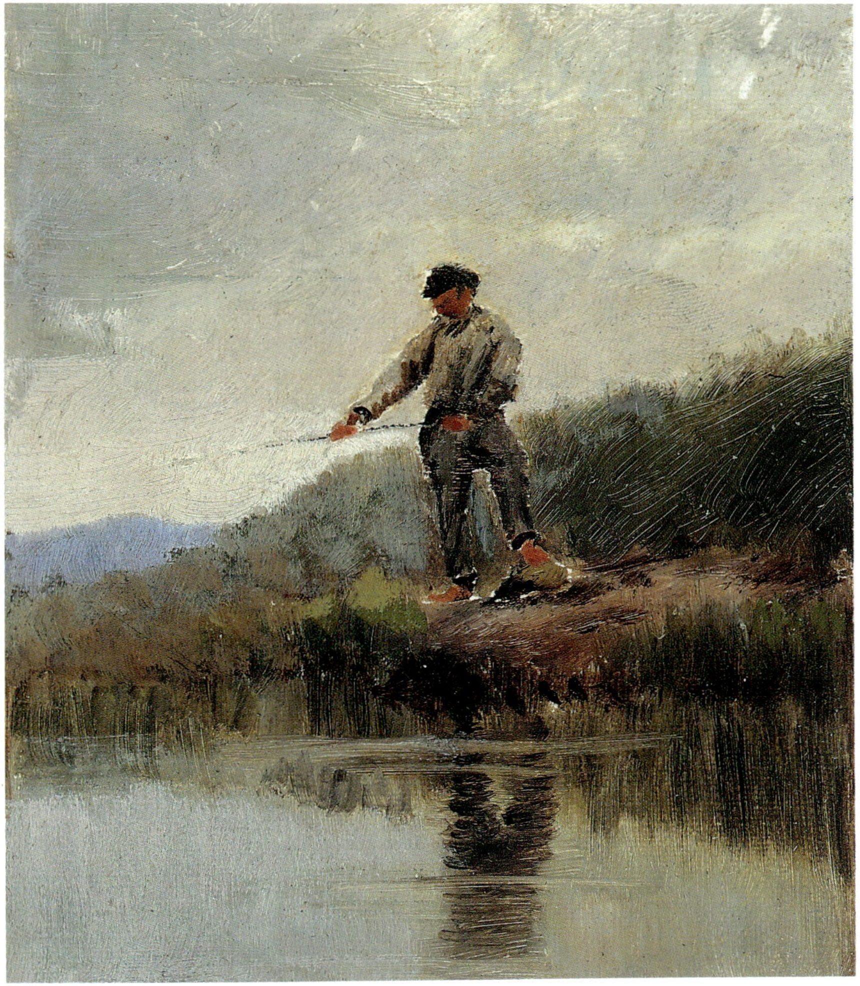

YOUNG FISHERMAN, c.1880.

Oil on paper mounted on panel, 6 1/2 x 5 1/8 inches. *Young Fisherman* resembles the work of fellow Maine painter, Winslow Homer.

NOTES, Chapter One

[1] City of Rockland, *Deaths*, vol. III, p. 171.
[2] James H. Mundy, *Presidents of the Senate of Maine, from 1820*, Augusta, Maine: Secretary of the State of Maine, 1979.
[3] Obituary of N. A. Burpee, *Rockland Courier Gazette*, Dec. 13, 1887, p. 7.
[4] *Journal of the Senate of the State of Maine*, 1858, 1866, Augusta, Maine.
[5] Neal R. Pierce, *The New England States: People, Politics, Power in the Six New England States*. (New York: W. W. Norton & Co., 1976) p. 373.
[6] *Journal of the Senate of the State of Maine*, 1867, Augusta, Maine, pp. 5–6.
[7] *Rockland City Directory*, 1868.
[8] *Rockland City Directory*, 1871.
[9] Obituary of N. A. Burpee, *Rockland Courier Gazette*, Dec. 13, 1887, p. 7.
[10] Alice Frost Lord, "Rockland Artist Never Sought Fame He Merited," in *Rockland Courier Gazette*, [1940s]. It is clear that Lord had access to Burpee's sister, Carrie Burpee Shaw, and other primary sources for this article. Many of the details of Burpee's life can be substantiated by other documents or by circumstantial evidence. In the absence of other evidence, Lord is considered by this author to be authoritative. Hereinafter referred to as "Lord."
[11] Obituary of Mary Jane Partridge Burpee, *Rockland Courier Gazette*, Dec. 1, 1908, p.3.
[12] *Rockland Courier Gazette*, Feb. 8, 1877, p. 2.
[13] Lord; Cyrus Eaton, *History of Thomaston, Rockland, and South Thomaston, Maine*, Hallowell, Maine, 1865.
[14] Edwin L. Brown, "William P. Burpee," obituary, *Rockland Courier Gazette*, Dec 19, 1940. There is evidence that Brown, a painter, was a good friend of Burpee's, and that where there is no evidence to the contrary, his obituary should be taken as authoritative. Hereinafter referred to as "Brown."
[15] *Rockland Courier Gazette*, May 9–10, 1876.
[16] Brown.
[17] Lord. It should be noted that the Boston City Directory lists a William P. Burpee as early as 1851 as a trader [who is later in produce]. There is no evidence that the artist is in the Boston City Directory before 1882; however, the provisioner does not appear in the 1867 directory and it is possible that the artist came to Boston in 1868 and replaced a relative/namesake. It is fairly certain that the artist had cousins in the Boston area.
[18] John Wilmerding, *William Bradford,* De Cordova Museum, Lincoln, Massachusetts, 1969.
[19] Henry T. Tuckerman, *Book of the Artists* (New York: James F. Carr, 1966) p. 553.
[20] Wilmerding, op. cit., p. 29.
[21] Wilmerding, op. cit., p. 11.
[22] Wilmerding, op. cit., p. 22.
[23] For aesthetic and visual similarities compare Burpee to the works illustrated in Linda S. Ferber and William H. Gerdts, *The New Path: Ruskin and the American Pre-Raphaelites*, The Brooklyn Museum, New York, 1985.
[24] Barbara Novak, "On Defining Luminism," in John Wilmerding et. al., *American Light,* National Gallery of Art, Washington, D.C., 1980, pp.23–29.
[25] *Rockland City Directory*, 1882.

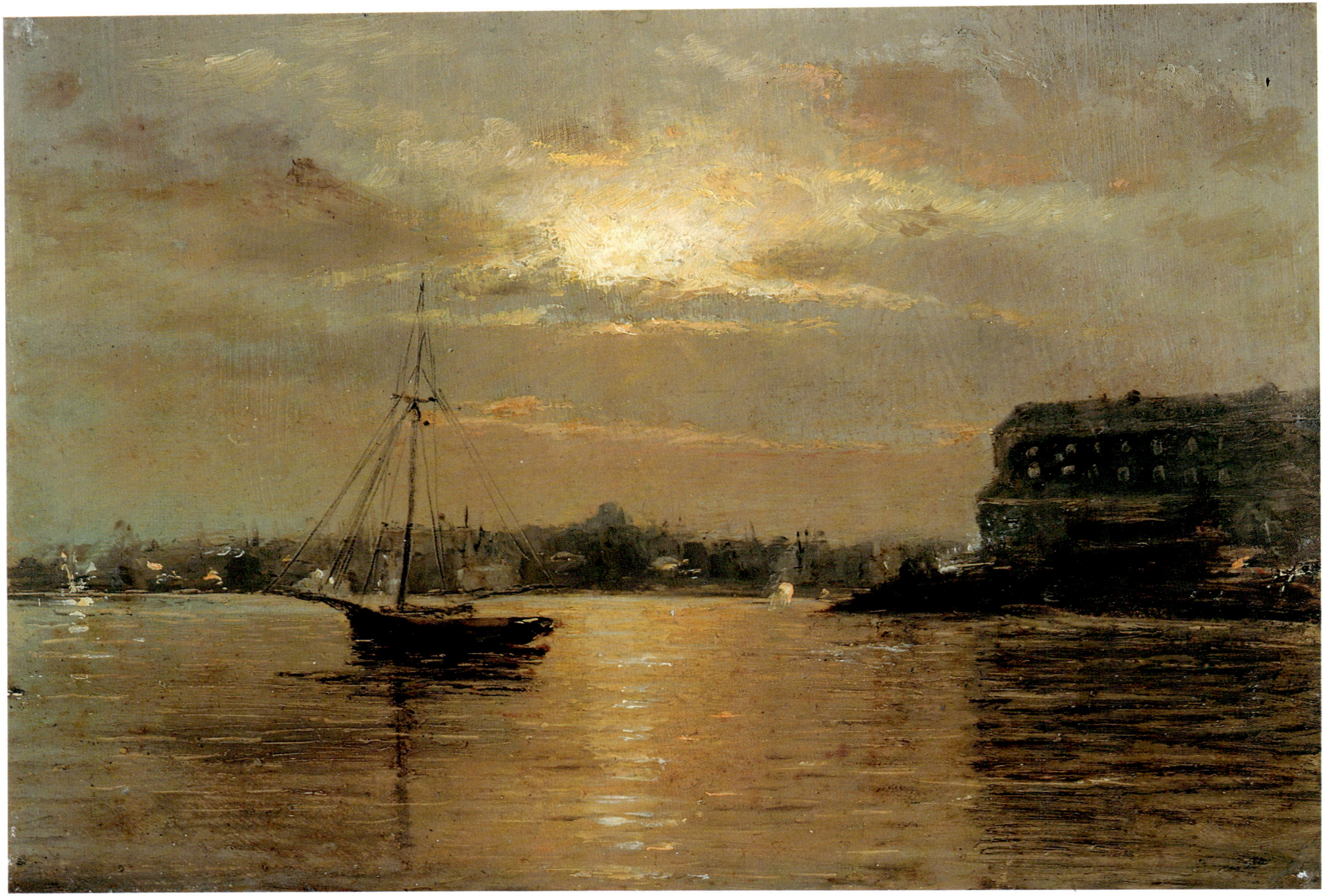

CHAPTER TWO

Move to Boston (1882 – 1897)

Burpee might have been attracted to Boston, among other reasons, by a 22–painting exhibition of William Bradford's paintings of the Arctic and Yosemite held at the galleries of Williams and Everett, art dealers, in November of 1881. A reviewer of the show pointed out Bradford's prolonged absence from the Northeast by stating that Bradford had bought the ship *Panther* 13 years prior, and spent seven years in the Arctic and subsequently six summers in Yosemite. Bradford's critic might have been describing many of Burpee's Luminist paintings such as *Sails at Sunset* (p. 14) when he wrote of a Bradford picture, "The vivid rose-color and deep magentas multiplied in quantity by the water reflections make the pictures glow like coal fires."[1]

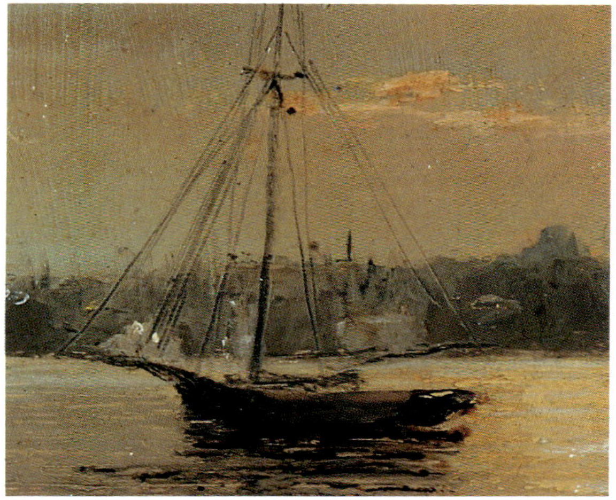

BOSTON FROM CHARLESTOWN, c.1882.

Oil on paper mounted on panel, 5 3/4 x 8 3/8 inches.
The Luminism that Burpee expressed in the previous decade continued into his first Boston pictures.

Burpee first appears with a Boston business address in 1882 at 48 State Street, boarding at 747 Tremont Street. From various family accounts we are told that he arrived in the city that year at age 36.[2] We must presume that in his first Boston years he was primarily engaged in bookkeeping and accounting; to all evidence, he lived a modest lifestyle. We can also posit that he was increasingly taking a part in the artistic life of Boston.

The Boston that Burpee entered in the early 1880s was burgeoning financially, physically, culturally, and artistically. Although the art organizations that would help to advance his career centered around the Back Bay, he lived in the South End most of the time. Since the Civil War the South End had been eclipsed as the fashionable new district by the Back Bay, and some of its developments never fully recovered from the financial panics of the period. Therefore rooms to let, apartments, and boarding houses abounded, and Burpee took advantage of these lower costs and always maintained his residence in the city in the South End.

Boston was a major art center in the late 19th century. The Massachusetts Institute of Technology building where drawing and watercolor were taught was in the area of Copley Square, the Museum of Fine Arts was directly on the square, and the Boston Art Club had broken ground one building off the square on Dartmouth Street in 1881. Described in anticipation by one writer as: "Fronting on the grand square already surrounded by

Trinity Church with its great tiled tower, the Art Museum with its broad terra-cotta bas-reliefs, the new "Old South" with its lofty campanile and Byzantine lantern, and blocks of towering French apartment houses the new art club will be emphatically "de son temps", a monument to the sumptuous "solid" period in which old Boston is settling down to the luxurious enjoyment of the well-earned fruits of generations of thrift, enterprise, industry and cultivation." The edifice was budgeted at "not far from a hundred thousand dollars. Is there another art club anywhere in the New World or the Old?" It promised to provide "the luxurious privacy of the club proper and the public use of the gallery for periodical exhibitions."[3] In the same article the author described the simultaneous construction of a grand gallery in the Back Bay for the Massachusetts Charitable Mechanics Association, "an immense structure, no less than six hundred feet long, built of brick and stone which will include, besides the art gallery, a great hall for meetings and concerts." The next year after Burpee's arrival the new Massachusetts Normal Art School building was begun (the school had opened in 1873 to train public school teachers in art, but had expanded to offer courses for artists; the new building opened in 1886 on the corner of Newbury and Exeter Streets); and the Boston Public Library was begun on Copley Square in 1887. The School of the Museum of Fine Arts had opened next to the museum in 1877, and the Cowles School of Art (1882) had just opened on Dartmouth Street. Painting or modeling in clay was an accepted social accomplishment as well as a way of making a living. Many Bostonians of old and respected Brahmin families, as well as the general population in Boston and other parts of the country, accepted the principle that art in general, and painting in particular, was an acceptable pursuit for a young man or woman. The "Athens of America" was in an unprecedented period of building, including great public buildings, and many of those erected in the area of Copley Square in the period when Burpee entered Boston housed galleries for art exhibitions or classrooms for teaching art.

The Back Bay, as well as Beacon Hill and the South End, was filled with artists' studios. Indeed, today, walking through these areas of Boston one has only to glance up at the north sides of buildings to see the tall studio windows of ateliers of the past. Large buildings were built incorporating studios as a major part of their rental space, and many private houses had upper floor studios either for rent or for the artist in the household. The larger edifices included the Harcourt Studios, the Studio Building, St. Botolph Studios, the S.S. Pierce Building, and the Grundmann Studios (named after the first artist-director of the School of the Museum of Fine Arts), adjacent to the Museum of Fine Arts and Trinity Church. The latter was the site of the meetings of the Boston Art Students Association, which gave an annual festival in Grundmann Hall; and the square was the site of the Artists' Ball.

The Boston Art Club was not the only artists' society in the Back Bay; there was the St. Botolph Club (1880), known for its sophistication, innovation, and exclusivity; the Paint and Clay Club, which attracted many of

BOSTON ART CLUB, c. 1883.

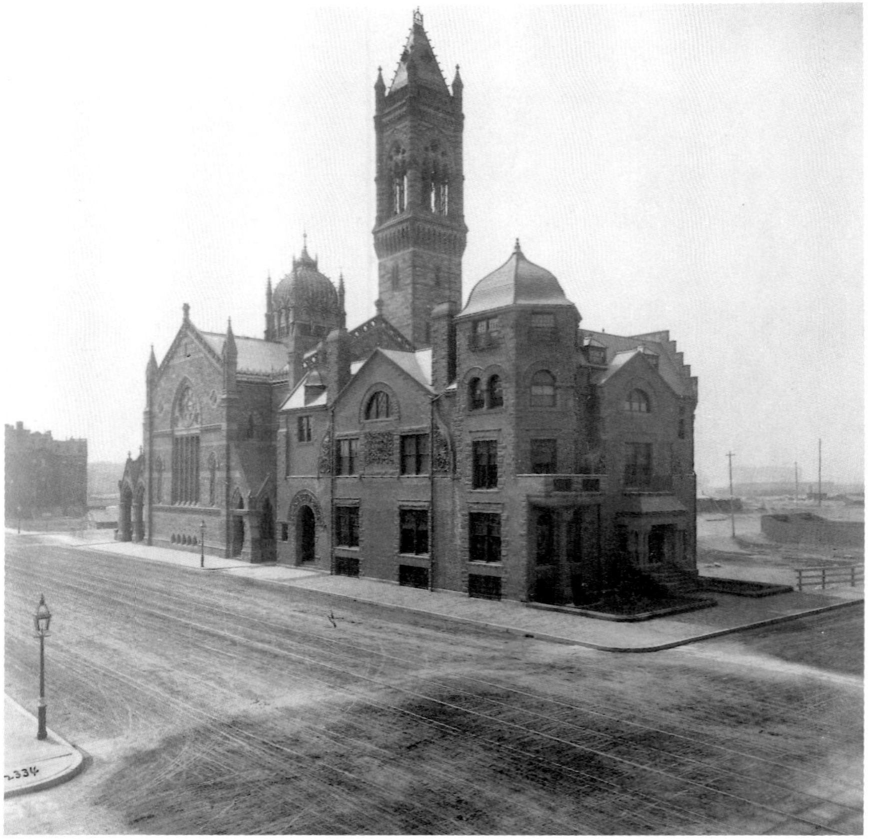

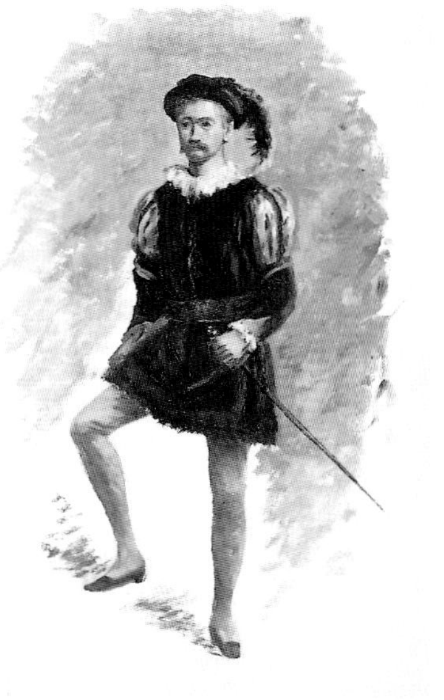

COSTUMED MALE FIGURE, 1887.

Oil on canvas, 17 1/2 x 12 1/8 inches.
This study, done on February 15, 1887, represents one of the last of a year of such studies made at the Boston Art Club.

the younger artists; and the Boston Society of Watercolor Painters (1888). The Boston Art Students Association (1879) was originally formed by alumni of the museum school, but in 1891 it opened its membership and in 1901 changed its name to the Copley Society. The Association of Boston Artists (1880) aided its artist members in selling paintings; in addition, the New England Manufacturers' and Mechanics' Institute (1879) ran annual fairs during the 1880s and 1890s with an ambitious art department.

Burpee began to take classes at the Boston Art Club, first doing costume and figure studies from life in oil between May 1886 and April 1887, and later, in 1891 and 1892, regularly attending the every-other Friday life classes where he learned to produce creditable academic male nude drawings in charcoal.

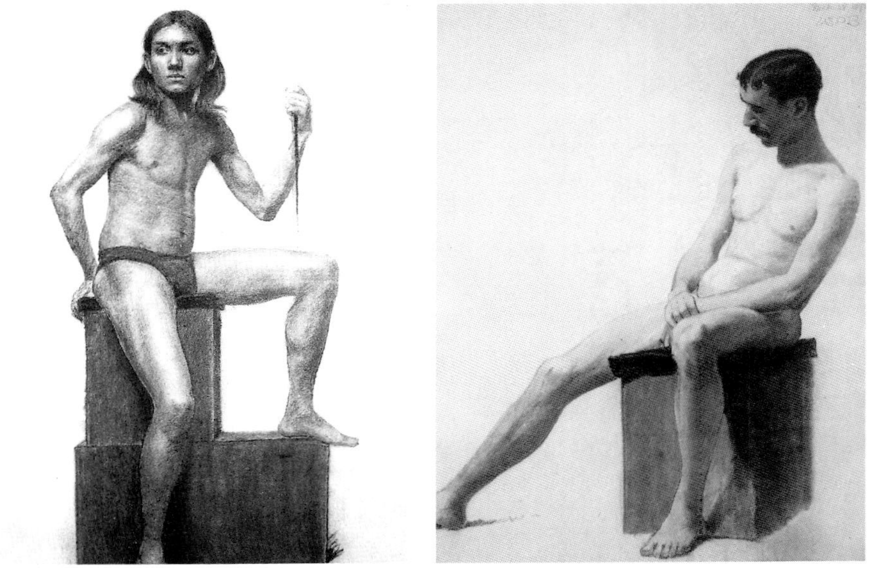

TWO FIGURE STUDIES, 1892.

Each charcoal on paper, 24 1/2 x 19 inches.

The Boston Art Club, the oldest art club in Boston, was very active when Burpee began to attend classes and seek out the other artists associated with them. By 1881 the club had more than 800 members, although only 100 were artists. In the new clubhouse they instituted a regular series of exhibitions including semiannual exhibitions of the work of members and other contemporary artists. The first, usually in January, was dedicated to oil painting, and the second, normally in April, was devoted to watercolor and pastel. In addition there were many special exhibitions that showcased either a single painter or a group of artists. The clubhouse was a site for exhibitions of work by other art organizations as well, and the Boston Art Club membership generally took the lead in forming committees to send art to exhibitions and fairs in other cities.

On the Beaches at Swampscott and Lynn

It was almost certainly at functions at the Boston Art Club that Burpee met painters with similar interests in landscape and seascape: Charles Woodbury (1864 – 1940), C. E. L. Green (1844 – 1915), E. A. Page (1850 – 1928), Thomas Clarkson Oliver (1827 – 1892), Edward Burrill (b. 1835), Nathaniel L. Berry (b. 1859), Ross Turner (1847 – 1915), George Wasson (1855 – 1932), Hendricks Hallett (1847 – 1921), Walter L. Dean (1854 – 1912), and John J. Enneking (1841 – 1916). Woodbury, Green, Page, Oliver, Burrill and Berry all had connections to Lynn or Swampscott, Massachusetts, by birth, residence, or marriage (as had Burpee's mentor, Bradford).[4]

With its easy rail access to Boston and its striking coastline with wide beaches and granite bounded points, the coast at Lynn and Swampscott attracted Burpee. His earliest dated, documented painting in the Boston area is *View of Nahant Bay and Egg Rock from Lynn Beach*, dated September 1, 1885, and with the notation that the oil study took the artist two and one-half hours. The painting included most of the salient features that were to be the elements in Burpee's beach paintings during the next decade: a working fisherman, the local dories (both at sea and beached), and the wide beaches. It is difficult to find comparable beach paintings by the other Lynn artists that date with certainty to as early as 1885, which suggests that Burpee may have led or at least influenced the other painters in their eventual choice of the beach, dories, working fisher families, and the fishhouses as subjects for their work.[5] From Nahant and Lynn in the south to Marblehead and Salem in the north and the rocks and beaches of Gloucester and Cape Ann, Burpee painted the life of the sailors, dorymen, the fishermen and wives and children, clamdiggers, netmenders, and lobstermen at the edge of the sea.

The focus of Burpee's studies in paint was the series of broad beaches which were nearly adjacent — Short Beach at Nahant, Lynn Beach, and Fisherman's Beach (including King's and Blaney beaches) at Swampscott. Burpee certainly gravitated here because of his affinity for the subject, but for two other reasons as well. By 1880 three railroads made regular connections between Boston, where Burpee lived, and stopped only blocks from the beaches in Lynn and Swampscott that he would choose to paint; and Burpee had begun to associate with a group of painters who were working on Boston's North Shore from Revere Beach in the south to Marblehead in the north and most of whom traveled to Cape Ann and

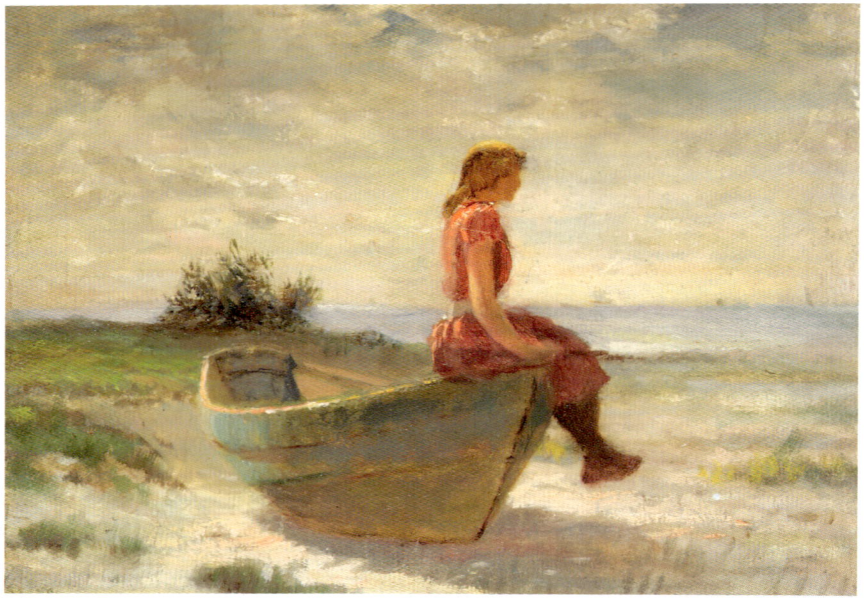

left

FISHERMAN'S DAUGHTER, c.1892.

Oil on paper mounted on panel, 12 3/4 x 9 inches.
Burpee captured the emotional quality, much as Homer did before him, of the hopes and fears of the fisherman's family.

opposite

DORIES ON LYNN BEACH, early 1890s.

Oil on paper mounted on canvas, 11 3/8 x 16 inches.
Burpee utilized the oatmeal color and texture of the paper for tonal effect in this atmospheric study of returning fishermen.

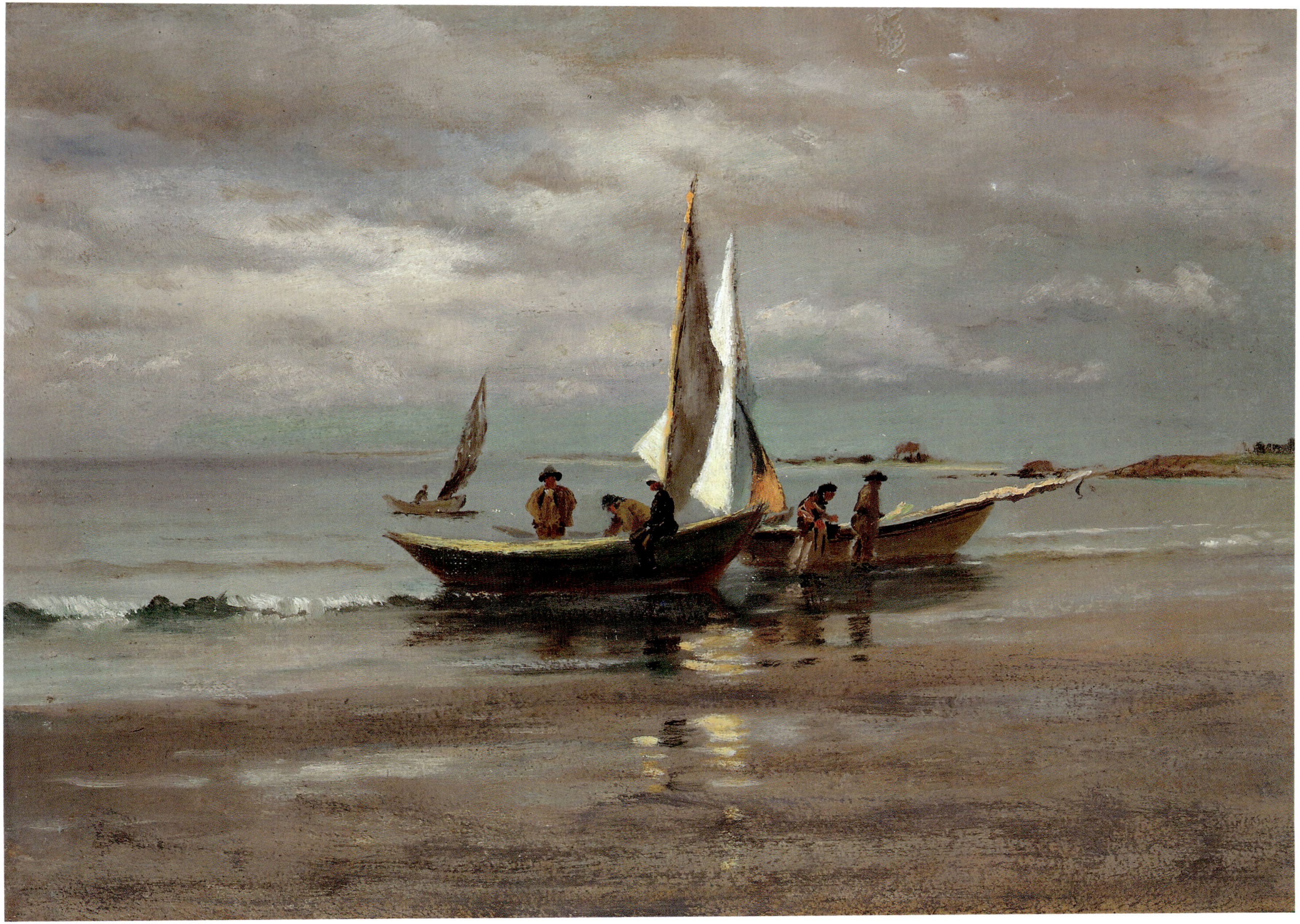

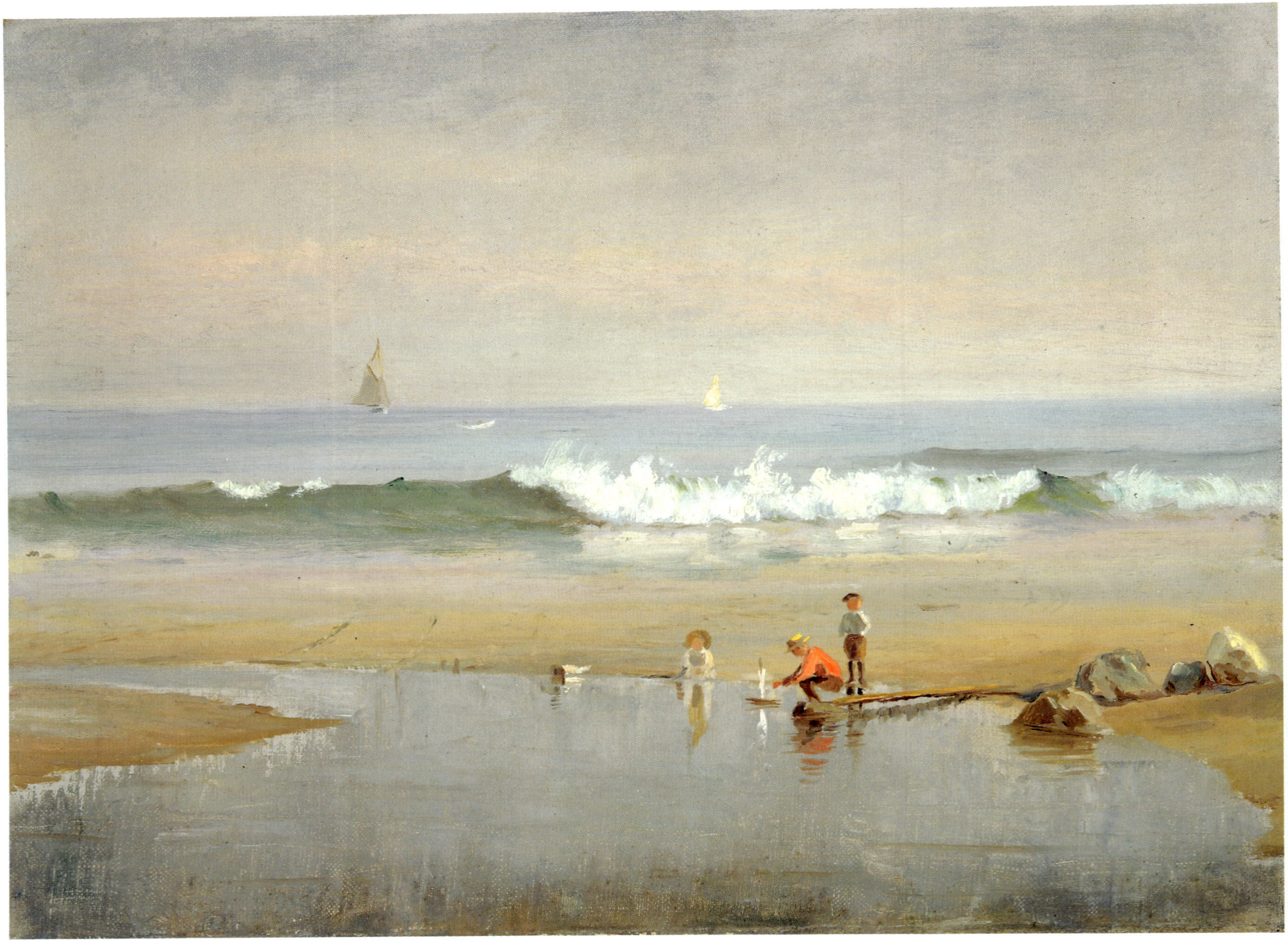

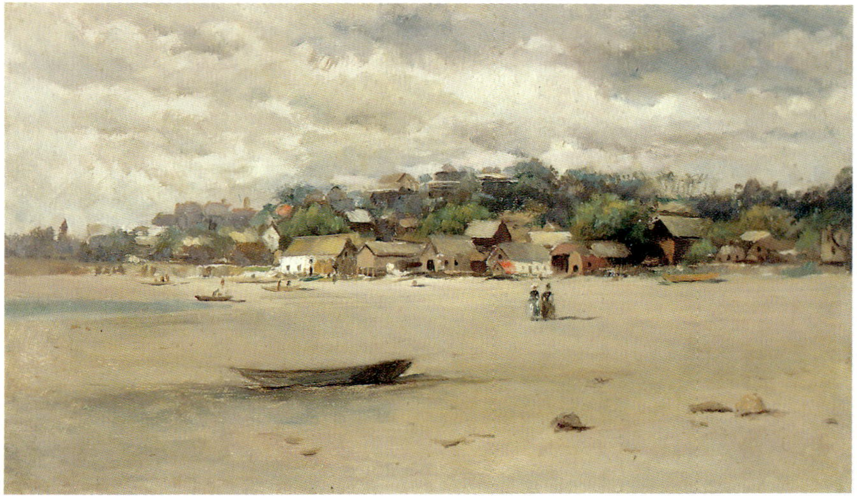

Gloucester in search of additional littoral subjects. A striking comparison can be made between Burpee's *Shore View, Swampscott*, c. 1888 and Woodbury's *Shore View, Swampscott – Lynn*, 1888 as well as other works by Burpee and the works of these North Shore painters. Here he found endless opportunity to describe weather, time of day, and water and sky effects in paint. They all centered their work on the beaches of Lynn and Swampscott and were exhibiting regularly at the Boston Art Club. This situation gave him easy access to his chosen subject and proximity to other painters equally taken with the beauty and the possibilities of painting these great stretches of sand bordered by granite outcroppings and teeming with active working families making their living from the sea.

The dories and dorymen were unique to these beaches, where a few designers had refined traditional dories to add sails, centerboards, and manageability to match the fishermen's needs to the site of the broad sand beach. A word is perhaps necessary to add some understanding of Burpee's fascination with the Swampscott/Marblehead dory. The particular design in

above

SHORE VIEW, SWAMPSCOTT, c. 1888.

Oil on canvas, 10 1/8 x 17 inches.
Charles Woodbury and others of the North Shore painters were addressing this subject at precisely the same time that Burpee painted this picture. From the collection of the William A. Farnsworth Library and Art Museum, Rockland, Maine.

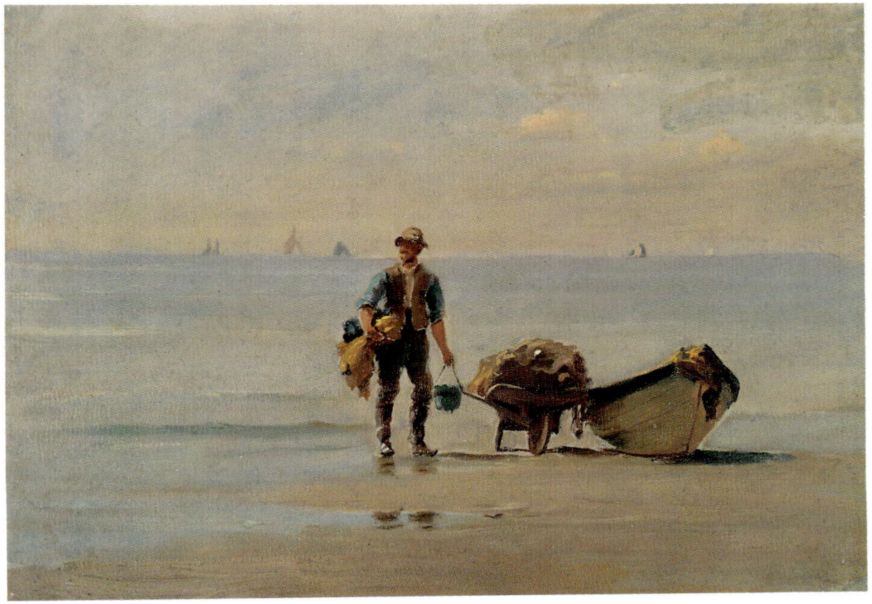

right

THE FISHERMAN'S RETURN, c. 1895.

Oil on paper mounted on panel, 7 1/2 x 11 inches.

opposite

SAILING IN A TIDAL POOL, c. 1892.

Oil on canvas, 11 x 15 inches.
Children at the shore were a major focus of Burpee's art for nearly two decades.

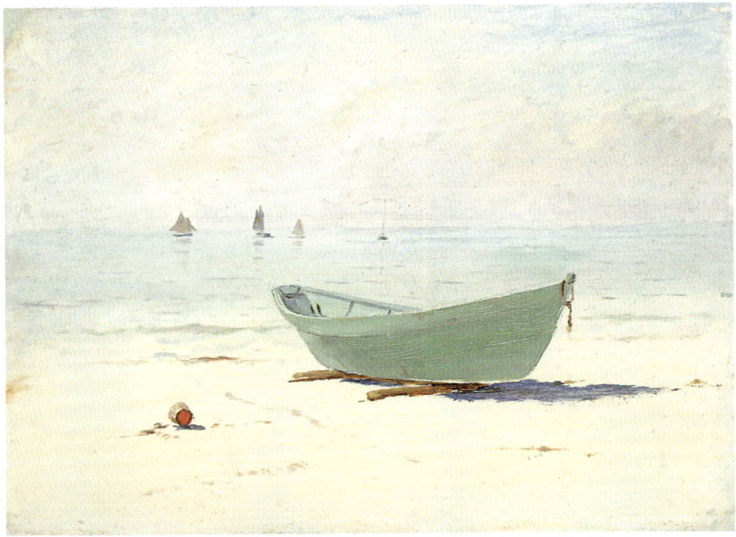

use in the 1880s had been developed on Boston's North Shore in the prior half-century. The boat was used as a lifeboat and tender on larger vessels and as a seaworthy oceangoing fishing vessel in its own right on the coasts where it was built.[6] Sails were added to save rowing home the catch, and centerboards were added for stability. But the configuration of a flat-sided, flat-bottomed affair with a narrow stern remained. The designer-builders became local legends — Emmons and Small in Swampscott and Chamberlain in Marblehead — and local boys took to racing them, especially during summers at Nahant. Whether sailing at sea or beached, they were picturesque and caught the artist's eye; and Burpee painted them, along with the life of the beach, for over a decade.

What effect artists outside this little group of Lynn Beach painters had on Burpee in the 1880s is unclear, but Winslow Homer had been addressing similar subjects in the 1870s and 1880s in Gloucester and was well-known as an exhibitor in Boston as well as being personally known to many of the artists in Burpee's circle at the Boston Art Club; and the visual similarity of Homer's work to Burpee's through the 1890s suggests an influence. Homer's *Green Dory* (1880) (Museum of Fine Arts, Boston) compared to Burpee's *Green Dory* (c. 1891), and Homer's *Prout's Neck, Mackerel Fleet at Sunset* (1884) (Museum of Fine Arts, Boston) compared to Burpee's *Coastal Sunset* (c.1905) (p.65) make clear a relationship between the two painters in subject, style, and palette. Similarly, Eugene Boudin, the French painter of the beach and coast at Trouville, may have been known to Burpee through collections in Boston,[7] and would certainly have been known to him through the one-man exhibition at J. Eastman Chase's Gallery in Boston in May 1890.[8] Works by Boudin's contemporary, Emile Louis Vernier (1829 –1887) seem even more relevant. There is strong evidence that Vernier's paintings were known to Boston dealers and collectors in the last quarter of the 19th century.[9] Boudin and Vernier had both had paintings exhibited in the 1883 Foreign Exhibition in Boston. Like Burpee and his Lynn Beach colleagues, Vernier addressed the subject of the working fisherfolk on French beaches; whereas Boudin confined his beach paintings exclusively to the bathing "swells" on an outing to the seaside.

In addition, in the same period A. T. Bricher, F. A. Silva, and William Trost Richards were painting on the New England coast and exhibiting and selling their works in Boston. These latter-day Luminists, with their paler light of the shore, may have influenced Burpee in some of his lighter palette paintings such as *The Lincoln House, Swampscott.* Burpee

left

THE GREEN DORY, c.1891.

Oil on paper mounted on panel, 9 5/8 x 12 5/8 inches.
The Green Dory is probably closely related to Burpee's *Swampscott Dory* which he exhibited in 1892.

opposite

THE LINCOLN HOUSE, SWAMPSCOTT, c.1892.

Oil on canvas, 11 x 16 inches.
The closely held tonal values in this painting of a popular summer resort hotel compare to coastal views by F.A. Silva and A.T. Bricher.

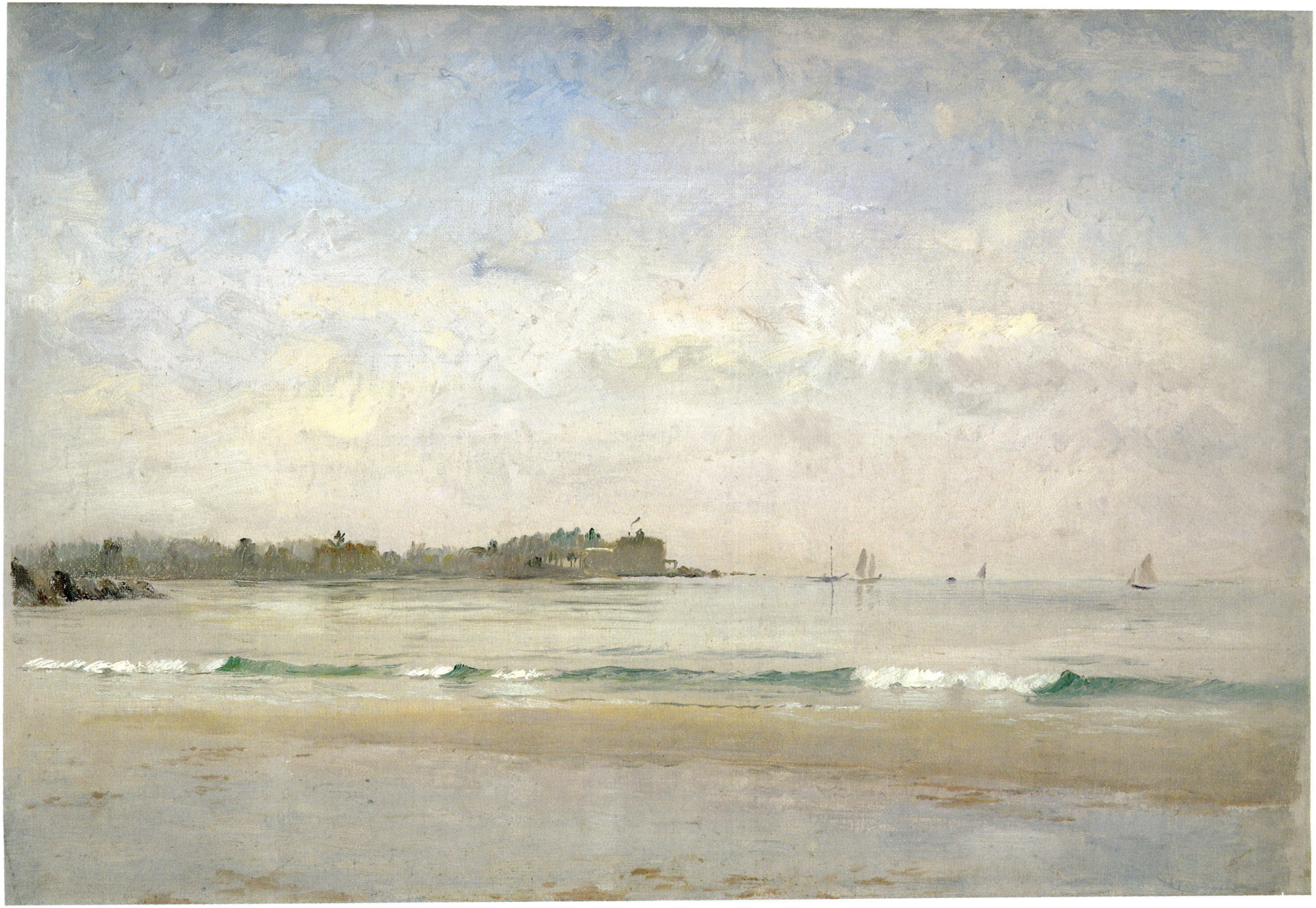

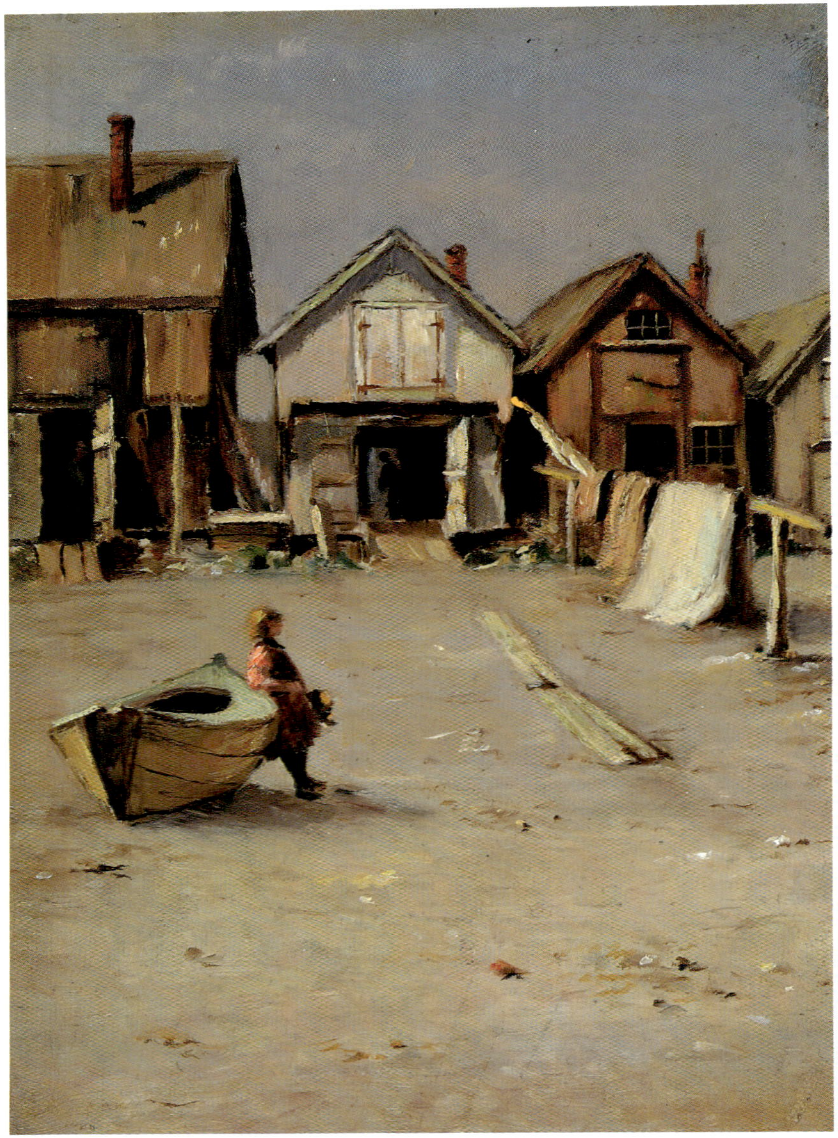

was clearly experimenting in tonal and close value effects and introduced his interest in Tonalism and nocturnes in that beach painting and in his watercolors, *Moonrise by the Sea* and *A Sunset Study*, which he exhibited at the Boston Art Club. By 1892 he certainly knew Arthur Wesley Dow (1857 – 1922), who was beginning to develop his own theories about color, tone, and composition from his hometown of Ipswich, Massachusetts and his studio in Boston.[10]

Impressionism in Boston

Burpee's growing interest in light effect and close value study may have resulted partly from his increasing knowledge of the work of Claude Monet. Monet's work became known in Boston shortly after Burpee's arrival there. There were three works by Monet (*Custom House Station, Dieppe* ; *My Garden* ; and *Tide at Varengeville*) shown in 1883 in Boston in the Foreign Exhibition; at least one Monet was owned in Boston by 1889;[11] and in 1892 the St. Botolph Club presented the first noncommercial exhibition of Monet's paintings up to that time. Of all the Impressionists, American or French, over the next 20 years, Monet's style of painting in oil would be the most influential on Burpee's oil painting technique and method of viewing light effects on ordinary landscape. Monet's influence is not surprising; his increasing popularity in the next decades among Americans in general and Bostonians in particular, to the exclusion of many of the other Impressionists, may have been a result of the American artists' and patrons' predilection for pure landscape. This tradition of patronage reached back to the early Hudson River School. Burpee had naturally developed in America's plein-air tradition; and the growing admiration of his fellow Americans for Monet's pure landscapes would have led Burpee to find in Monet a model for the direction of his painting for the rest of his career.[12]

Impressionism underwent a critical change from the late 1880s to the 1890s in Boston. At first the paintings of the so-called "impressionists" were derided by some of the critics. By the mid-1890s the term had become an accolade. The view of Boston Impressionism at this point might be best described by the French critic S.C. de Soissons, who wrote a small book on Boston artists in 1894. In it he wrote:"Here began the artistic careers of such painters as Inness, Hassam, Grant, Sprague, Pierce, Wright, Metcalf, Davis, Thomas W. Dewing, etc... " He explained the origins of Impressionism in France:

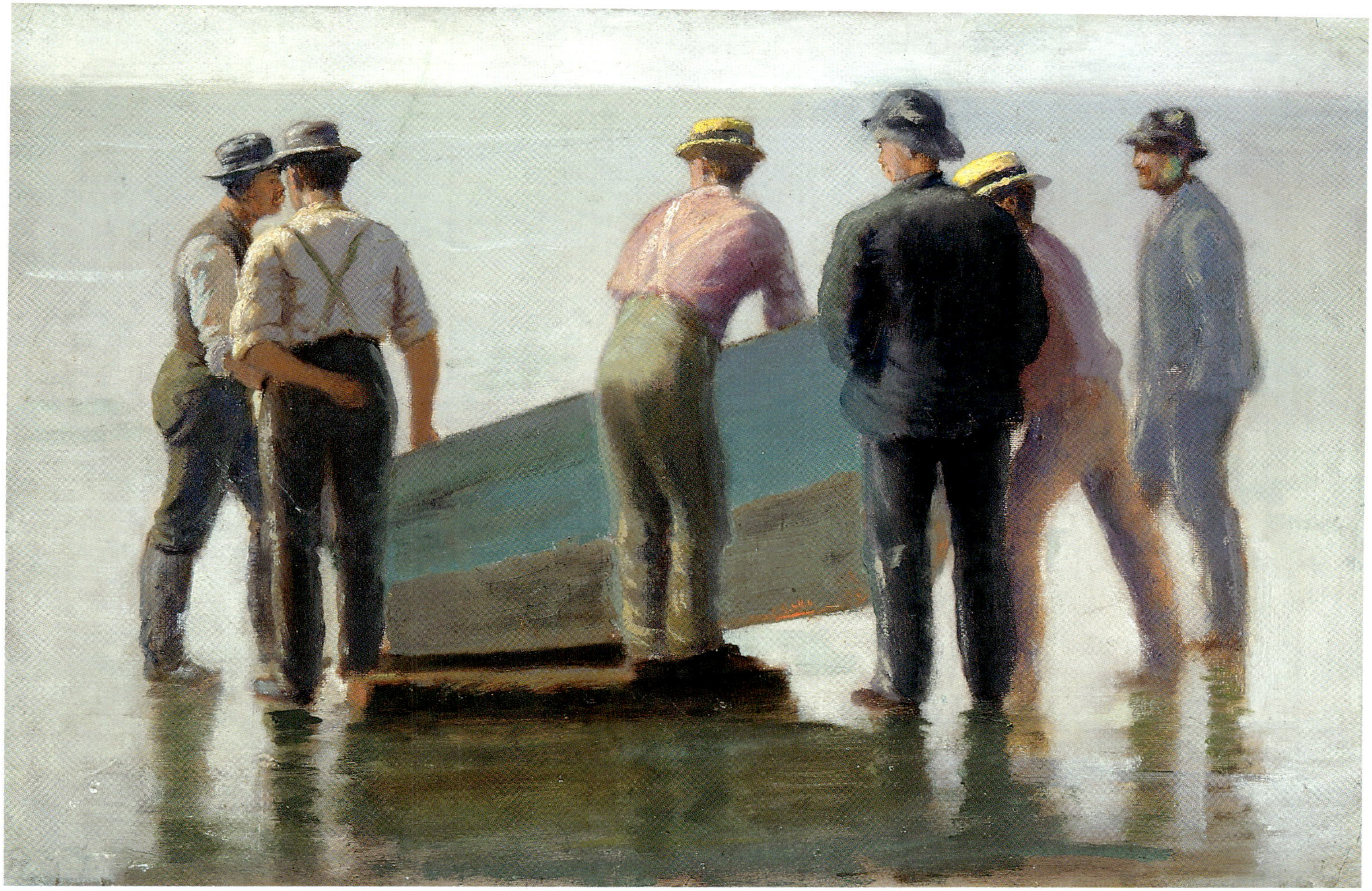

opposite, left

FISH HOUSES, KING'S BEACH, SWAMPSCOTT, c.1888.

Oil on canvas, 9 1/4 x 7 inches.
In 1888, C.H. Woodbury painted nearly identical studies of fish houses on the Swampscott beaches.

above

MY FRIENDS AT SWAMPSCOTT, c. 1892.

Oil on paper mounted on canvas, 12 x 18 1/2 inches.
While typical of Burpee's subject interest of this period, the scale of the figures in this work are much larger than usual.

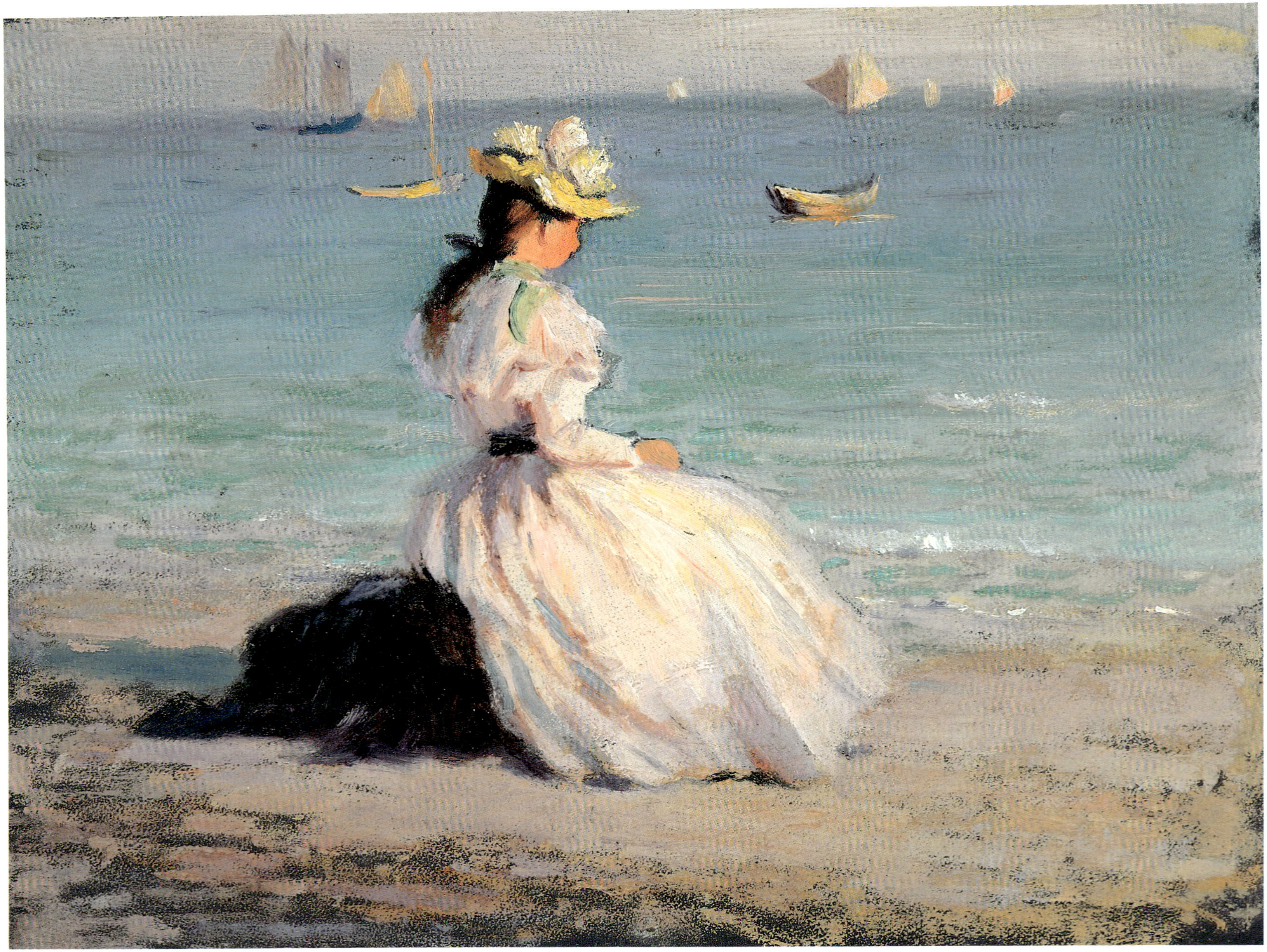

Then rose up Claude Monet, who remembered the rule of Leonardo da Vinci, "One color is light, two colors tone, three colors mud," and started to paint with pure colors, but in such a way that he does not mix them, but lays them beside one another, slightly blended together, and so he produces sunny, bright, brilliant, and rich pictures. His method is adopted by such painters as Sisley, Pissarro, and many others.

So was originated the school called impressionistic — why, no one knows.

Speaking about this school or direction, there is no need of saying that impressionism does not mean anything new, that every artist is an impressionist, because he paints his impressions, etc. It is necessary to state that by impressionism we understand the direction of painting which eliminates the use of black and bitumen, which executes pictures with pure colors not mixed together, but laid down one beside another, and which tries to fix the subject upon the canvas as it is seen by the artist as a certain moment in a certain light, if possible, as soon as the artist sees it, or, if afterwards, always after the impression received at the moment when he decided to paint a picture. The superiority of painting executed after the impressionistic idea is clear. The coloring is richer, livelier, and more brilliant, and the consistency of it is stronger, because it is known that bitumen and black are not of long duration and eventually turn black, so the pictures painted with them are darkened from year to year, until finally many of them are hardly recognized as masterpieces of a few years ago.[13]

SUMMER AT THE BEACH, c.1895.

Oil on paper mounted on panel, 9 x 11 5/8 inches.
Burpee's Impressionism asserts itself in this figure painting and relates not only to Monet's painting, but to work by his Boston colleagues Benson, Tarbell, and Hale who were committed figure painters.

Increasingly over the next decade, Burpee joined the movement in Boston and in Europe that both French and Americans now called Impressionism, and he learned from observing paintings made by both French and Boston artists. To a large extent he practiced the simple principles set forth by de Soissons. By the late 1890s, Burpee identified himself as an Impressionist.[14]

A Professional Artist

It was during this time of tremendous opportunities for expression of and exposure to new ideas that his father died on December 11, 1887. Burpee was now 41 years old. He was, according to family tradition, still working as a bookkeeper, but was investing much of his time in his art. He had lived a modest lifestyle that would continue up to his death, and he had saved his money. His father left him a one-eighth part of the Burpee Block on Main Street in Rockland, together with a share of the N.A. and S.H. Burpee furniture business. The income from the legacy together with his own savings and the final impossibility of disapprobation from his father led W.P. Burpee to list himself the next year (1888) for the first time as "artist" in the Boston City Directory. He maintained a position in bookkeeping and accounting up to the point of his departure for Europe in 1897, but from 1888 on he seems to have identified himself primarily as a painter.

In 1889, Burpee took his first separate studio in the S.S. Pierce building just off Copley Square. The next year he moved to the nearby studios at 135 Huntington Avenue, where Joseph DeCamp also had his studio. In 1892, Arthur W. Dow and Theodore Wendel also moved into studios at 135 Huntington. It is clear from later correspondence that Burpee met and became friends with many of his fellow artists who had studios in the same buildings that he occupied. DeCamp later painted his portrait (p.3) about 1903, which he probably gave to Burpee or exchanged for a painting. Burpee moved into the Harcourt Building at 23 Irvington Street in 1893.

building, with more than 30 studios, also housed Frank W. Benson, Edmond Tarbell, F. H. Richardson, Helen Mary Knowlton, W. W. Churchill, Laura Lee, F. D. Williams, and Jacob Wagner. The latter clearly became a friend of Burpee's, and Burpee was deeply distressed at Wagner's death in New York in 1898.[15]

In the mid–1890s several of these artists moved to the nearby St. Botolph Studios (Benson, DeCamp, Tarbell), but the proximity of all of these buildings, including the Grundmann Studios (where Dow moved in 1894), made studio visits from artist to artist, the formation of friendships, and the exchange of ideas exceptionally easy in this small community.

In 1890 Burpee exhibited for the first time at the Boston Art Club in the January exhibition of oil paintings; not surprisingly, the subject was *On the Beach at Swampscott,* and the work was well received.[16] In 1892 he followed up by exhibiting *Swampscott Dory* (p. 86) and *On the Saugus Marshes*, and began later in the year to exhibit his watercolors. From then on in the 1890s he exhibited regularly in the Art Club exhibition of oils and consistently in the watercolor exhibition.

Burpee's becoming an artist member of the Boston Art Club in 1894 or 1895 meant that Burpee fit the club's definition of "professional artist" as one "who follows his profession as his principal occupation in life."[17] The Boston Art Club was the most public of the Boston art organizations and became his base for his entire Boston career. The artist members included traditional painters (Nathaniel Berry, Albert Bierstadt, Thomas Hill, A. T. Bricher, Benjamin and J. Wells Champney, Edward L. Weeks, John R. Key, Henry Sandham, Frank Shapleigh, and Edward C. Leavitt), Impressionists (John J. Enneking, Childe Hassam, Henry H. Gallison, Abbott Graves, William J. Kaula, Ernest L. Major, Frank D. Millet, Charles S. Parker, Frank H. Richardson, Robert W. Vonnoh, Charles Copeland, and Charles H. Turner), and marine painters (Walter L. Dean, Hendricks Hallett, William F. Halsall, Melbourne Hardwick, Marshall Johnson, Walter F. Lansil, and William E. Norton). Burpee took part in a club life that included lunches and dinners, entertainments, and opportunities to meet the nonartist members, who included many of Boston's most prominent men in business, the professions, and society. In the next two decades, Burpee took an increasing part in the exhibitions of the club, almost to his last year of membership, 1913.

The list of exhibition subjects he showed at the Boston Art Club encompassed Burpee's interests in painting in the 1890s. In addition to the Swampscott and Saugus paintings, he exhibited works of Marblehead (1893) and Brookline (1894). He may have begun work as a bookkeeper at The Country Club in Brookline as early as 1892. The Brookline subject suggests that he was working there by 1894, and he moved from Boston and gave up his studio in the Harcourt Building to live with George C. Burpee and his wife at 12 Kent Square in Brookline in 1896. He remained living there and working at The Country Club until his trip to Europe in the summer of 1897 ended his career in bookkeeping and accounting. It ended his exhibition schedule for four years as well, since he last exhibited before his departure at the 56th Boston Art Club Exhibition in April 1897.

Whether or not his decision to make a break and go to Europe was occasioned by the difficulties of his job at the prestigious club, it must have been a relief to unburden himself of the position. The club dues never seemed to cover expenses. He stated, "I had hard work when I was there, making out one unsatisfactory report after another, year after year. There was always a good deal of growling and some of it seemed to be on account of the bookkeeping."[18] Resigning relieved him of the strain and added to his enjoyment of the freedom that he would find in travel. After years of working in business, saving and investing his money, both earned and unearned, he could support himself comfortably from capital investments and from his family legacy without needing income from the sale of paintings. And, after years of waiting, he was going to make a European tour.

THE ARTIST'S STUDIO, c.1890.

Oil on canvas mounted on card, 14 3/16 x 11 1/4 inches.
The interior of Burpee's studio, probably at 135 Huntington Avenue, shows a woman standing among the artist's many matted and framed marine studies.

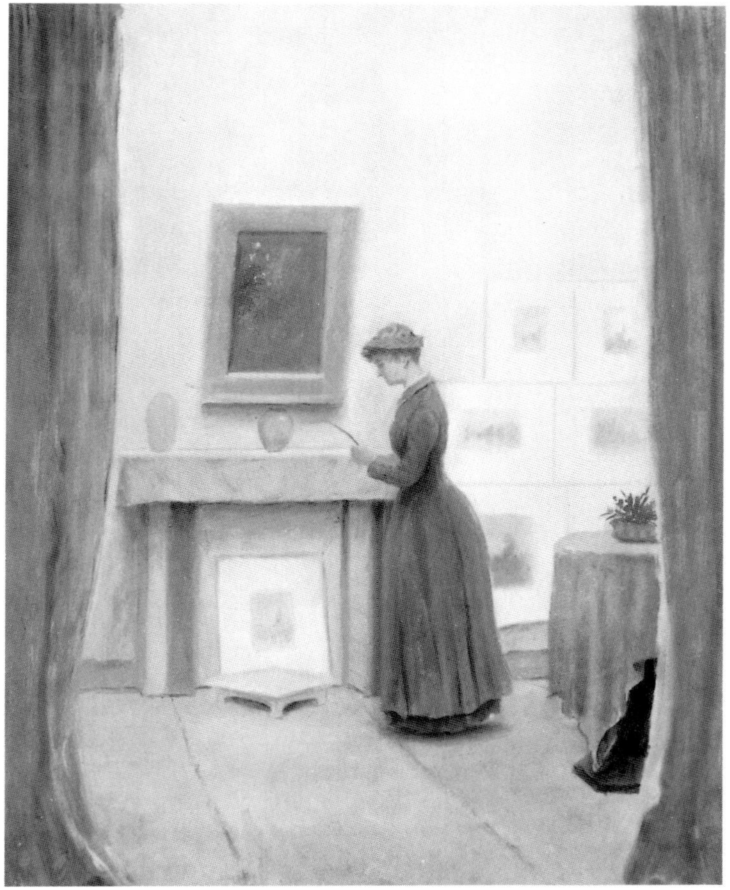

NOTES, Chapter Two

[1] Alpha in *Art Amateur*, vol. 6 (Nov. 1881), p. 115.

[2] Interview between D. Roger Howlett and Margaret Shaw, May 10, 1988, hereinafter referred to as Shaw Interview. Shaw says that Burpee moved to Boston at age 36, which would be confirmed by his appearance for the first time in the Boston City Directory in 1882.

[3] Greta in *Art Amateur*, vol. 5 (July 1881), pp.30 +.

[4] This group of painters seems to have been very friendly with each other as evidenced by a letter in which Charles Woodbury wrote to Ross Turner on Oct. 13, 1886, "Saw [C.E.L.] Green tonight, and we will be over Sunday in accordance with your kind invitation" (Ross Sterling Turner mss. collection, Essex Institute, Salem, Massachusetts), and as reported by Greta in *Art Amateur* , vol. 17, no. 5 (Oct. 1887), p. 93, "C.E.L. Green and Charles Woodbury are painting near Halifax for a month." For a more complete discussion of this neglected group of painters of the shore, see: Frederic A. Sharf and John H. Wright, *Paintings by Essex County Artists, 1865 – 1910* , Essex Institute, Salem, Massachusetts, 1971; Sharf and Wright, *C.E.L. Green : Shore and Landscape Painter of Lynn and Newlyn*, Essex Institute, Salem, Massachusetts, 1980; Joan Loria and Warren A. Seamans, *Earth Sea and Sky—Charles H. Woodbury —Artist and Teacher, 1864 – 1940* (Cambridge, Mass.: The MIT Museum, 1988) (see *Shore View, Swampscott —Lynn*, 1888, illustrated p.65); Paul M. Rowell et al., *Scrap Book,* Lynn Historical Society, Lynn, Massachusetts. This contains clippings of articles on Lynn and Swampscott artists that are often undated and unascribed, but are among the best sources of information on the Lynn and Swampscott painters.

[5] Peter MacLaddie, in "Veteran Artist Recalls City's Cultural Period," article in Paul M. Rowell, Scrap Book, Lynn Historical Society. Despite MacLaddie's comment, "a very prominent art critic made the remark 'Green was the first man to show the Art World the artistic possibilities of the common fishing dory'," there is no evidence that Green treated this subject before his 1888 exhibition of *King's Beach, Swampscott*.

[6] Fred A. Wilson, *Some Annals of Nahant Massachusetts* (Boston, Mass: Old Corner Book Store, 1928) pp.117 – 122.

[7] Cadart, the eminent Paris print dealer, had sold work by Boudin in Boston as early as 1867.

[8] J. Eastman Chase's Gallery, *Boudin*, May, 1890. Copy in Archives of American Art.
Art Department (of Massachusetts Charitable Mechanics Association) Foreign Exhibition, 1883. Boudin showed *Rotterdam*, *Fishing for Shrimps*, and *Marine on the Meuse*.

[9] Childs Gallery, Boston, has bought two separate paintings by Vernier that relate in size, palette, and subject to Burpee from collections that were formed in Boston in the 19th century, and which still bear their 19th-century Boston gallery labels. In addition the 1883 Foreign Exhibition in Boston showed Vernier's *Coast View*.

[10] Frederick C. Moffatt, *Arthur Wesley Dow (1857 – 1922)* (Washington, D. C.: National Collection of Fine Arts, 1977).

[11] Alexandra R. Murphy, "French Paintings in Boston: 1800 – 1900," in *From Corot to Braque: French paintings from the Museum of Fine Arts, Boston* (Boston: the Museum, 1979.)

[12] Frances Weitzenhoffer, "The Earliest American Collectors of Monet," in John Rewald and Frances Weitzenhoffer, *Aspects of Monet* (New York: Harry N. Abrams, 1984.)

[13] S.C. de Soissons, *Boston Artists: A Parisian Critic's Notes* (Boston: n.p., 1894) pp.22, 29–30.

[14] Burpee Correspondence AAA, March 27, 1898, Venice, to Mrs. N. A. Burpee.

[15] Burpee Correspondence AAA, July 3, 1899, London, to Mrs. N. A. Burpee. "Jacob Wagner, Artist," *Boston Transcript*, Nov. 7, 1898 .

[16] The Archives of American Art microfilmed a catalogue at the Museum of Fine Arts, Boston, which belonged to the critic William Howe Downes and in which there is a pencil notation (probably by Downes) next to this entry: "good."

[17] Boston Art Club, Constitution, Bylaws and list of members, 1913 et al. Burpee is listed in the Blue Book of Boston as a member of the club first in 1895, but he may have been admitted in 1894 after that year's book was compiled. His membership continued unbroken through 1913.

[18] Burpee Correspondence AAA, Jan. 5, 1899, Capri, to Mrs. N. A. Burpee.

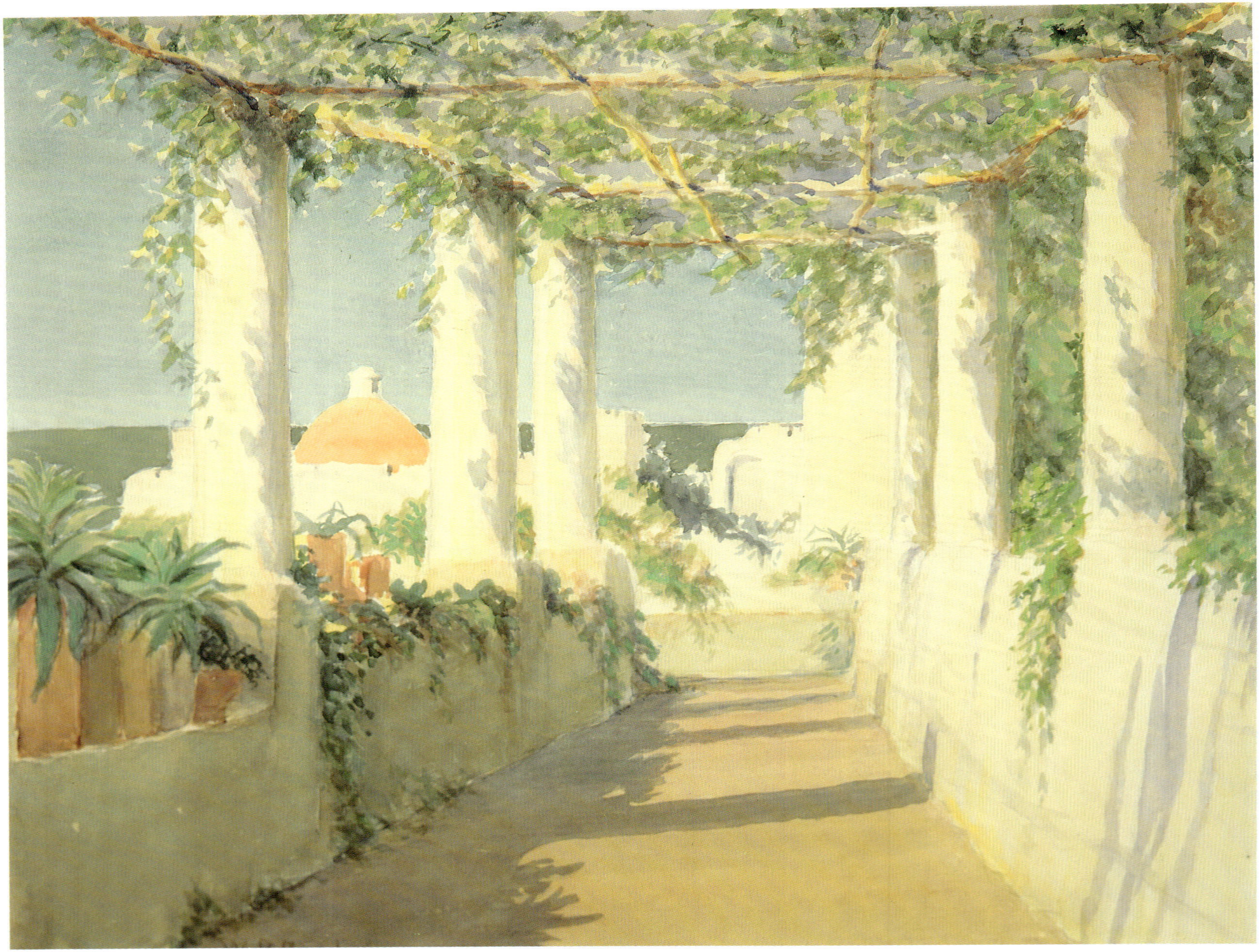

CHAPTER THREE

The Beautiful, The Grand, The Historic Past: Cycling Through Europe (1897 – 1899 & 1900)

In the middle of 1897, Burpee resigned his position as bookkeeper at The Country Club in Brookline, closed his studio, visited his family in Maine, and booked passage on the North German Lloyd's steamer *Werra* from Hoboken, New Jersey, to Gibraltar with the intention of bicycling through Europe. When he departed on October 23, he was 51 years old and had dreamed of visiting the sights and museums of Europe all his life. Most of his artist friends and colleagues of the Boston Art Club had preceded him there, some by many years. After he arrived and began to travel he wrote that it "has equaled my anticipation, and this is much, for my anticipation had been augmented by years of waiting. I have been too much employed in sightseeing to paint, but have made some little souvenir sketches and drawings, of no value, perhaps, to any one but myself."[1] The character of the trip seems to have remained, with some exceptions, for his pleasure, expansion, education, and sightseeing more than to settle into painting. He carried a Kodak camera and made photographs that he clearly intended to use in his art, and he recorded at intervals drawings, studies, and watercolors that he was making to record the sights.

He wrote copiously from Europe to maintain contact with his family in Rockland and friends across the United States, and the Archives of American Art preserves more than 325 pages of letters written between October 1897 and July 1899. These give a full picture of a very different grand tour from what most conventional views of the European tours of Americans of the period encompass.

Burpee planned from the outset to travel by bicycle. The modern bicycle, with equal sized wheels, chain, sprockets, and pneumatic tires had been developed and widely marketed in both America and Europe in the decade of the 1890s. Rockland papers were filled with notices of cycle competitions and races as well as the advantages of the bicycle for exercise and transportation, and the *Rockland Courier Gazette* carried a weekly column entitled "Astride the Wheel." Naturally, he sent his trunk on ahead to a stop where he intended to stay awhile and where he could refresh his clothes and other supplies. He did his research, bought Baedeker and Ruskin, and with the "stopover" plan of the steamer lines, sent his disassembled bicycle on to Naples, while he disembarked at Gibraltar on November 1. After two nights on Gibraltar he took a boat for Tangier, where he stayed at the Hotel Bristol. He had plunged himself into the most disparate experience from life in Rockland that he could manage.

PERGOLA, CAPRI, 1898.

Watercolor on paper, 14 x 18 inches.
Burpee made studies, a watercolor and an oil painting of this feature of the houses of Anacapri.

In the evening [I] went to [a] Moorish Cafe and to a house where our party was handsomely entertained by two dancing girls, one of whom, about fourteen years old, was a perfect type of Moorish beauty and posed and danced very gracefully. In the morning to the Moorish market where a motley crowd buy and sell everything made and raised in that country. Snake charmers there were, and veiled women selling all kinds of roots, nuts, and berries and planted goods.

In the PM took the camera and made some exposures of the streets and gateways or archways. Next took a muleback ride to the suburbs where are the Consular residents and some of the finest houses, also the wretched huts where slaves live, the poorest of the earth's poor. It was one of the most interesting experiences of my life — but had to have an end.[2]

Spain

Burpee sailed in a rough passage to Cadiz on November 7, which seemed refreshingly clean and modern to him after Tangier. He went on to Seville, where he stayed at the Hotel de Paris which was "truly a haven of rest, and the jolly table — full of Spaniards, Frenchmen and Americans, with really superb cuisine gave me great delight. The table d'hote of seven courses, was, at first a puzzle for me to negotiate. I got several cooks to get me an English beefsteak instead, and so with soup and fruit made a nice little dinner.[3]

As with tourists in every generation, Burpee discovered that the expenses of traveling can be unexpected and more than anticipated.

Armed with my camera, I strolled through the main streets, taking many views. It was necessary to hire guides through the crooked labyrinth of the cities, and also find certain points of interest hard to discover. The expenses of guides, and gratuities and fees make a goodly sum and amounts to more than one usually counts upon. At some of the hotels there is the head-waiter, then the under-waiters, chamber maid, "boots," concierge or porter, elevator boy and door-keeper. After you get out of the house there is the omnibus driver to remember. You will thus see that one needs plenty in order to really enjoy traveling. [4]

In Seville he went to the cathedral, which was under scaffolding, the Alcazar "full of the most entrancing beauty," the Roman ruins, and the picture gallery where he was especially impressed by the Murillos. He was developing and printing film as he progressed in his travels. In the next two weeks he visited Cordova, Granada, and Rhonda, returning to Gibraltar on Sunday, November 21, for a night's rest before embarking on the *Kaiser Wilhelm II* for Naples.

Italy

Arriving at Naples on November 25, he remarked:

It was just like the pictures I have read about when at last we steamed into the world famous bay, just as the sun was rising to glorify the day and tip the hills and villas with warm glowing light. Farther down it crept until all the city was exceeding fair in its pervading glow and the picturesque boats and boatmen with many colors to enliven the scene made quite a perfect picture in whatever direction you looked. It was some time before the sun got round to illumine the streaked sides of Old Vesuvius with its rosy beams and the smoke issuing from the crater was quite steamy and cloudlike in its character. It seems strange, so white, when I have always seen it described as dark and smoky. It is as white and pure looking as the clouds. Today it had been blowing down the side of the mountain almost as far as the sea (like this [drawing]) and it looks quite absurd as though it was burlesquing a little for us. Yesterday afternoon it was radiant in the glowing sun and the happy-looking bright little villages scattered along its edge laughed at danger.[5]

He went through customs and settled in the Hotel Brittanique and went for his bicycle:

> The annoyance I suffered on account of my bicycle at Naples was unexpected. My card of membership from Paris was sent promptly to meet me on arriving. When I applied for the letter, I was told there was none. I went a second time, but in vain. Then I wrote to Paris. I thought I would make this attempt. So I went again to the same offices and inquired — when the letter was promptly delivered. It had been there a month. I felt like swearing. I was waiting to enter my wheel free by means of the card, and had to pay storage. Armed with my card as a member of the Touring Club of France I went to the Custom House for the bicycle. I was told there was a deposit due of $8.00. I said no, that it should come through free. So they gave me a paper to sign, and I paid for making it out, and I paid for storage, and the bus driver took it to the hotel where I unpacked it and put it in order.[6]

His bicycle was outfitted with a brake and he noted that he needed a license for riding in Italy. Burpee was also very aware of the recent history of the unification of Italy under Garibaldi and Mazzini and noted a house that had been presented to Garibaldi. The hotels, he said, were not yet filled, the season being in the winter, and would not fill until January. He had met Mr. and Mrs. Anson Mills from Woodstock, Vermont on the *Kaiser Wilhelm II* ; they were also planning a cycling tour, and Burpee now joined them.

> I got my bicycle from the Custom House, where it was stored while I was in Spain, and today being fine, tried it for a fine spin along the Corso Vittorio Emmanuale [where the Hotel Britannique is situated, and rode with Mr. Mills] down hill through the long tunnel at Posilippo, and away toward the seashore at Cumae, and by the main road which skirts the rocky, precipitous coast, which presents some very grand scenery. This afternoon the surf ran high, and the sun just setting glorified it with light and gilded the heights and made the pink and yellow and white buildings resplendent. It was perhaps the most beautiful ride I ever had.
>
> I entered my wheel here as I became a member of the "Touring Club de France." I am wearing the badge which came with my card and letter. There is also a book called the Annual which every member gets. I have met some Americans in the forwarding office who ride, and they have been most unusually kind in loaning us maps, telling us about all the roads and the best way to manage on a tour. Mr. Mills bought a couple of maps and books to go with them published by a "Union" at Turin, which shows routes from Naples to Rome, and also the routes in northern Italy all about Milan, Turin, Genoa and Venice, and also the Italian side of the Alps, and we have had quite a good deal of amusement in puzzling out the Italian words. In fact we have understood it pretty well. The Millses have Dayton wheels, enamelled red brown, very nice machines, 1897 make. We are planning our trip to Sorrento, Capri, Amalfi, Salerno and Cava. They have visited Pompeii, but I have it in prospect. We intend to leave tomorrow for Sorrento, and will take our wheels for the road along the coast is magnificent, and the scenery of surpassing beauty.
>
> The Museum was visited last week, and there we saw the interesting frescoes from Pompeii and Herculaneum, as well as the marbles and vases. Sunday we went up by the funicular railway to the top of the hill just back of the hotel where is the town of Vomero, and the castle and convent of San Martino. Then we looked through the rooms of the museum, at the paintings and relics, and then went to the window balconies from which we had a splendid view of the bay, Naples, Sorrento, Capri, Ischia, and the great city below. Naples has to have a million inhabitants, and the streets, so narrow and crowded with people, are full of most picturesque sights. We make almost daily visits to the sea and never tire of watching the fishermen and their boats. Every day,

> almost, there is the arrival of some big steamer, now a Lloyd or Hamburg American from New York or the north bound for Egypt, and now a steamer going to N.Y., Sicily, or Algiers or Malta.[7]

Later that day, Burpee continued:

> I haven't time to see all the many things I want to see about here, because I am determined not to overdo the thing. It is not like a world's fair. All these things have historic interest, and I feel that I would like to devote say a week to one room full of things in gallery or museum, and I am only stopping here for two short weeks.[8]

After Naples, Burpee and the Millses explored Pompeii, Herculaneum, and the towns of the Amalfi coast and embarked from Sorrento for Capri and the Blue Grotto. They settled into the Hotel Pagano where he met his first artist, a Russian. While the Millses explored the castles and ruins on the heights, Burpee went down to the port to begin to paint the subjects he loved best: "When the North Wind blows I go down to the little beach in the south where there are sheltered spots, and sit down to paint the fishing boats and quaint houses and bright colored sea."[9]

He spent Christmas at Capri and returned to Naples to depart by cycle for Rome on the last day of 1897, and after a difficult trip reached Rome and settled into the Pension Marley, "where we are quite 'en famille' with a pleasant hostess and a number of Americans, some of whom hail from Boston, and where we form a very happy community. After each morning and afternoon kind inquiries go the round 'Where have you been this morning?' etc. and we compare notes and tell of things one must see before he leaves Rome. The city is little as I expected it to be, in fact it is very hard to form a conception of such a jumbled-up place, new and old side by side and sometimes one built on top of the other."[10]

Burpee was fascinated by the pace of life in modern Rome and by the profusion of wonders to be seen there:

> Next day was Sunday, and we hurried to the Vatican where we saw the beautiful statuary of which you have seen the pictures. Only the statuary and wall paintings were to be seen for they have a way of locking up whatever doors they choose, and doling out to you piecemeal for the small sum of one franc such views as they think best. In the afternoon Mr. Mills and I went on an excursion awheel through several of the streets and out of the gate to the park of the Borghese Villa or palace. The next day we all went to the Sistine Chapel , to view the Raphael pictures in the room named after him; also the Loggia and got a first view of Michelangelo's frescos in the chapel itself, and a glimpse of the interior of "San Pietro." St. Peter's appears to disappoint almost everyone by its outside architecture, but within it is simply perfect, so rich, so beautiful, nothing overdone, nothing tawdry, but in perfect architectural taste, with all its immensity of space, its magnificent chapels, its grand altar and wonderful arches. . . .

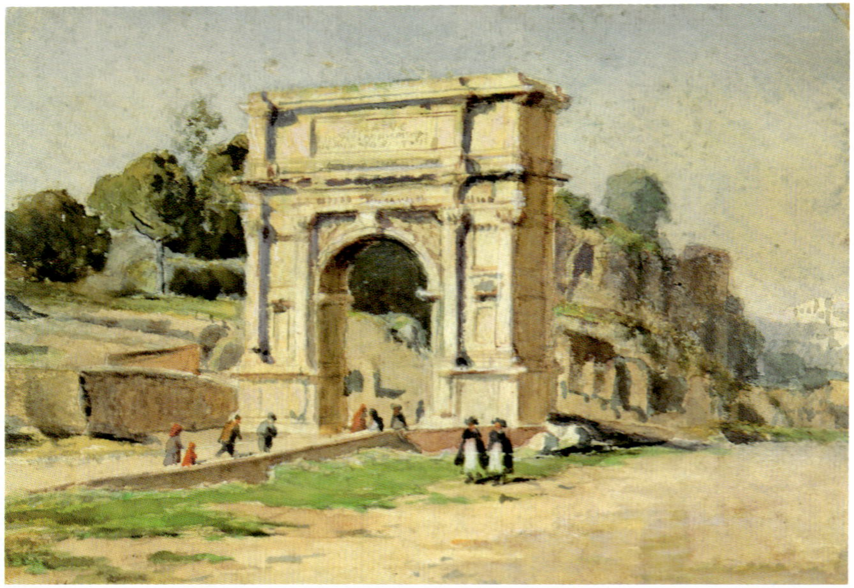

ARCH OF TITUS, ROME, 1898.

Watercolor, 6 1/4 x 9 1/8 inches.

> We have visited a few of the most important of Rome's 365 churches. The most beautiful are St. John in the Lateran, Santa Croce in Gerusalamme, San Maggiore, St. Paul outside the wall and San Lorenzo.
>
> We have yet to see the last two. They all abound in celebrated paintings and relics. The Croce has the most of the latter including the biggest piece of the true cross. At Della Nunti the nuns sing. At Arichaeli there is the old dungeon where Peter was imprisoned, also the pillar to which he was chained. I was glad to escape from the terrible place. These old underground rooms are never ventilated, and as you enter when the sacristan has unlocked the door, you breathe an atmosphere that, to use a vulgar expression is enough almost "to knock you down." For this reason I have avoided the catacombs, and, on account of the danger of a chill I have failed to see the damp Colosseum by moonlight.[11]

He went to the Colosseum, the Forum and out to see the tombs along the Via Appia and the Campagna. He remarked:

> Pictures of the Campagna are out of style, and the artists nowadays, paint always something else. The Italian models who used to throng the steps of the "Trinita", go elsewhere, and only a few of these picturesque costumes are seen there now.
>
> The arches are a source of great pleasure as we view them at morning or noon or in the evening glow and after twilight. That of Constantine with its three portals is most admired. But, the arch of Titus is also very beautiful.

He noted, "We find the English travellers like to be let alone. They keep to themselves, and read books and show themselves unsocial towards Americans. Still I would say they are polite when one addresses them or pulls them out of their moods." [12]

In early February the party left Rome for Florence by bicycle, passing through Civita Castellane, Narni, Terni, Spoleto, Assisi, and Perugia, where Burpee wrote, "I particularly enjoyed the study of the paintings in the Pinacoteca showing religious work of the 4th century and down to the time of Perugino and his school. I passed the house where this artist lived."[13] He arrived in Florence about February 7 for a three week stay. Armed, as generations since have been, with Baedeker and Ruskin, he confronted the trials and treasures of Florence.

> [We arrived in] this lovely City on the Arno where we are now spending the beautiful February days in its Galleries and churches or rambling about and through its narrow streets. I am simply overwhelmed with the splendid privileges which the art student finds here, and wish I might live here. But there is my plan to see all these different countries, and I am somewhat "torn in my mind" as Dr. Hale says, to decide just what is best. For my soul's good I want to travel. For the Good of Art I want to stay in Florence and Venice and Paris and paint.
>
> I have already visited the "Uffizi," "Pitti," and "Museo" and Santa Croce, Duomo, and Maria Novella. Tomorrow, Sunday, I am going to the "Pitti" and "Uffizi" for the second view. The river by morning and evening light has been very beautiful, and if it were warmer, out of doors I could certainly make some pictures. February is half gone and when March comes in I look for a chance to sketch.
>
> I have seen hundreds of charming "Motifs" since my arrival in Italy, but I cannot paint out-of-doors. When the sun shines I might have perhaps an hour or two, but it usually takes so long to get where I want to paint that I cannot do anything worthwhile.[14]

Burpee had a running dialogue with his Ruskin book in Florence:

> I take up Ruskin once in a while to learn how hurriedly I am

doing the churches and Picture Galleries. At Santa Croce I went by a marble pulpit called the most beautiful in all Italy, simply because there was so much else to demand attention.

Giotto's Chapel, too, which Ruskin thinks the most perfect ever built, I went into and gave only a few minutes not appreciating its proportions or its frescos. But, on reading about it I went again and again. Ruskin spent five weeks studying one wall in the Spanish Chapel of Santa Maria Novella! What can one do who has only five days, or say ten, for the whole of Florence? I see others doing just as I do and not seeing even as much, but it is really too bad, when every square foot deserves notice.

When there is so much to see and so little time, one really does not know what to look for, and often takes a general view of the whole, getting no impression whatever of any detail. And it is a pity when so much of that detail is exquisite.[15]

Burpee recorded in detail Ruskin's description of the marbles on the side of Giotto's Tower at the Duomo and the added understanding that it brought him. On the other hand, Ruskin's condescension finally got to the American artist:

While I do not accept his dictation about things he does not like — because he shows himself narrow, I must confess that those he admires, he admires for cause. He has a certain right to lecture, but he should not do it as though he had a stupid audience, who are dull of apprehension, and willfully blind. He well knows that only now and then a man has the unlimited leisure of opportunity which he has had to study the *Stones of Venice* and the architectural gems all over Europe. Why should he treat with illy concealed scorn those who, for want of time, hurry by these beautiful works of art?[16]

At the end of February Burpee left Florence for Siena, Empoli, and Pisa, where he stayed at the Washington Hotel and where he was deeply impressed by the grouping of buildings around the Cathedral. He noted, "Those who wrought had patience, skill, and above all the religious devotion to do perfect works and so their monuments stand, the marvels of the ages."[17]

From Pisa he went to Venice in early March, settling in at the Casa Kirsch Pension on the Grand Canal with a room that overlooked the water. "This City by the Sea," he wrote, "is a superb jewel indeed, fulfilling all demands and the lovely waterways with the gliding gondolas and crafts of every shape and size almost — so still, and volatile, would do your nerves good. No dust, no noise — a lubricated happiness."[18] As with other cities, in Venice, Burpee set out to do the sights, but he was, as in Florence, especially interested in seeing the paintings in the public places, and here, at last he settled into some painting of his own. On March 23 he wrote:

It was raining today, so I went to the Accademia for a fresh view of the splendid pictures. These are superb examples from the hand of Titian, Veronese, Bellini, the Bonifacios and others who belong to the Venetian School and a number of Tintorettos which I admired greatly. Many of them are very large, as for instance the Supper of the Levites by Paul Veronese, the Assumption by Titian and the Crucifixion by Tintoretto. The coloring in all these is very sumptuous and Tintoretto and Bellini are very rich, whereas Titian's are strong and painted with great power. I was quite amazed by the splendor and magnificence of the collection and must needs go again to fix some of the beautiful portrayals more securely in my memory.[19]

After stepping through the sights of the main islands Burpee ventured out into the lagoon and the islands of Murano and Torcello following Ruskin's *Stones of Venice*. After exploring the early buildings on Torcello, he wrote:

Time was short as the boat returned in two hours, so, I returned to Mazzorbo where the steamer was lying at her wharf and had a very very happy time in this highly colored and picturesque old town which more than any old town which I was ever in made me long to stop and sketch the handsome color in the houses and dresses of the inhabitants. As an Impressionist I was filled completely full of motives of all the primitive colors and felt that they fairly ran riot.[20]

Burpee made the requisite bows to tourism with nighttime gondola rides on the quiet canals and listening to the bands and the clock tower in the Piazza San Marco on Sunday evenings. After more than a month he departed for Padua and from there went to Switzerland and the Italian lakes (Como, Lecco, Maggiore) before settling into Milan where he spent

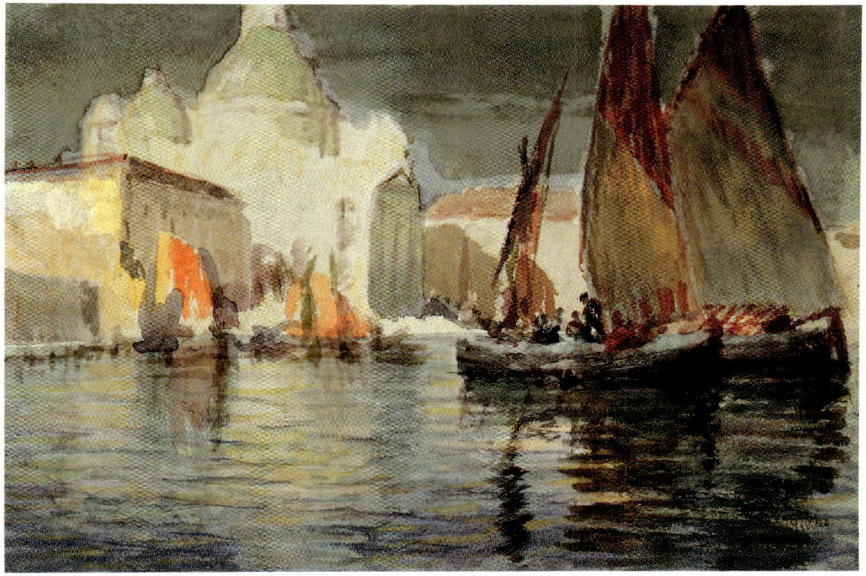

VENETIAN WATERS, 1899.

Watercolor, 2 9/16 x 3 13/16 inches.
As an Impressionist, Burpee was excited by the colors of Venice and its outlying islands.

Easter week and viewed the processional services at the Cathedral. Bellagio, especially, was interesting to Burpee, because, as he remarked, "Ever since I saw the old scene painting at Rockland on the drop curtain [in the theater], with 'Bellagio' upon it, I have wanted to visit this beautifully situated place."[21]

On April 23, he took the train to Milan, commenting that the rain had kept him from bicycling for more than a week. He received a great pile of mail, correspondence, and back issues of the *New York Herald* which acquainted him with the American perspective of the troubles building between the United States and Spain over Cuba and the Philippines. "Today is the day [April 23, 1898] when the trouble is to begin, in hot headed war-rush and war-cry. I hope the sequel will be less terrible than I fear it may be. It has hindered my enjoyment of travel."[22]

He noted in Genoa that "the statue of Columbus which Mark Twain has written about in his *Innocents* stands near the entrance to the station." His hotel, the Hotel Milan, was near the station as well.

There are many foreigners here. They are coming from Nice and Cannes, Menton and Monte Carlo where the season is almost over, and from the north down to Rome and Naples on their way toward America. The travel is greater from the north as such a large number of Germans and English are taking their Spring and Summer trips — and Americans who came to London and Paris and Hamburg and are on their way home. The English and Germans are very fond of sightseeing, and its cost to them is not half what it is to Americans as they do not have to pay $200 for a passage to and fro across the Atlantic . . . . They have to rush about, though, and lose no time. I am a month behind my schedule now, but I have enjoyed not being obliged to hurry away from a place and the impressions have sunk deep, and been a great joy. I look back upon the three weeks in Naples, the three weeks in Rome and a similar period in Florence and Venice, as very very happy ones when I was absorbing the long looked for ministrations of Art and beauty like a flexible sponge and felt repeatedly filled to overflowing.[23]

France

In Milan, he visited the cathedral and Leonardo's *Last Supper* and noted the richness of the shops and the quality of musical events. Despite his desire for slow travel, he struck north by bicycle for France, passing Ventimiglia, Menton, Nice, Cannes, Toulon, and Marseilles along the coast and then heading inland to "the old towns in 'Provence,' Aix, Arles, Tarascon, and Avignon . . . . Then on to Lyon, Macon and Dijon, busy thriving cities and through Fontainbleau to Melun, and by train to Paris,"[24] finally arriving in mid-May 1898.

"After all these months," he wrote, "I have at last arrived in this beautiful city which to many is the most attractive city in the world." He took a room at "a home-like little hotel and pension where a number of Americans are stopping kept by an English lady — so the quiet and rest is very refreshing. The great 'Louvre' is just opposite over across the Seine and the quarter is so busy that one seems to be in a maze of cabs, omnibuses and bicycles everywhere . . . . Yesterday I went to see the Luxembourg where pictures by artists still living are hung. When they are dead, the pictures will be carried to the Louvre. The salons are both open, and held in the same building. I expect to visit them tomorrow."[25]

Burpee was increasingly distressed by the Spanish American War and noted that some Americans were returning home. He cannily surmised, "It is entirely outside of my sympathy, and I can not understand how it occurred unless the Newspapers expected a rich harvest by the war operations."[26] Nonetheless he wanted to continue with his program:

> After fixing myself up a little I made a call on two sculptors who are here, former friends in the Harcourt Building. One is Mr. [Cyrus] Dallin [1861 – 1944] who has been here two years and the other is Mr. [Bela] Pratt [1867 – 1917] who has also been here two years.
>
> They have both received 'honorable mention' from the Salon jury which is of course a very coveted honor and next to receiving a medal. Mr. Pratt was married while I was in Brookline and immediately came to Paris. I met his wife, who was exceedingly pleasant, and soon the baby returned from his outing in the carriage and I had a delightful call. Then I went to see Mr. Dallin. He invited me to stop to dinner, and I had a charming evening with conversation and discussion. I also made a call on Mr. [Frank H.] Richardson [1859 – 1934] who is a painter. He used to be in Harcourt too. Has now been in Paris studying and painting for 5 years. He has a picture in the Salon. So you can see I had a 'red letter' day.[27]

After about a month in Paris, Burpee took off for a fast tour by bicycle in the French Alps and across Switzerland. He arrived in Switzerland about June 20 and covered most of the major towns and sites of the area, by both bicycle and train. He returned to Paris to celebrate Bastille Day there, and by the first of August he had settled into Barbizon.

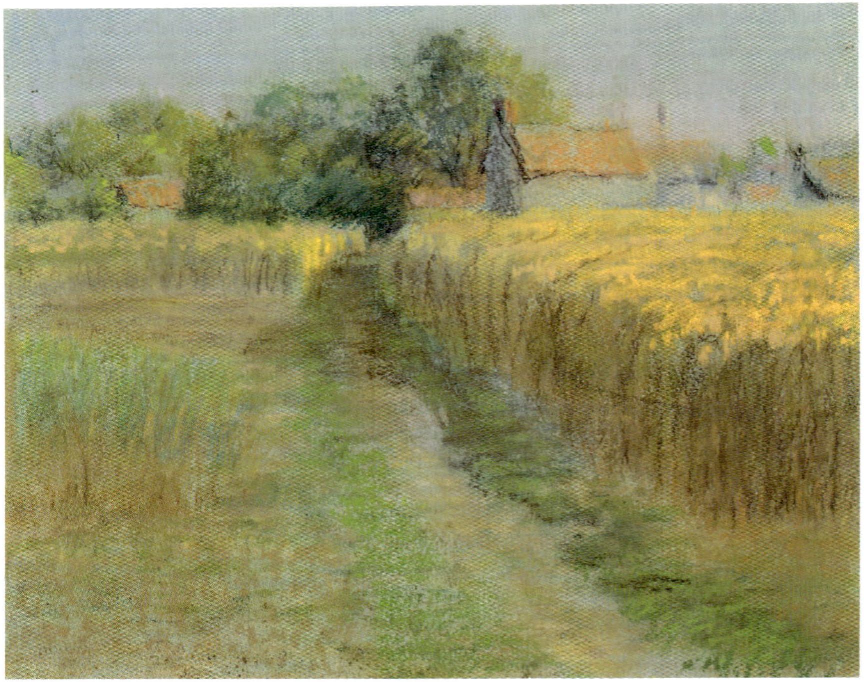

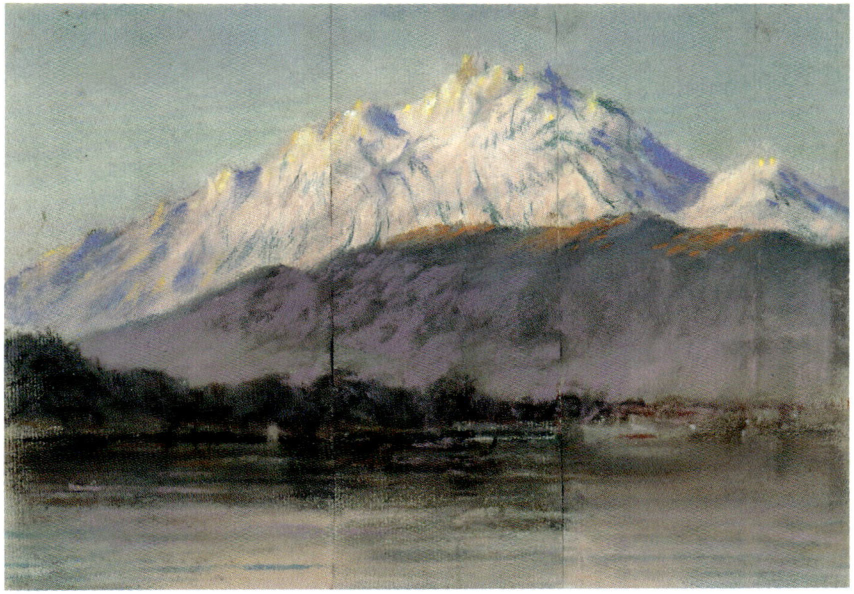

above

MONT BLANC.

Pastel on paper, 7 1/2 x 10 5/16 inches.
Burpee visited Mt. Blanc in early summer 1898, but may have returned in early 1906.

left

GRAINFIELDS, FRANCE, 1898.

Pastel on paper, 7 1/2 x 10 3/4 inches.
Burpee spent most of the summer of 1898 in Barbizon and went to nearby Chailly with its "great haystacks surrounded by miles of grainfields."

The last month of summer is very sweet in this locality this year. The lovely warm days and cool nights, the busy harvesters, the beautiful full moon, all conspire to make it quite an ideal country. The people live to a good old age. Madame tells me that the dame who posed for the woman in Millet's *Angelus* has recently died.

Womankind is very busy here, working in the fields with the men and doing the simple work of the house. I see them every day gathering the wheat into bundles, and bringing home gleanings and green stuff from the gardens. The painters are beginning to be in evidence. I saw five today out sketching. I was in the fields making studies and have just now returned from following a flock of sheep to their fold watching their movements and enjoying the superb evening and twilight picture motives.

Since I have been able to talk Italian and French, I have avoided the hotels where Americans stop and have begun to live just as the natives do, at much less expense. It takes some time to learn how to understand all their customs, and one only does it by leaving his compatriots and mingling with the people, or by doing as one of my traveling acquaintances did, hire a guide by the month and learn from him. That artist I met in Capri lived on two francs a day, (40 cts) and he lived with an artist near Paris for 3 francs a day.

Today I went to Chailly, another town in the vicinity with great haystacks and surrounded by miles of grainfields. The grain being near ripe is of a very rich color, and the harvest is in full swing. I am watching the sunsets, but most of them are dull on account of clouds. I look for a brilliant one as the grain looks lovely in such a gold and red light. . . . I saw the studio where Millet painted. His son owns it now and lives opposite.[28]

The automobiles are now a great feature. In Paris there is

quite a stir about them and many are being made and sold. Some of them have little chariots in behind so that the automobilist can give his friends a ride, and some are really quite large wagons like an omnibus or a coach and hold four or six persons. We have a great many here as it is a beautiful run from Paris, and one can return the same day. I have seen some quite elegant-looking turnouts. They cost from three hundred dollars upwards. (I am writing of all classes.) This is not much more than a horse and wagon. They seem to steer very easily and accidents are rare or no more frequent than with carriages. But they are heavy and accidental run-ons are apt to be more serious.

Barbizon is a restful place, one that a person might come to for a few days, and stay a few years. There is so much to satisfy the soul and nature is so kind. The atmosphere is peculiarly sweet and wholesome and the forest seems to breathe strengthening odors from the pines and firs.[29]

Return to Italy

After returning to Paris and spending early September there, Burpee made an important decision; it was time to work again. "When I arrived back in Paris I longed to stay there and study, but on the whole I considered that the time would better be spent [in Sorrento], where I longed to paint last winter."[30] So he took the train through France and the Mt. Cinis tunnel into Italy to Genoa, where he caught a steamer for Naples and then traveled on to Amalfi; and in late September 1898 he arrived at Sorrento and the Hotel Grand Bretagne, where he had been nearly a year before. He was told there by a Neapolitan gentleman about the beauties of Sicily and the warmer climate, and thus planned to spend some time in Sorrento and Capri and, when the weather got colder, to go on to Taormina.

At Sorrento he got out his watercolors and began to paint. After a few weeks he moved to Capri and after three days to Anacapri where he remained until the last day of 1898. There he settled into a routine of painting watercolors and studies in oil. He fell in love with the jumble of walls and windows that made up the local domestic architecture.

The beauty of the houses, artistically, is that they are built by the natives who cannot afford to hire masons, and the result is the walls are quite always out of plumb, the windows not on a level, the sides not square, the arches uneven and lop-sided, and a general devil-may-care irregularity which is a delight, at the same time giving no end of perplexity as to the drawing and perspective. Indeed, I am not sure that it would not be well sometimes to throw perspective to the winds and paint just as the builders builded.

The village of Anacapri is very attractive to paint. I have found a few children of whom to make studies, and in fact my hands are quite full just now.[31]

He made studies, a watercolor and at least one oil of a pergola with white columns covered with vines looking to the sea (p. 36).

Besides the courts with pillars and vines, which I have described in my letters, I have mostly worked on three pictures — one, a Sunrise on Ischia with the village of Caprile in the foreground in shadow. Another is a moonlight scene in one of the principal streets, which is really nothing but a pathway along the bed of a torrent, grass-grown and full of picturesque rocks. The third is an interior or inner court of a house near the church. They are all as difficult as I have attempted. The sunrise, of course, only gives me a few minutes, and as for the moonrise, I can only study and guess and remember as well as I can, for I cannot paint out of doors so late. But the difficulties will be of excellent benefit to me. I went to Capri one fine day with several of my sketches of last December when I was here, walked down to the Piccola Marina and impressed them much. There were three other artists there, as it is a favorite spot.[32]

Inevitably, travelers compare their new sights with the familiar ones of home. Burpee was no exception. In writing home about the Bay of Naples he said,

The stretch of this gulf is like Penobscot Bay in largeness. For instance, Ischia from Naples is about where Fox Island is from Rockland. From Naples to Pompeii, which I have indicated is 16 miles — to Castellamare — about as far as from Rockland to Belfast. The whole sweep is about 100 miles and the towns and villages contain nearly one million inhabitants! The Apennines form a grand background, some of them snow-covered in winter. From Sorrento to Capri is about ten miles. Vesuvius is about 4300 feet high or nearly twice as high as Camden Mountains as seen from the point. Ischia is about the same height at Migunticook. Anacapri is about half again as high as Dodge's Mountain, and the view at sunrise or sunset is something wonderfully fine.[33]

He was happy in Capri and for the second year in a row spent Christmas there, where he was welcomed as a friend in several families. But the north winds blowing across the lofty heights of Anacapri convinced Burpee "to leave for the 'Sunny Climes.' I went down to Capri and stopped a week, nearly, in a pleasant pension facing the south and on the slope. Then I got up before light, and took the steamer for Naples."[34] There he finally climbed the slopes of Vesuvius before taking the steamer for Messina and shortly arriving at Taormina in Sicily, where he lodged in the Hotel Victoria in the company of four other artists — two Danes, one Norwegian, and one Frenchman. The Norwegian, Mimi Falsen (1861 – 1957) was 37 years old and traveling with Miss Petersen, one of the Danish artists.[35] She and Burpee struck up an immediate and strong friendship. He settled in for nearly four months at Taormina and the surrounding villages. "Some think it the most beautiful scenery in all Italy, and I enjoy going out to see the sunrise on snow capped Etna, or to watch the gathering shadows, as the warm rays of the setting sun turn crimson and gold."[36] He visited the Greek ruins in the area. He noted that picturesque models could be hired very cheaply, but that they tended to overcharge most foreigners. "I get along very well, however, because they take me for a German, and the people know full well not to expect much from a German. . . . Miss Falsen told me that she had a picture in the World's Fair at Chicago. She speaks English quite well and French very well."[37] In late February he wrote, "Just now we are in the season of the almond blossoms. All around and above us the little trees which have been so somber and grey, have put forth their beautiful pink flowers until it seems like the smiling of heaven upon the landscape far and wide. It was a great surprise to me as I did not know the trees were 'Almonds,' and I had not heard about there being so many of them. . . . In morning, at noon and towards sunset the glorious light is caught by the shining petals until ones sees everywhere a picture of fairyland as it were."[38] The almond blossoms were to form the basis for studies and exhibition paintings, as were the local fishermen: "We have been down to the seashore several times on excursion, but it is rather too hard a descent and climb for frequent visits. Giardini, the coast town here, is in some

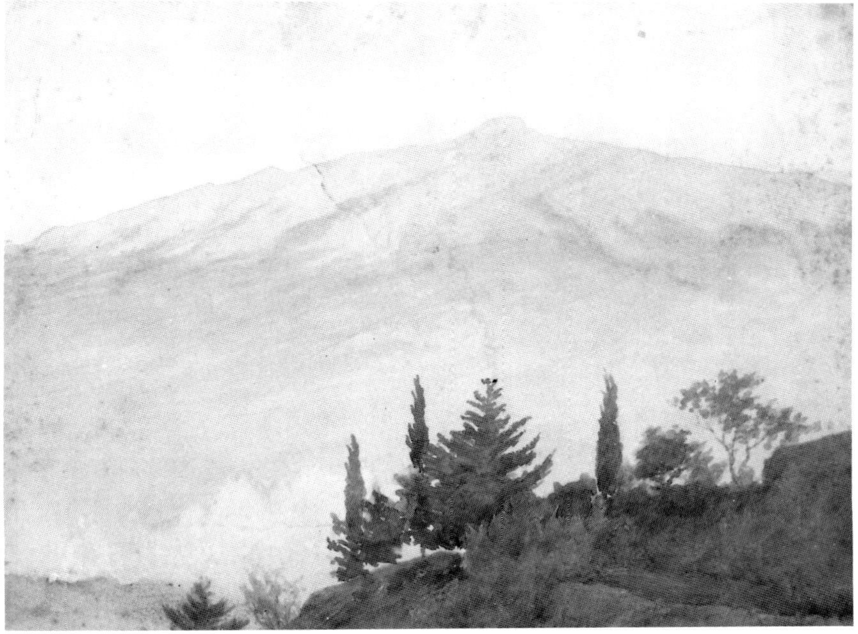

CAPRI, 1899.

Watercolor, 10 1/4 x 14 1/8 inches. Signed and dated. Capri became Burpee's retreat in Europe for rest and for work. He was taken into local families and spent both Christmasses abroad there.

respects as interesting as Taormina, and I like especially the fishermen, busy with boats and nets, as are my friends at Swampscott."[39]

Burpee became fond of the Larsen family from Copenhagen. The father reminded him of his dead brother, Frank, grown older. He remarked on Larsen's kindness. The various foreigners, mostly northern Europeans, formed a compatible group. "We all met at the room of Fraulein Schneekloch on the eve of her departure and had a little Champagne collation with games and songs by Mlle. Falsen, the Norwegian, who sat on the bed and sang more beautifully than ever before. She has been painting with me lately and we have become quite friendly. She tells me about her home life, by way of entertainment at table, and I tell her of my home life in America, so different."[40]

The Voyage North and Home

He left with difficulty the friends he had made at Taormina and departed for Naples April 4, to paint in Venice. His friends felt he was hard on them leaving,

> especially the Norwegian artist who sat by my side at table and has been like a "sister" to me. I helped her in her painting very much, and in that way became very interested. So to comfort her a little (?) I told her if she came to Naples, I would not hurry from there as I had planned. Well, I had a fine time wandering about, with two visits to the grand old museum — especial satisfaction among the Pompeiian and Herculaneum curios — a visit to Cape Posilippo, San Martino on the Hill (monastery) and Herculaneum and San Sebastiano before the smoking slopes of old Vesuvius. I felt in so much better health than when I first arrived, after the long trip across the ocean and through Spain, that I enjoyed it more this time than at first, and I was very glad.[41]

Burpee and Miss Falsen went on to Rome to paint and draw. They were there by April 13, his 53rd birthday: "My birthday was quite happy. I was with Miss Falsen in Rome and she made a chocolate breakfast in her room. I went out and bought some eggs and bread and butter, and thus she gave me a birthday cake or 'pasta' as they call it here and she had also kindly bought me a handsome necktie, which we both admired in Naples. So you see I had quite a celebration."[42]

He met up with the Larsen family, and "Herr Larsen bought one of my watercolors to hang up in his house in Copenhagen. It was a view of Etna — morning, truly one of my best."[43] And the Larsens gave him a photograph of their family taken in the courtyard of their hotel in Rome.

He left the Larsens and Mimi Falsen in Rome and went on to Florence, where he revisited the principal art treasures and reached Bologna by April 19. He was apparently having a touch of homesickness, and the endless grind of a European tour was wearing him down. A summing – up was in order. He remarked, "I am here to break the journey, which is a rather tiresome one, and tomorrow I go on to the fair 'City of the Sea' hoping for a chance to paint in weather warmer than last year, when I was there. To retrace my steps in this way and visit again the scenes I first looked upon a year ago is very satisfying, and gives me a feeling of content and completeness of travelling. . . . I have been in the very best of health — I have felt as though I were in the 'Prime of Life.' "[44]

He went to Venice on April 25 and remained there until about May 19. To his mother he wrote:

> It will seem to be a great change to leave this lovely Square of St. Mark's with its smooth and beautiful pavement, its border of palaces, its crowd of happy Venetians and foreigners intermingling, and its shining church — like a veritable crown of gems, and come home to the muddy streets and dilapidated fences of Rockland. But you see, I shall not be compelled to look always at the mud and the dirty fences, for in a twinkle of the eye, I can scale the heights of memory, and look down on these lovely scenes of Venice, Rome, Naples and Sicily, and they shall always be mine, and then when I do descend to earth again, as it composes the Rockland "Strata" I shall have your dear face near mine and look into the eyes that have watched over me all these long years and embrace the loving sisters and nieces.

And then Miss Falsen, the Norwegian, who has been truly like a sister to me. We have many a laugh together because I tell her of my own sisters who "brush me up" a little now and then, when they think I am getting "moss grown" or try to jerk me out of a bad rut in the path which I have followed too long. She thinks they have not been kept enough in remembrance and sees many things in me that are not as they ought to be. As the Northern people are very free in speaking their minds, you can imagine that I get a symbolical "box on the ears." She and Mlle. Petersen, the Danish artist, were both with me in Venice, but have now left for the North by way of Munich and Berlin, one to go to her home in Copenhagen, and the other to hers in Christiania.[45]

Before they left, Burpee and Mimi Falsen went about Venice together. "One night we went out together with Miss Petersen in a gondola and there were several serenading parties on the water with many colored lanterns and the sights of the palaces twinkling in the water below. It was quite like a dream. Then we went into some of the smaller canals full of dark and mystery, and so quiet. Can you imagine a city without dust and noise, with the musical water-waves, and silent-floating boats, sweet and still and beautiful?"[46]

The long journey, in which Burpee had expanded his horizons and deepened his artistic sensibilities, was now drawing to a close. He left in late May for Paris, where he saw the salons for 1899. From there he went on to Brussels, Amsterdam, and Hamburg. He visited the Rhine country and Holland, where he spent several days at Dordrecht before crossing the channel from Flushing to Queensboro, arriving in London July 1. He saw the major sights of London, but by this time his attitude had changed. "I shall be able, I think to limit my sightseeing, as I have seen so much, that it fails to assume the importance which attached to it at first. . . . It is said that every steamer from America is full of passengers and that they have to wait for steamers in New York."[47] He booked passage from Liverpool on July 22, 1899, on the first crossing of the new Leyland steamer *Winifredian* which arrived in Boston at 5:00 p.m. , August 1 to the celebratory tooting of steam whistles. He did some needed business in Boston before going, after 21 months, home to Rockland!

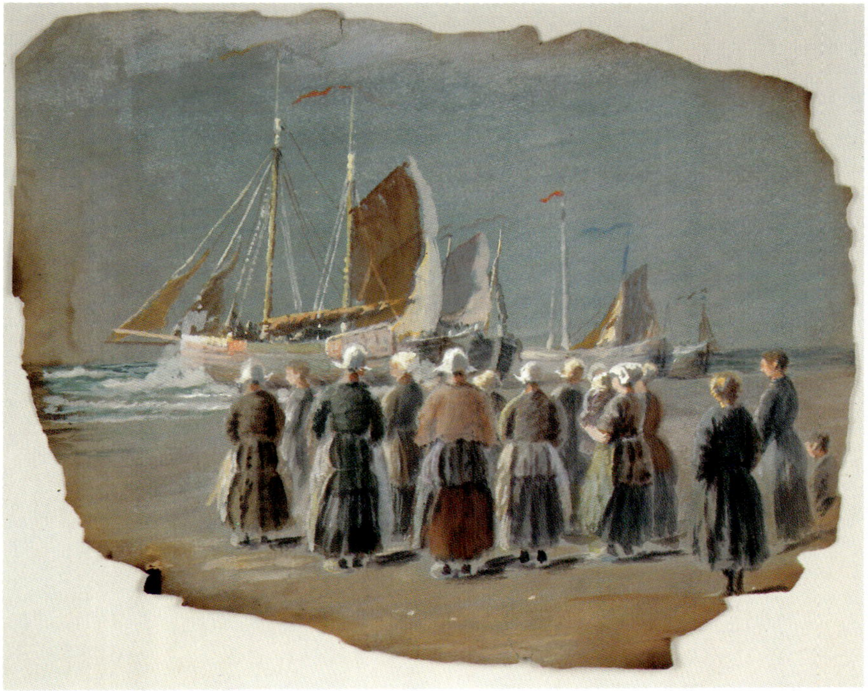

KATWIJK WOMEN GREETING THE FISHING BOATS, 1900.

Watercolor and gouache, 10 1/2 x 13 inches.
This brilliant and complex figure group was badly scorched in the 1904 Harcourt studio fire.

Holland, 1900

What transpired in the next few months is still not clear, but Burpee seems to have returned to Europe for the summer of 1900, when he settled into the little Dutch town of Katwijk just north of The Hague.[48] Katwijk had been a magnet for American painters with Bostonians among their number. In 1900 Melbourne Hardwick exhibited *Sorting Fish — Holland* and Charles Gruppe (a Boston painter born in Holland) showed *Low Tide — Beach at Katwijk* at the Boston Art Club. Burpee and Frank

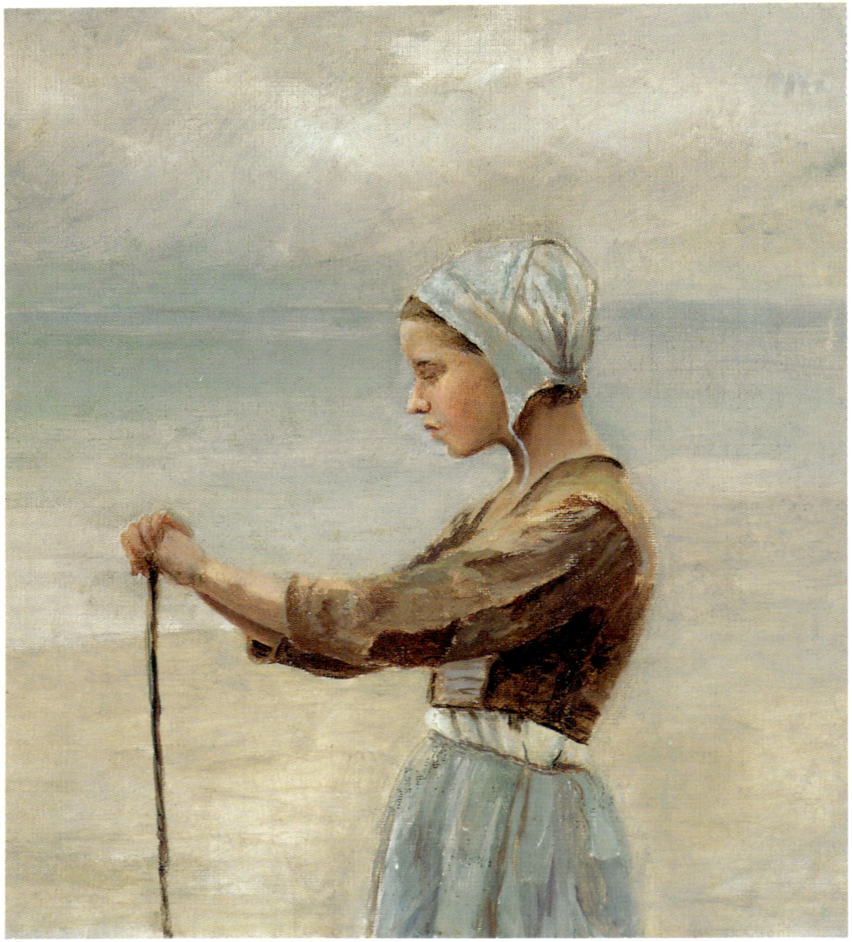

H. Richardson both exhibited watercolors of the old church at Katwijk the following year, and it is easy to speculate that they were both in Katwijk in the summer of 1900. Indeed, with Burpee's oft–stated longing during his prior trip to Europe to "limit my sightseeing" and settle down and paint, an invitation from one or more of his fellow members of the Boston Art Club to return to Europe and concentrate on painting in this small seaside fishing village would have led to this trip. It proved very productive in pastels and watercolors with great atmospheric effect of the gray slickness of the North Sea beaches and in beautiful studies of the women and children in Dutch costume on the beaches. The site, not very different from the beaches at Lynn and Swampscott, proved to be both familiar and exotic with the formal problems of beach, water, and figures that he had worked out earlier, enhanced with the exotic costumes and the complex figure groups that he chose to employ in these paintings.[49]

The Dutch modern painters were in popular ascendancy in the United States as well as Europe; they were regularly being shown in Boston. Burpee may have wished to work on the same sites and to have an opportunity to meet some of them. In the Boston Art Club 1901 watercolor show Dutch subjects were shown not only by American artists; William Howe Downes wrote that "with their works are shown a few modest but choice specimens of the art of the modern Dutch painters — Mauve, Israels, Bloomers, Weele. One of the things that is incidentally emphasized by this juxtaposition is the extent to which the more imitative of the American painters are influenced by the Dutchmen."[50] Burpee seems to have valued his Katwijk works, because he continued to exhibit them throughout his following Boston years including sending *Evening Katwyk* to the Art Institute of Chicago in 1907 and showing work from Katwijk in his studio exhibition of 1911.

The European experience and the European work in painting, watercolor and pastel must have lent Burpee a new confidence in the value of his art and his opinions on art. He returned to Boston with a markedly increased exhibition schedule and soon was called upon by his colleagues to judge their work for Boston and national exhibitions.

DUTCH GIRL ON THE BEACH, 1900.

Oil on paper mounted on panel, 9 1/2 x 8 1/2 inches.

opposite, right

BOATS ON THE BEACH, KATWIJK, 1900.

Watercolor, 4 3/8 x 5 5/8 inches.
As with so many of Burpee's watercolors of Katwijk, this shows the scorching of his 1904 studio fire.

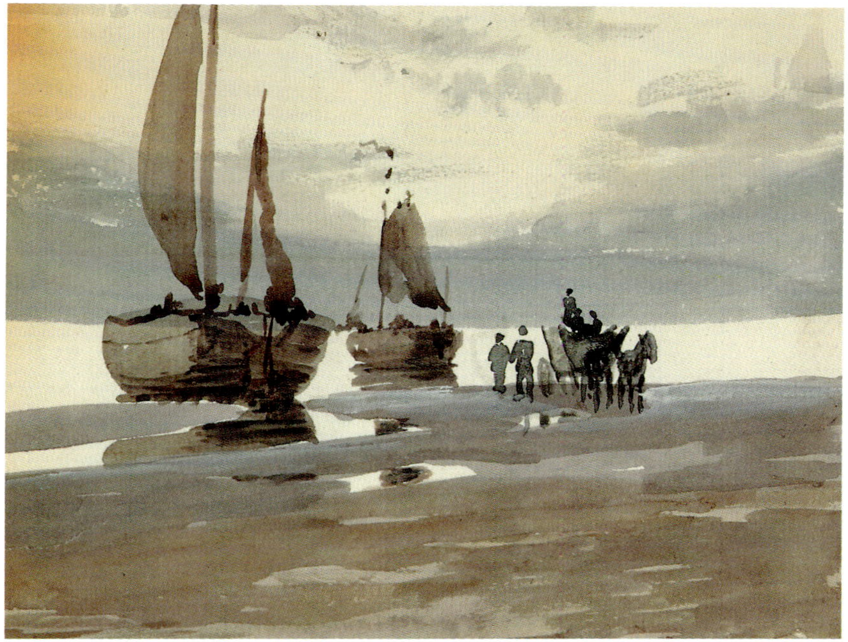

NOTES, Chapter Three

[1] Burpee letters, Nov. 7, 1897, Cadiz, to Mrs. N. A. Burpee (his mother). The William Partridge Burpee Papers at the Archives of American Art (#2336) holds letters from his trip of October 1897 to July 1899. They will be cited here as "Burpee letters, AAA" followed by the following information, if known: date, location, to whom sent.
[2] Burpee letters, AAA, Nov. 7, 1897, Cadiz, to Mrs. N. A. Burpee.
[3] Burpee letters, AAA, Dec. 21, 1897, Hotel Pagano, Capri, no addressee.
[4] ibid.
[5] Burpee letters AAA, Nov. 26, 1897, Naples, to Carrie Burpee Shaw.
[6] Burpee letters AAA, Dec. 21, 1897, Hotel Pagano, Capri, no addressee.
[7] Burpee letters AAA, Dec. 6, 1897, Naples.
[8] ibid.
[9] Burpee letters AAA, Dec. 1897, on Hotel Pagano stationery from Sorrento, no addressee.
[10] Burpee letters AAA, Gennaio 28, 1898, Roma, no addressee.
[11] ibid.
[12] Burpee Papers AAA, [Feb. 1898], Florence, to Hattie Sawyer, "Impressions: The Hill Towns".
[13] ibid.
[14] ibid.
[15] ibid.
[16] ibid.
[17] Burpee letters AAA, March 2, 1898, "Jottings from Pisa".
[18] Burpee letters AAA, March 13, 1898, Venice, to Carrie Burpee Shaw.
[19] Burpee letters AAA, March 23, 1898, Venice, to Mrs. N. A. Burpee.
[20] Burpee letters AAA, Sunday, March 27, [1898], Venice, to Mrs. N.A. Burpee.
[21] Burpee letters AAA, April 20, 1898, Hotel Como, Milano.
[22] Burpee letters AAA, April 23, 1898, Genoa.
[23] ibid.
[24] Burpee letters AAA, May 16, 1898, Paris, to Mrs. N. A. Burpee.
[25] ibid.
[26] Burpee letters AAA, May 16, 1898, Paris, Dear Ed.
[27] Burpee letters AAA, June 1, 1898, Paris, to Mrs. N.A. Burpee.
[28] Burpee letters AAA, Aug. 1, 1898, Barbizon, no addressee.
[29] Burpee letters AAA, [early Aug. 1898] Barbizon , no addressee, with map.
[30] Burpee letters AAA, Sept. 27, 1898, Sorrento, to Mrs. N.A. Burpee.
[31] Burpee letters AAA, Oct. 25, 1898, Anacapri, to Mrs. N. A. Burpee.
[32] Burpee letters AAA, Nov. 18, 1898, Anacapri, to Mrs. N.A. Burpee.
[33] Burpee letters AAA, Dec. 15, 1898 Anacapri, to Mrs. N. A. Burpee.
[34] Burpee letters AAA, Jan. 18, 1899, Taormina, my dear Emma.
[35] Probably Anna Sofie Petersen (1845 – 1910), who had been well trained, was noted for her travels in Italy, and was a champion of realism in Danish painting.
[36] Burpee letters AAA, Jan. 18, 1899, Taormina, my dear Emma.
[37] ibid.
[38] Burpee letters AAA, Feb. 20, 1899, Taormina, to Mrs. N. A. Burpee.
[39] ibid.
[40] Burpee letter AAA, March 13, 1899, Taormina, dear sister.
[41] Burpee letters AAA, April 19, 1899, Bologna, to my dear Emma.
[42] Burpee letters AAA, May 5, 1899, Venice, to Mrs. N. A. Burpee.
[43] ibid.
[44] Burpee letters AAA, April 19, 1899, Bologna, to my dear Emma.
[45] Burpee letters AAA, May 5, 1899, Venice, to Mrs. N. A. Burpee.
[46] Burpee letters AAA, May 5, 1899, Venice, to Mrs. N. A. Burpee.
[47] Burpee letters AAA, July 2, 1899, London, to Mrs. N. A. Burpee.
[48] A large number of the Katwijk watercolors were scorched in a November 1904 Harcourt studios fire. Burpee exhibited a Katwijk picture as early as 1901, yet he traveled swiftly through Holland in 1899 and mentioned that he planned to go to Amsterdam and that he spent several days in Dordrecht and departed Holland from Flushing. This hardly indicates the time to create an entire body of Katwijk pictures. The only dated picture yet discovered of a Dutch boy standing at the coast, a key to the dating of the Katwijk work, (in a private collection in New Jersey) is signed followed by "/00", indicating 1900.
[49] Mr. Jan Peter van Brakel of the Oud Katwijk Historical Society could not find Burpee in the Katwijk hotel lists for this period which indicates that he was staying in a pension, as he had earlier in Europe.
[50] Archives of American Art MB505 6864, William Howe Downes' manuscript notes on the cover of a copy of the 66th Boston Art Club exhibition catalogue.

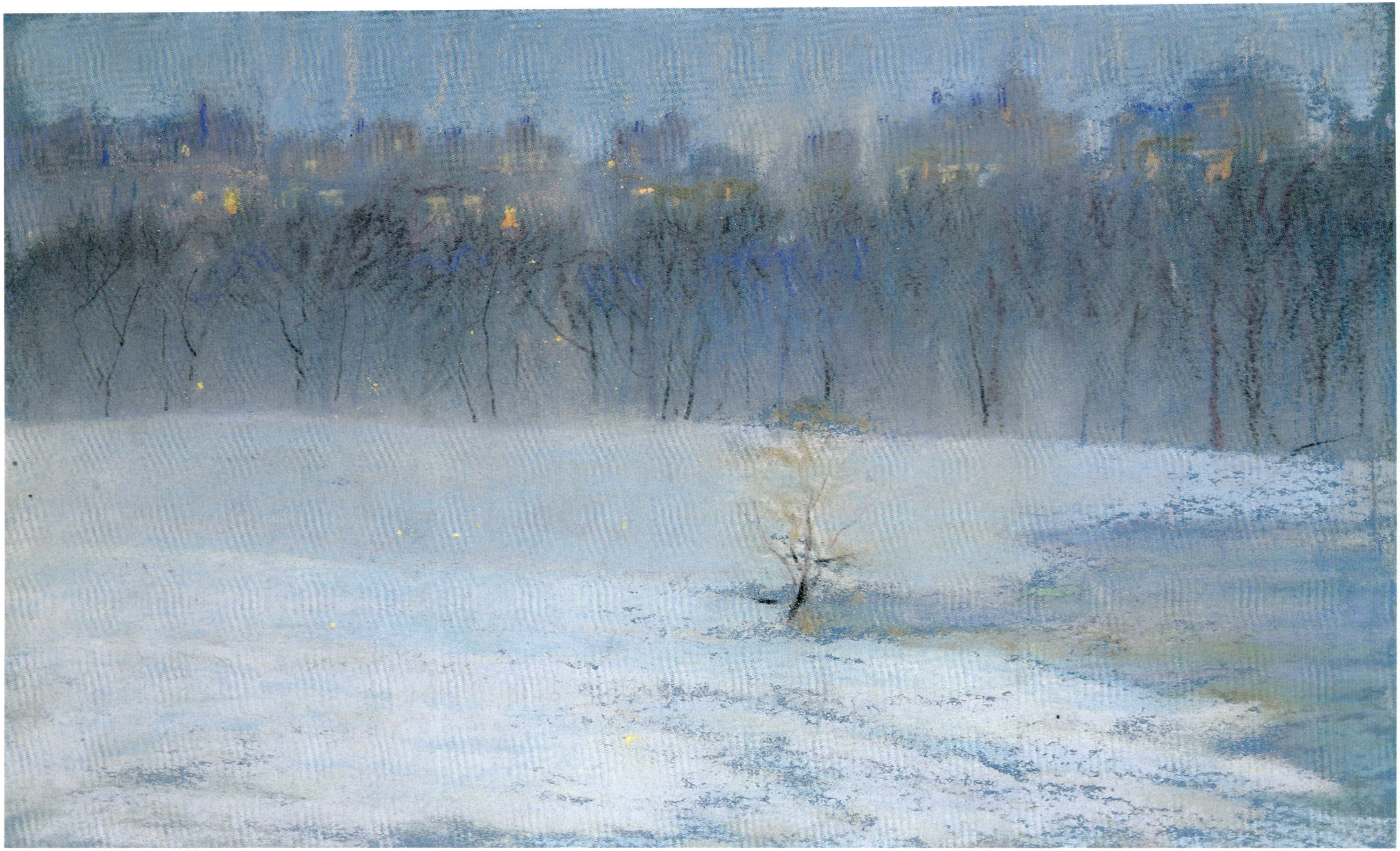

CHAPTER FOUR

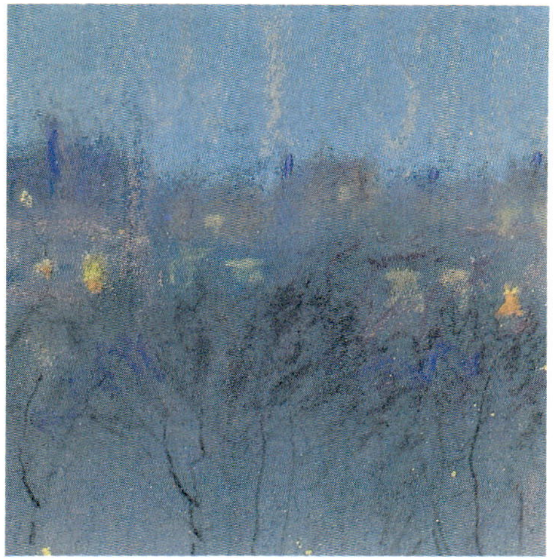

Artistic Maturity and Return to Boston (1900 – 1913)

The impact of nearly two years in Europe on Burpee had been great. It had given him the advantages of cosmopolitan travel and a perspective on Boston, Maine, and New England from abroad. He had been able to visit the great public collections of Italy and France and to associate with artists from many other countries. His evolution as an artist in the first years of his return was swift. The American mannerisms that related to the Luminists and to Bradford disappeared from his work , and he increasingly adopted the Tonalist and Impressionist principles that had been incipient in his work since the early 1890s. He had become not only, in his own words, a "globe trotter," but an artist who had adopted an international view.

He was far from the only American artist to visit Europe. Indeed, most of his closest colleagues in the Boston art community had gone there before him; but he was increasingly to have a point of view that took him away from New England provincialism in attitude, if not in subject. This loss of provincialism was seen by some critics of the time as a loss of innocence and of a distinctly American viewpoint, inevitable as that transition might be.

WINTER ON BOSTON COMMON, c.1904.

Pastel on paper, 8 1/16 x 13 3/16 inches.
In the 1904 show of the Boston Society of Watercolor Painters Burpee exhibited a similar pastel, *Winter Evening*.

William Howe Downes, a Boston art critic, reflecting on the exhibits of the painting of many countries at the Louisiana Purchase Exposition in St. Louis in 1904, wrote:

> The first tour through the 156 art galleries here suggests the disturbing question, whether one consequence of these vast international expositions may not be a certain rapprochement or growing-together of the nations, and a corresponding loss of national individuality. I shall, ask, then, what, after all, are the specific characteristics which distinctly and unmistakably separate the nations in art, the peculiar, the unique "notes"? Are we not already on the way to lose or greatly modify such of these as exist or are conceived to exist? We see the Europeans striving to adopt to their aesthetic purposes Japanese and Chinese modes of expression, while the Orientals, for commercial ends, readily take up with European styles. And will not the process of levelling up and levelling down , of smoothing off rough edges and corners . . . go on with increasing momentum until the arts of tomorrow are as cosmo-

politan as agriculture, transportation, commerce, education or a page of Henry James? . . .

It is the time and place for us to confess that American art is more than ever eclectic. Sargent and Whistler and Alexander, the painters; French and Paul Bartlett and Bitter, the sculptors; Cass Gilbert, C. Howard Walker and J. Knox Taylor, the architects, are all accomplished artists — the word is too lukewarm — they are remarkable, exceptional artists; but, whether we like it or no, [an unbiased outsider] will not be able to tell whether our architecture, sculpture and painting possess any nationality; there will be no evidence that they grew out of any peculiar local conditions or any inborn racial instincts, or met any need peculiar to the nation. . . .

We in America, like the French, are given to the notion that a literary or episodic picture or sculpture is necessarily a relatively cheap sort of art; that an illustrative painting or relief is a lower form of art, so to say; and that the religious, moral, historical or humorous element in plastic art is extrinsic, a vulgar appeal for popularity.[1]

Burpee's early Luminist paintings and the beach pictures of the 1880s and 1890s are clearly identifiable as New England painting, as well-executed as they are and as well-trained as he had become. But in going to Europe, seeing, thinking, talking with his peers, reading and discussing ideas then current in art, Burpee had eaten of the fruit of the tree of knowledge and could never return to the coast of Maine or the beaches of Lynn with the same viewpoint. While Downes took a mildly pejorative view of the internationalization of contemporary art, Burpee probably would have seen it as part of the progress toward perfection of his art and part of his self-realization and self-revelation through painting.

Even if Burpee had not gone to Europe, by the 1880s Europe was coming to Boston; without a thoroughgoing retreat to Maine it would have been difficult to blind an artist to the French Impressionist paintings being shown, sold, and collected in Boston. Whistler and Sargent, supreme Internationalists, were being lionized. Boston led the American romance with things Japanese, and the galleries regularly exhibited the work of contemporary Japanese painters. If Downes decried the loss of narrative and "subject" in the work of sophisticated American artists, he did so because he recognized (perhaps more presciently than he realized) that artists were choosing to leave subject behind. From his narrative figure paintings of Lynn beach and his carefully worked out compositions of Dutch men and women at Katwijk, Holland, Burpee moved to paintings in which light, color, and abstract composition were the intended subject. "Excellence of color and atmosphere," remarked one critic; "Good feeling, an echo of introspection," said another.[2] Of this trend in Boston painting in general, one critic wrote, "The modern, outdoor, atmospheric school gives the dominant tone; its ascendancy is greater than ever . . . so this school is affecting all vital modern painting. There is doubtless, much more to be achieved, but the greatest step forward in painting since the technical triumph of the old masters has been in this."[3] Burpee's cosmopolitanization had begun before he had left for Europe. Now it would become complete.

Burpee reestablished himself in the Harcourt Building in Boston in 1901. Presumably he was settled into Studio 27 by April 6 when he attended the opening of the 64th Exhibition of the Boston Art Club, the

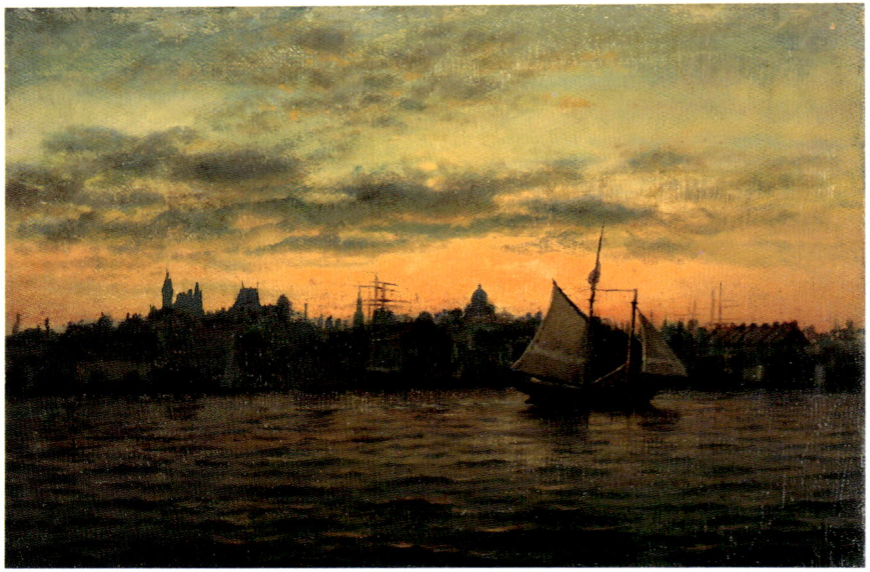

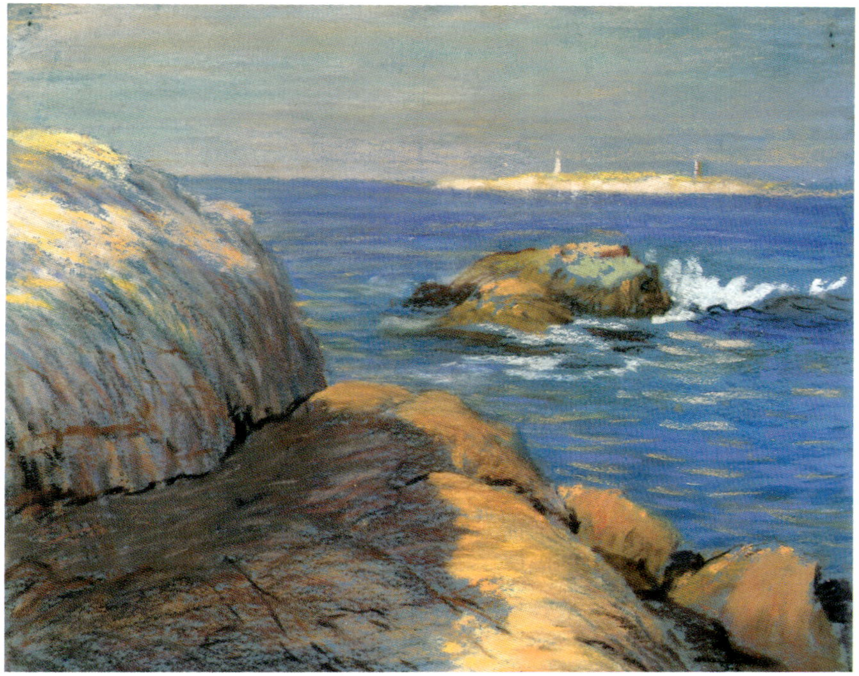

THATCHER'S ISLAND, EAST GLOUCESTER, c.1903.

Pastel on blue paper, 10 x 12 1/4 inches.

opposite

BOSTON HARBOR — SUNSET, c. 1905.

Oil on canvas, 7 7/8 x 11 7/8 inches.

annual watercolor exhibition at which anything except oil paintings could be shown.[4] The growing number of European subjects in Boston exhibitions is evidence of the ease with which Boston artists steamed across the Atlantic. One reviewer noted of this exhibition, "Two interesting pictures of the old church at Katwijk, Holland are neighbors here; they are signed by Frank H. Richardson and William P. Burpee. It is possible to see, in examining the two works together, how two painters can approach the same subject from entirely different points of view, and yet both make successful pictures."[5]

This painting and one of the two others he exhibited, *St. George of the Seaweed — Venice*, indicate the use that he was to make, through 1904, of the studies that resulted from his extended European trip. In the next three years he exhibited oils of *Pergola at Capri*, *Early Morning — Capri — Ischia*, *Island of Capri — Sunrise*, *Sunset in Holland*, and *Almond Blossoms*; as well as works on paper of *Early Summer — Capri* and *Nocturne Mt. Etna*. During the same period he continued to revisit subjects that he first discovered two decades before: *Sunrise — Point Shirley* [Revere], *At Swampscott*, *Thatcher's Island — East Gloucester*, and *Fishing Station — Coast of Maine*.

It appears that he went to the Gloucester area regularly as evidenced not only by exhibition titles, but by pastels that date from this period of Thatcher's Island and the Annesquam Lighthouse. Cape Ann was another artists' colony in New England; or better put, it was central to a collection of small artists' colonies at Gloucester, Rockport, and Annesquam and across the Annesquam River at Essex and Ipswich. The artists who summered there provided an extension of the collegial atmosphere of the Boston Art Club and the other Boston societies and clubs, since most of them were from Boston or belonged to Boston clubs and had their major exhibitions there.

Increasing Exhibitions

The openings of the January (oil) and April (watercolor) showings of the Boston Art Club were glittering affairs in formal dress. One was described in April 1902 as follows:

> A notable gathering of artists, financiers and prominent literary people visited the Boston Art Club last evening and enjoyed a private view of its 65th exhibition of paintings. The reception was tendered by the members and friends, and a group of some 200 admired the handsomely decorated walls, which reflected every credit on the "hanging committee" for the harmonious effects which resulted from its efforts. Then too, the hall had been sufficiently arrayed with palms and shrubbery so as to exclude from view the orchestra, under the direction of Mr. S. Bessell, which combined the

delights of music with those of art and blended the evening's affair into one of perfect harmony. Every one had a complimentary word for the artists, and their work.[6]

These were not only a showcase for the best works of the artist members of the club, but an opportunity to hang their works beside the best works from other American cities and from Europe. In January Burpee's paintings could be compared to oil paintings by Claude Monet, Eugene Boudin, and Fritz Thaulow. In the 65th exhibition Burpee's work hung in the company of American works on paper by Winslow Homer, Childe Hassam, William Merritt Chase, J. Alden Weir, and Everett Shinn, and of foreign works by Anton Mauve and Genjiro Yeto; and in this company his work received favorable critical notice.[7]

Beginning with the Boston Art Club April exhibition of 1902, Burpee became a member of the jury of admissions for the show, along with Thomas Allen, Charles Copeland, William Kaula, Melbourne Hardwick, Francis Draper and Hendricks Hallett. He judged watercolors, pastels and other works on paper for the club regularly through 1905, when he also was on the jury of admissions for oils. The composition of the juries changed with each show. Some of the other artists who juried with him during this period were sculptor Cyrus Dallin and painters Ernest L. Major, John J. Enneking, Horace Burdick, Charles Franklin Pierce, Scott Carbee, J. A. S. Monks, and Sears Gallagher. His acceptance in the Boston Art Club and the increasing ratification by his peers may have led him to list himself, for the first time, in the *American Art Annual* (a predecessor to *Who's Who in American Art*) in 1903. He must have begun to feel a greater part of the round of openings and exhibits in Boston.

Summers at Cape Ann or in Maine, after the formality of the season of art in Boston, provided a relaxed counterpoint for a large number of professional Boston painters. Many of his group at the Boston Art Club decamped to Cape Ann in this period. In addition many other painters from New York and the midwest joined them. In the first years of the twentieth century Gloucester and its environs welcomed Frank Duveneck, John Twachtman, Joseph DeCamp, Childe Hassam and many others as summer residents. A.W. Buhler was more or less permanently installed at Gloucester as was George Harvey at Annesquam and Arthur W. Dow at Ipswich. In November 1903 Burpee exhibited *Thatcher's Island, East Gloucester*, the first of what were to be many exhibition pictures of Cape Ann subjects.

It is also clear that Burpee regularly returned to Rockland, Maine, and to the family house there, and that he began to explore the shoreline of the Maine coast in summer and winter. In the summer of 1903 he was working there and doing studio paintings from studies made in the winter. At least one of the paintings that he would send to St. Louis the following year was painted then, probably in the loft studio at 43 Park Street.[8]

St. Louis Worlds Fair

The year 1904 would prove the most exciting of Burpee's career. New Year's Day saw the opening of the Boston Art Club's 69th exhibition, where Burpee exhibited oil paintings of *Sunset in Holland* and *Fishing Station — Coast of Maine*. In late January he submitted an oil painting, *Snow Covered Rocks at Sunset*, and a pastel, *Winter Sunset*, to the Massachusetts Committee for the Department of Fine Arts of the Louisiana Purchase Exposition, mentioned earlier. The judges of oil paintings —Thomas Allen, Frank W. Benson, John J. Enneking, Hermann Dudley Murphy, Sarah C. Sears, Edmund C. Tarbell, and Frederick P. Vinton — accepted 71 of the 246 oils entered by Massachusetts artists; and the judges of watercolor painting and pastels — Edmund H. Garrett, Joseph Lindon Smith, and Charles H. Woodbury — accepted 44 of 130 submissions in their field. The Massachusetts Committee's decisions were ratified by the national jury, which met with them in Boston.[9] To Burpee's surprise, both of his entries were accepted.[10] All of the accepted works of art were exhibited to the public at Walter Kimball & Co. from February 3 – 13. A reviewer suggested that the exhibit represented the majority of the artists of greater Boston "who may fairly be said to have arrived."[11] The Boston public was deeply interested

SNOW COVERED ROCKS, c.1903.

Oil on canvas, 29 1/2 x 36 1/2 inches.
This is probably very much like the oil painting which Burpee exhibited and sold at the St. Louis Worlds Fair.

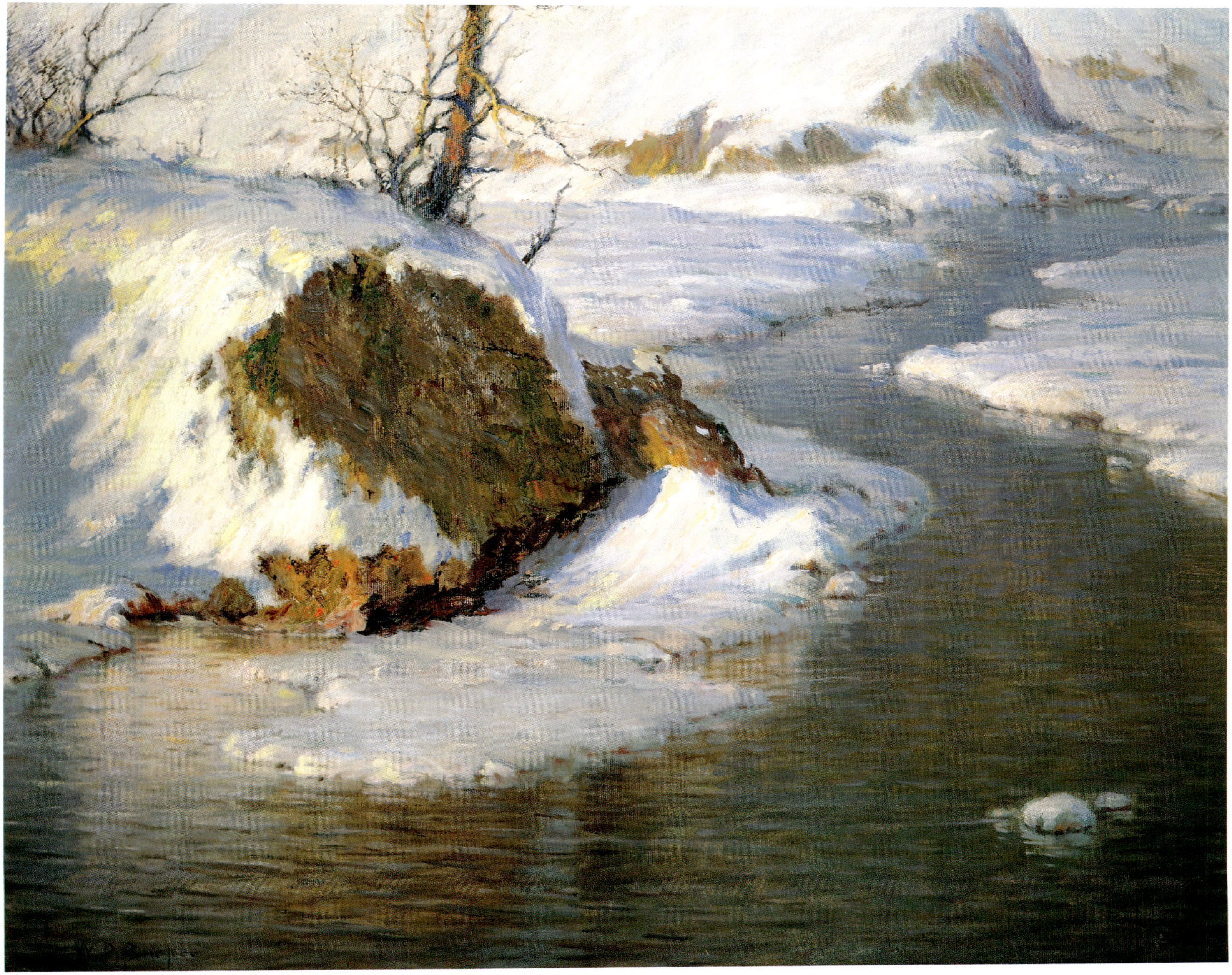

in these artists and in the Massachusetts entries for the fair; 2,542 people paid admission during the 10 days the works were on view. Immediately following the Boston showing, the entire exhibition was packed by Doll & Richards and forwarded by rail to St. Louis for the Louisiana Purchase Exposition.[12]

During the period when the Exposition works were on view, Thomas Allen, president of the Boston Society of Watercolor Painters, opened the Society's 16th exhibition at the Boston Art Club. In this small organization, fourteen exhibitors showed 129 works in watercolor and pastel. *Boston Transcript* singled out the group sent by Burpee: "The most interesting group of pictures is that by Mr. Burpee, who sends ten works. His *Winter Evening*, a view of the Tremont-street mall of the Common, looking towards Boylston street, is an exceptionally well-painted example of an interesting class of pictures; and his *In Wooded Depths*, an upright composition, representing the famous hemlock woods in the Arnold Arboretum, is an exquisitely observed and closely rendered painting of that wonderful place."[13]

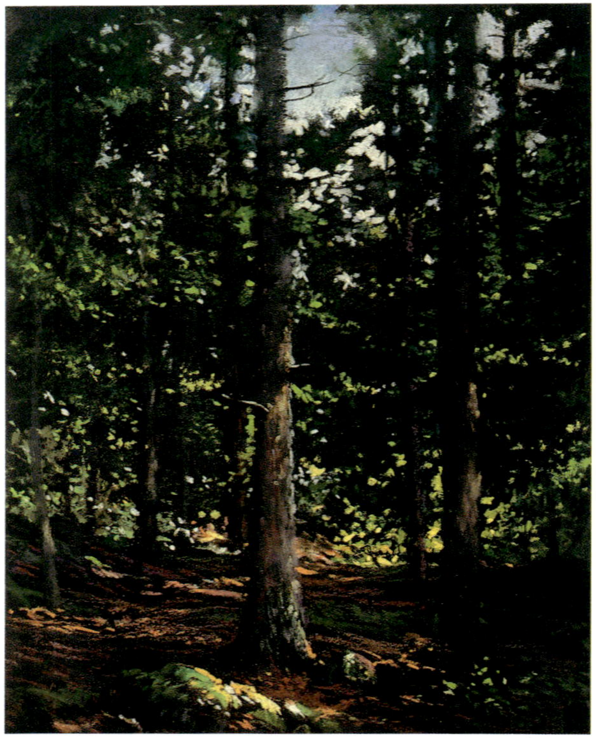

Similarly the reviewer for the *Boston Advertiser* wrote: "Mr. Burpee forces the note in *Pines at Sunset* in which light is literally flung, and *Mountains of Sicily*, too highly complected. Good feeling, an echo of introspection, is in his *Moonrise*; the round moon rises partially from a cloud bank and sends its rays in tremulous luminosity across the water."[14]

For the first time Burpee was beginning to be singled out for high praise, not just noted among his peers, and the praise from the critics came for his work in pastel. Although pastels were rarely granted exhibitions of their own in this period, they were beginning to take over a larger part of the exhibitions of the various watercolor societies throughout the country. Practitioners in pastel as diverse as Whistler, William M. Chase, Laura Hills, Ross Turner, and A.C. Goodwin were exhibiting work to favorable Boston notices.

Burpee seems to have discovered pastel as a medium and to have begun to perfect the use of it in Europe; increasingly in the first years after his return, pastel replaced watercolor as Burpee's medium of choice for works on paper. This tendency would certainly have been augmented by the favorable reception for the work.

Pastel painting methods, as they were discussed in the *Art Amateur*, suggested that nearly neutral, pale tones should be selected for the papers. Although Burpee sometimes followed that method, more often, and in many of his most successful works in pastel, he chose papers of intense shades. Two of his favorites were black and electric blue.

Traditional reports from Burpee's family indicate that he actively resisted selling his work; and it appears that he valued his exhibition

HEMLOCKS, c. 1904.

Pastel on black paper, 14 x 11 1/4 inches.

opposite

STREAM IN WINTER, c.1905.

Pastel on black paper, 4 1/8 x 7 5/16 inches.

pieces. From the few prices that he is known to have asked for them, he is noted as having priced and sold his pictures from $300 to $1,000.[15] Both reports fit well with the news on August 6, 1904, in the *Rockland Courier Gazette* that he had "sold one of his paintings at the St. Louis Exposition for a very handsome sum." This was undoubtedly the oil *Snow Covered Rocks at Sunset*.[16] Eventually he would sell the pastel *Winter Sunset* as well.[17] Halsey C. Ives, chief of the Department of Art for the fair, had the express intention of serving the artist during this exposition with every opportunity for sales, and at least for Burpee, the approach worked. Of the 150 works of art sent by Massachusetts artists, nine sold, two of them by Burpee. C. T. D. Fox, superintendent of the Exhibitors' Bureau of Sales, indicated that 120 paintings worth $70,000 had been sold out of the American section.[18]

In September and October the international jury, chaired by Thomas Allen (1849–1924) of Boston, convened in St. Louis. The majority of the 50 or so members of the international jury for the fine arts were American, but members of every important foreign nation were represented except for France, which had declined to exhibit. Allen was a nearly unique combination, even for his time, of businessman, committed artist, and public-spirited gentleman who gave his time, talent, and money in the service of the arts. Allen was known as "Boston's Millionaire Artist." He had inherited a fortune from his father, who had been a congressman and president of the Missouri Pacific Railroad. Involved with every arts organization of which Burpee was a member, he served as vice president of the Boston Art Club, president of the Boston Society of Watercolor Painters, and president of the Paint and Clay Club, as well as chairman of the Massachusetts committee for the fair, and he was appointed chairman of the international jury of awards for the fair itself. He had served in a similar capacity as a judge for the Columbian Exposition in Chicago in 1893 and the Tennessee Centennial in Nashville in 1897. He would later serve as vice president of the Boston Art Students' Association (Copley Society) and trustee and president of the Museum of Fine Arts, Boston. He was also chairman of the School of the Museum of Fine Arts and was deeply interested in its students. He was a regular exhibitor at the Boston exhibitions as well as at other museums, clubs, and fairs in the United States.

Allen was three years Burpee's junior. They must have known each other reasonably well, since the membership of the Boston Society of Watercolor Painters remained only a few more than a dozen throughout the period in which each man was associated with it. William Howe Downes, the Boston writer, was evidently an admirer of Allen. He wrote that Allen "avers solemnly that he examined every work of art on exhibition in St. Louis, and is alive to tell the tale. His familiarity with three modern languages was of great service to him and to the jury at large, as a number of the foreigners did not speak nor understand English. He also had frequent occasion to act a peacemaker, when a little oil was needed on the troubled waters of the Gold Medal Sea. All in all, it may be guessed that the office was not entirely a sinecure. ... But, it is pertinent to say here that the method used by the jury on the fine arts was well calculated to insure ample deliberation, and to prevent any but the most evidently superior things from being even nominated for an award."[19]

By late October Burpee's pastel, *Winter Sunset*, had taken a bronze medal at the fair. Massachusetts had done well at St. Louis; gold medals were granted for painting to Frank W. Benson, Joseph R. DeCamp, Lucia Fairchild Fuller, George H. Hallowell, Laura C. Hills, and Frederick P. Vinton; silver medals to Adelaide Cole Chase, Charles H. Davis, Wilton Lockwood, Hermann Dudley Murphy, Walter Nettleton, Sarah C. Sears, and Charles H. Woodbury; bronze medals to Leslie P. Thompson, H. H. Gallison, Lilla C. Perry, Philip L.Hale, Charles Hopkinson, William H. Paxton, Walter L. Dean, William P. Burpee, and Hermann Dudley Murphy.

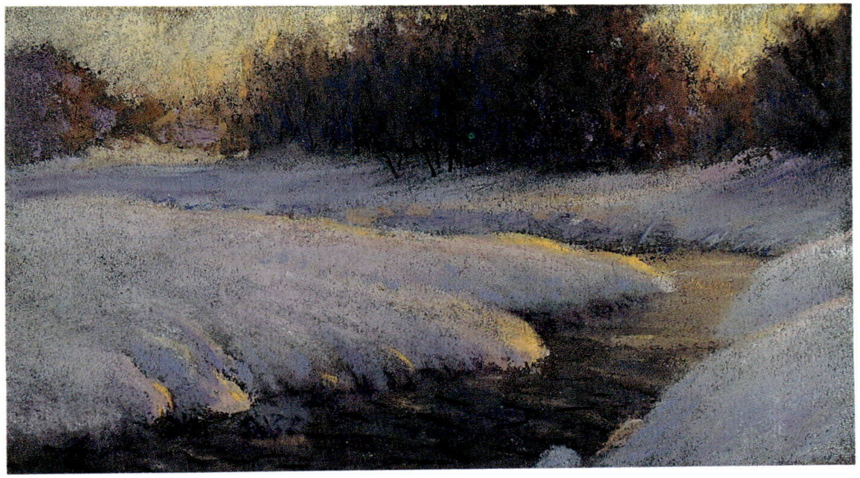

HARCOURT BUILDING FIRE

As seen from the foot of the Bridge on Irvington Street.
The Boston Globe, November 11, 1904.

Less than a week after the announcements of the medalists at St. Louis, the opening of the Semi-Centennial Exhibition of the Boston Art Club brought Burpee into prominence in Boston. Planned as a celebration of the 50th anniversary of the club, it was described as a " members' exhibition in which all of the living artist-members of the club, and many of the deceased members are well represented." Burpee received praise: "Mr. Burpee's several works are also to be remarked for their excellence in color and atmosphere."[20] Ironically, Burpee might not even have known about either the medal or the accolades for his work in the current Boston Art Club exhibition, because he was visiting his family in Rockland on October 25 and remained there until his return to Boston on Friday November 11.[21] Nonetheless, it was proving to be a glorious and memorable year; every exhibition that Burpee entered in 1904 was garnering him prizes and favorable notices.

Demise of the Harcourt Studios

That Friday evening, November 11, Burpee was in his studio at 23 Irvington Street, also known as the Harcourt Building. The structure was one of the large brick buildings that adjoined the tracks of the old Providence Railroad as they came through the Back Bay into Park Square. The Harcourt building was approximately 200 feet long by 150 feet wide and contained, in addition to a large area occupied by the Hutchings-Votey Organ Company, the Blanchard Manufacturing Company, and the George H. Walker lithographic press company, between 25 and 30 artists' studios. Burpee was apparently asleep in his studio in the building when, just before 11:30 p.m., night watchman George Comstock smelled smoke. He rushed up the stairs and found the premises occupied by Walker and Company in flames. He ran to the fire box on the corner of Huntington Avenue and Irvington Street and gave the alarm, and then notified superintendent J. F. Johnson who rushed to the building and, with Comstock, proceeded to awaken the sleeping inhabitants.[22]

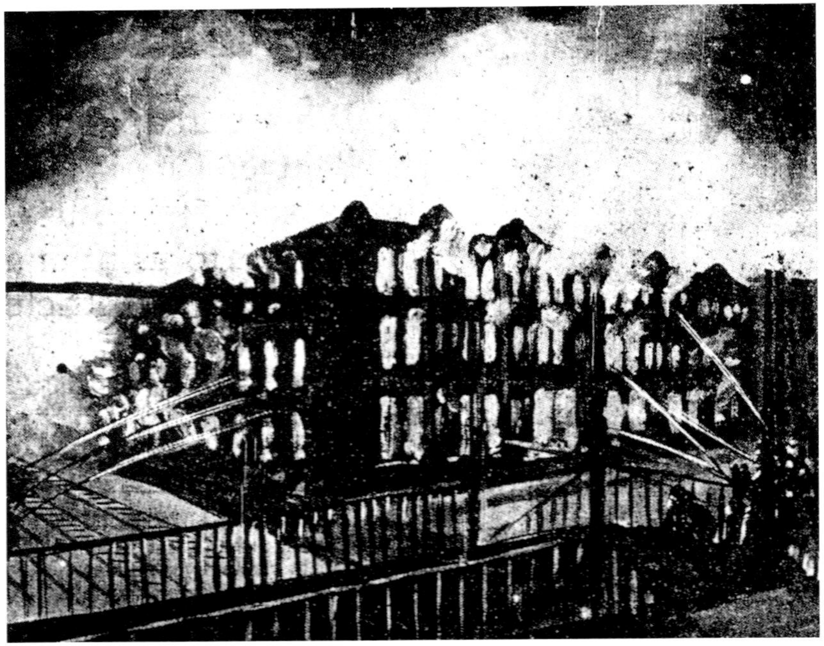

Burpee's own version was reported by the Rockland paper.

> Resting from the fatigue of his journey [after returning from Rockland, he] was suddenly warned by the odor of smoke and an alarming noise that something was wrong in the building. He went into the janitor's apartments and in a very short time the building was in flames fed by the abundance of combustible material. Mr. Burpee was forced to stand idly by and see one after another of the studios vanish in flames which carried with them the product of years of toil. Mr. Burpee not only lost all his paintings but all the money which he had there. Two artists who occupied the St. Botolph Studio nearby pressed their hospitality upon Mr. Burpee and at last accounts he was the guest of Charles Copeland, formerly of Thomaston. He has not sufficiently recovered from the excitement of the affair to formulate plans for the future. [23]

The fire burned for 19 hours and 58 minutes from the time the fire was reported until the "all out" signal was sounded by the fire department. The monetary damage was estimated at a half-million dollars, but that cannot begin to estimate the damage to the careers, hopes, and life work of the many artists whose paintings were destroyed in the blaze. According to contemporary reports:

> The building itself is now only a shell. Its outer walls remain, but its inside has caved in completely. Of the interior walls, there are only four minor ones which can present even a jagged and torn appearance. The interior of the once pretty Harcourt building is now very much like a scrap heap. About the scene of the night's fire many people gathered yesterday morning, and showed a lively curiosity of the remnant of a building.
>
> All Bohemia was there. Artists came around and gazed unhappily at the smoking ruin and wondered when they would get together again — where the inspiration for another picture would ever come. Models showed up for their usual engagement, and wept when they saw only relics of studios. Tech students pressed against the fire lines and stared hard at the police.
>
> The protective department, under Supt. Abbott, worked diligently to save as much of the contents of the building as possible. They took out of the basement a large pile of lumber and put guards over the more valuable property in the offices and studios.
>
> It is now settled that only nine persons were in the building when the fire broke out, and every one of this number is now accounted for. Had the usual number of occupants been in their rooms and studios, it is doubtful if all would have escaped the quickly spreading flames.[24]
>
> Among the artists who had studios in the building were Joseph DeCamp, W. W. Churchill, Henry Rice, Edith C. Swan, Ernest Fosbery, Arthur M. Hazard, William P. Burpee, Alice Stackpole, Ernest L. Ipsen, Felix Schmidt, Mary B. Hazelton, Mrs. Watson, Fred Williams, Mary L. Macomber, Laurin Martin, William M. Paxton, Martha Alford, Joseph H. Hatfield, Helen Paine, Mary C. Patten, Ella B. Smith, Elizabeth V. Taylor, Lizzie F. Wait.
>
> All the studios were well stocked with paintings as the exhibition season is just beginning, and their loss will be very heavy, [nearly] everything having been consumed.
>
> Mr. Paxton had 100 or more canvases in his studio, and like all the other artists, had all his studio implements there. Mr. Paxton has a number of paintings on exhibition at the St. Botolph Club, and these were thus saved. His insurance amounted to only about $1,000. His loss will be heavy.
>
> The total number of paintings cannot be accurately estimated, but it is safe to say that there were over a thousand and perhaps twice as many. The value of these paintings is indeterminable, but many of them would certainly have sold for $500 or $600.[25]

It was remarked that the loss to the artistic world of the city would be severely felt. No one must have felt it more strongly than Burpee. From his ratification in St. Louis he had attracted international attention. Now came the absolute devastation of the work in his studio. Evidence strongly suggests that he was able to salvage some work out of the studio, because a reasonable number of works on paper, all of which predate 1904, descended in the family with charred edges (p. 49). The vast number of smaller works that survive from his pre-Europe years with no suggestion of fire damage points to his having removed his studio contents, before he went to Europe, from his Harcourt Building studio and placed them safely elsewhere, probably in the family house in Rockland. He may have been luckier in this than others, for this most destructive of all Boston artists' studio fires is often cited as the reason for the paucity of pre-1904 paintings by Paxton and the rarity of work in general by Joseph DeCamp.

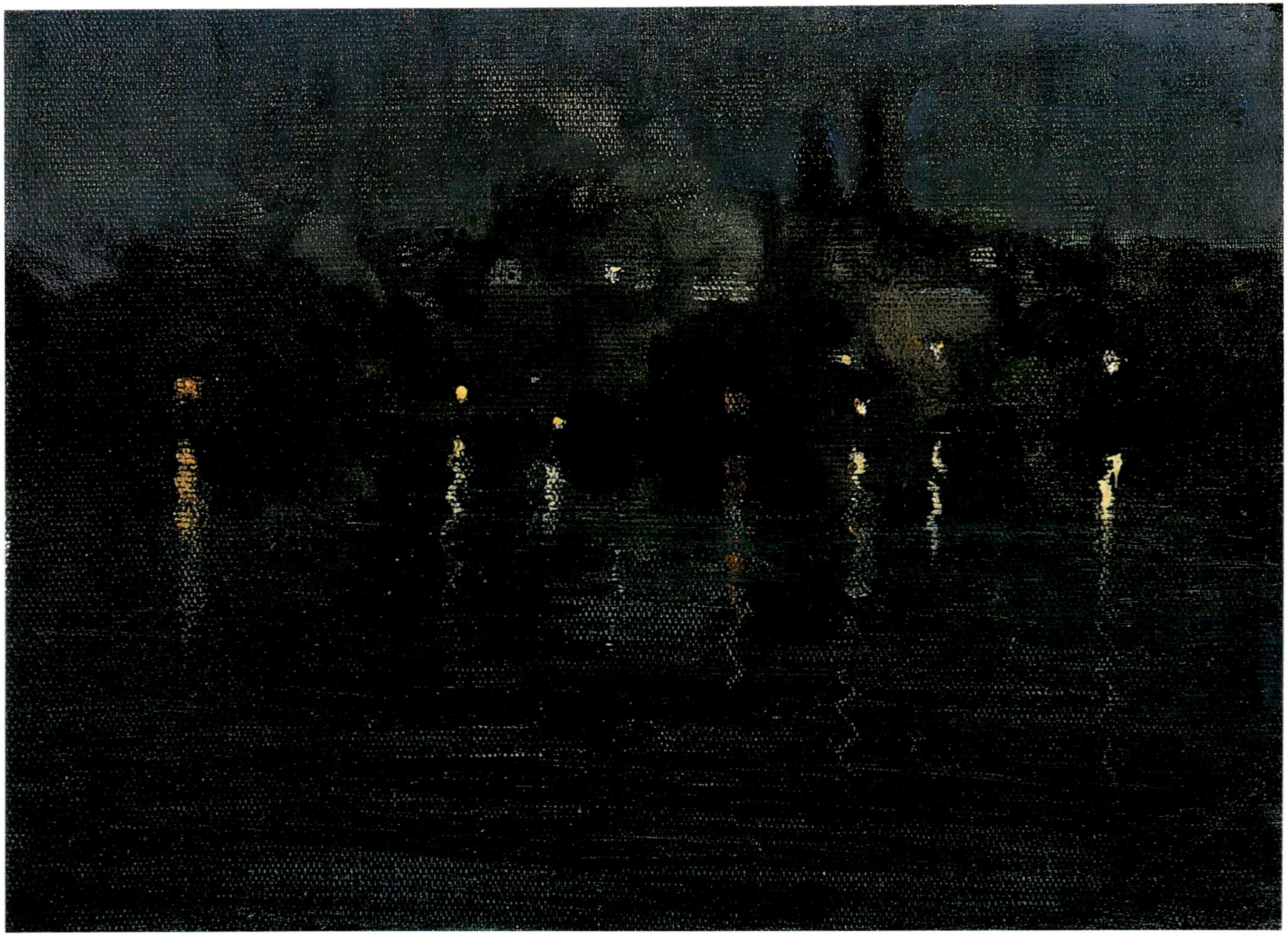

Although the fire was a devastating blow to the Boston artists' community, Burpee personally seems to have bounced back immediately; he exhibited eight works in three separate exhibitions at the Boston Art Club in 1905 and was on the jury of admissions for two of the shows. His *The Harbor Evening*, exhibited at the 71st show in January of 1905, was purchased by the club.

Whistler in Boston

In 1904 there was a major memorial exhibition of the works of James Abbott McNeill Whistler at Copley Hall in Boston. The four-week event, which opened February 23, was both a social and artistic tour de force.

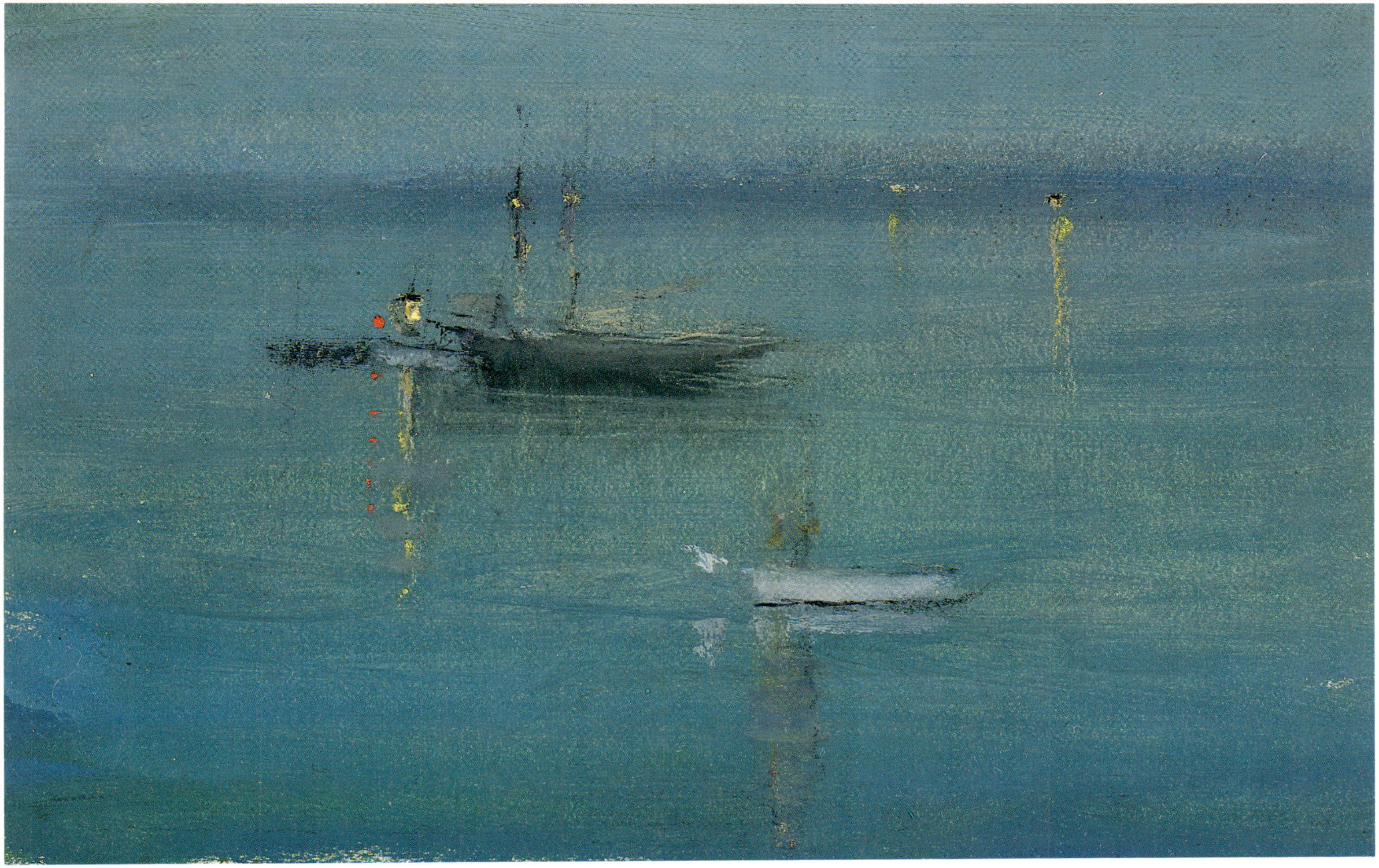

opposite

NIGHT EFFECT , GLOUCESTER, c. 1905.

Oil on canvas, 9 x 12 inches.
Burpee's vantage in East Gloucester provided this night view. As he had noted earlier, "I can only study and guess and remember as well as I can, for I cannot paint out of doors so late."

above

BLUE AND GOLD, GLOUCESTER, c.1905.

Oil on paper mounted on panel, 5 5/8 x 8 7/8 inches.
Burpee's long-standing interest in nocturnes, the 1904 Whistler exhibition in Boston, and Burpee's summers on Gloucester Harbor resulted in a series of glowing night pictures.

Many of the most prominent collectors in Boston, New York, Paris, London, Philadelphia, and Chicago were either organizers or lenders to the show. There were about 150 oil paintings, watercolors, and pastels as well as about 225 etchings and a large collection of lithographs and drawings. It was styled by the *Boston Transcript* as "the exhibition of the year" in which "the collection of Mr. Whistler's works is the largest, the most important, and the most representative ever brought together."[26] Even in Burpee's home town of Rockland, the exhibition merited a three-column review from a fellow Rockland artist. She noted that "Mr. Whistler's style of expressing himself on canvas and paper is so different from all others: and having taken in so many exhibitions both public and private where one sees so many pictures glowing with brilliant color, many being somewhat after the impressionist style; these low tones, subdued colors, rich and harmonious effects of Mr. Whistler's were a revelation and surprise, and an exceedingly agreeable and happy one . . . . Whistler's style is broad and his color schemes are very simple. In his drawings a few lines express much, and in color a few colors express a great deal more. Some of his pictures are simply entitled: *Black and Gold*, *Grey and Silver*, *Pink and Purple*, *Opal and Green*, *Rose and Red*."[27] The community of artists working in Boston responded in one degree or another, attending the exhibition, praising it and to a large extent, being influenced by it. Burpee seems to have been greatly moved by Whistler's work at this time, especially his close-value nocturnes, and we may suppose that the increased interest in this type of work is the result of the impact the Whistler exhibition had on him.

Burpee seems to have had much the same reaction to the exhibition as his Rockland colleague, in the sense that he was able to pose Whistlerian effects and tones against the brightness that was expected by the Boston public in plein-air Impressionism to develop a counterpoint within his own work. He was certainly not about to abandon his increasingly skillful use of broken color Impressionism, but the simplified palette of Whistler's nocturnes attracted him as an alternate mode. To be sure, Burpee had been attracted to the nocturne nearly 15 years earlier and had exhibited *Moonrise by the Sea* in 1892. Tonalist work seems to have become a staple for him by the end of the century, and he was always interested in the effect of light. But as he searched for new directions in the first part of the 20th century, Whistler's nocturnes seem to have become a model for a body of work. This attraction to the nocturne coincided with an increased amount of time spent in and around Gloucester and East Gloucester. Many of the oil paintings and pastels of the next ten years in the Whistlerian mode are either of Gloucester or seem likely to be so. Gloucester has a particularly distinctive skyline as seen from East Gloucester, and it appears regularly in Burpee's work. Burpee began to adopt Whistlerian titles as well: *Gray-Green Willow*, *Rose and Gold*, *Almond and Olive*, *Early Morning Effect — Gloucester Harbor*. The light and color sensitivity in Whistler's work was certain to appeal to Burpee, as was the great success of Whistler's pastels as Burpee increasingly became a master of that difficult medium. Whistler, however, worked from memory, and Burpee, in staying with his New England sensibilities, captured the essence of an observed moment of nature. While he may not have painted the night on site, neither did he compose as decoratively as Whistler might.[28]

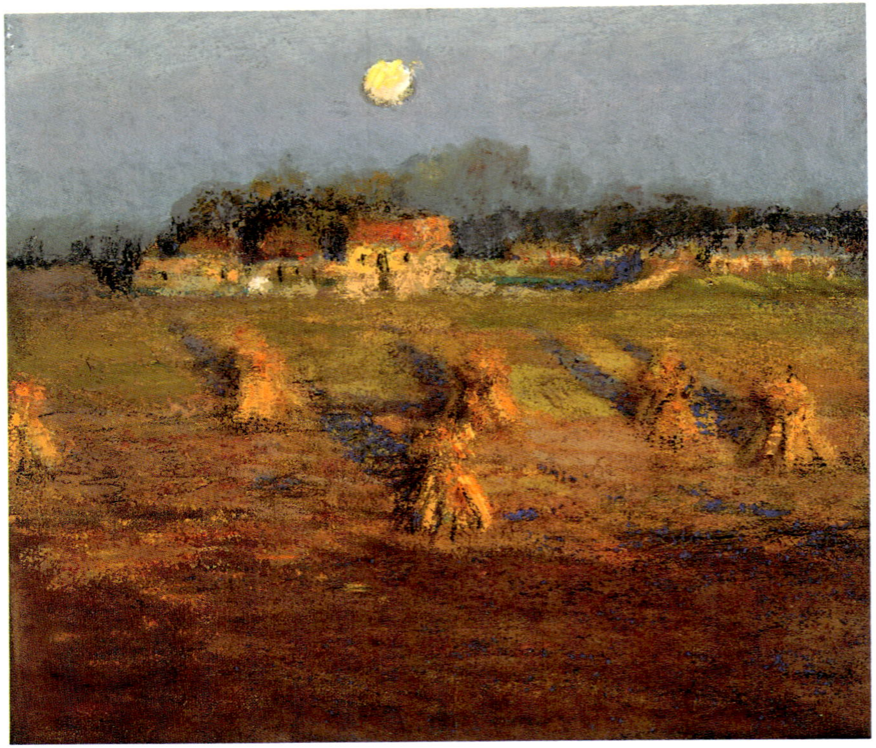

opposite

HARVEST MOON, c.1905.

Oil on black-ground canvas, 10 x 11 inches.
Burpee certainly knew Arthur Wesley Dow and his theories and work, and Burpee often adopted Tonalism for oils and pastels.

right

COASTAL SUNSET, c.1905.

Oil on paper mounted on panel, 6 x 8 1/2 inches.
Coastal Sunset demonstrates Burpee's growing sophistication and compares to Homer's Prout's Neck paintings as well as to works by Monet.

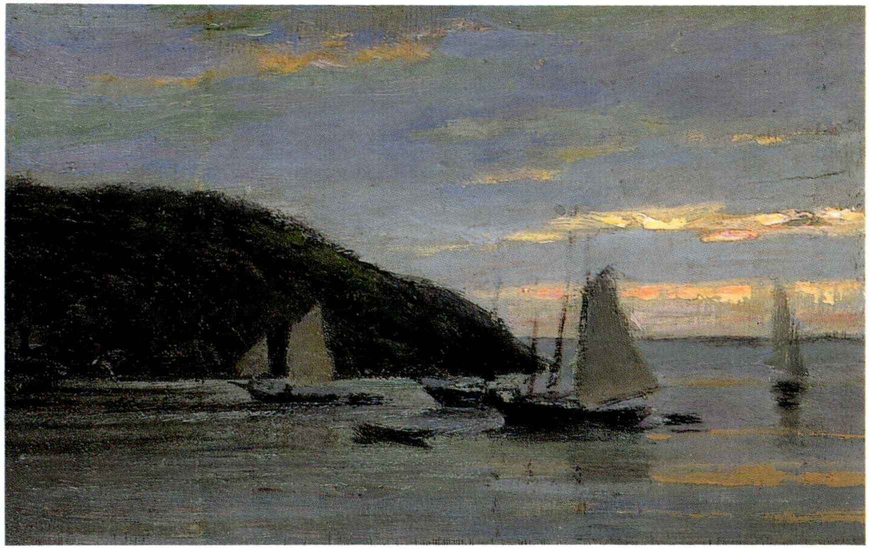

Maine and the Mediterreanean

In the summer of 1905, Burpee was again working in Maine; this time he had taken a "temporary studio" with E. H. Crie and was putting the finishing touches on a large marine subject of which one critic would note, "The scene is off-shore at Criehaven, where a great wave is rearing its huge bulk at a bar. Sea and sky, with the low sun lighting the foam of the breaking wave, are admirably handled" (p. 84).[29] Criehaven is a point on the western side of Ragged Island, the southernmost island in the Matinicus group, which is due southeast of Rockland. There the Crie family seems to have delighted in providing studio space to artist friends, including Burpee, Edwin Brown, and Burpee's friend and colleague Charles Copeland, who made numerous studies of the island and may have accompanied Burpee there.[30]

That same year the siren sound of Europe was calling for Burpee to return. He booked passage on the White Star steamer *Romanic* and left Boston October 28 for Ponta Delgada in the Azores. He had closed his Boston studio and, as he had done before his previous trip, retreated to his friends and family in Rockland, no doubt to visit and most certainly to store paintings in the loft studio at 43 Park Street. He told friends that on this trip he would stop at the Azores and winter in Spain and that he expected to go to Algeria, following the path of the White Star steamers, which would allow the artist to stop over at Gibraltar as well as in Algeria.[31] Burpee left paintings to submit to the Autumn Exhibition at the Boston Art Club which were shown from November 17 to December 2. The titles indicate a combination of landscape and seaside pictures, and one, *Sand Dunes at Sunset*, was noted by reviewers as "full of good qualities" that should "attract more than passing attention."[32] He also left an oil painting, *Sunshine and Shadow*, with the picturehangers Stedman Wilder & Co. for submission to the 1906 73rd Boston Art Club Exhibition. It was exhibited from January 6 to February 3, 1906, to good notices (and the comment that he was among the well-known names of the Boston contingent) while Burpee was wintering in Spain.[33]

His route to Spain with a planned stop in the Azores was probably prompted by the whetting of interest when he passed the islands in 1897. He had written, "I cannot describe with a pen the lovely beauty which we saw, made twenty times greater by the unusual effect of light and shade caused by the rain clouds which hovered over and near these islands. . . . I made a few watercolor sketches from my 'port hole' of bits of the Azores."[34]

Burpee's return to the Azores in 1905 lasted long enough (probably more than a month) to produce the studies for exhibition pictures over the next several years. He did not settle on the island of Pico, which he had described in 1897, but on the island of Sao Miguel in the northeast, the largest of the Azores. He stayed long enough at Ponta Delgada to provide studies for paintings and then went east to the town of Furnas. The valley there is a famous sight, and the town of Furnas is known for its mineral springs and geysers. In this quiet resort he had time to contemplate the strange vegetation and verdant beauty of the island and the people and architecture.

He went on to Spain where he seems to have spent most of his time in Granada, but titles exhibited after his return would indicate that he visited Toledo and revisited Rhonda. He had written in 1897 from the Hotel Washington Irving at Granada of his too-brief stay of two days, "The Alhambra, with its marvellous courts, baths, chambers, towers, et cet. was fully up to the largest expectations, and the Sierras covered with eternal snows were more beautiful than I can tell. But we had to leave and next we visited Rhonda, an old, old town sitting on a rocky precipice cleft by a stream, and a most charming resort for a painter of landscape as well as for one who loves street scenes and quaint houses. I had a happy time here for two days."[35] He had expressed the desire to return to "this most paintable place", and now was able to do so.

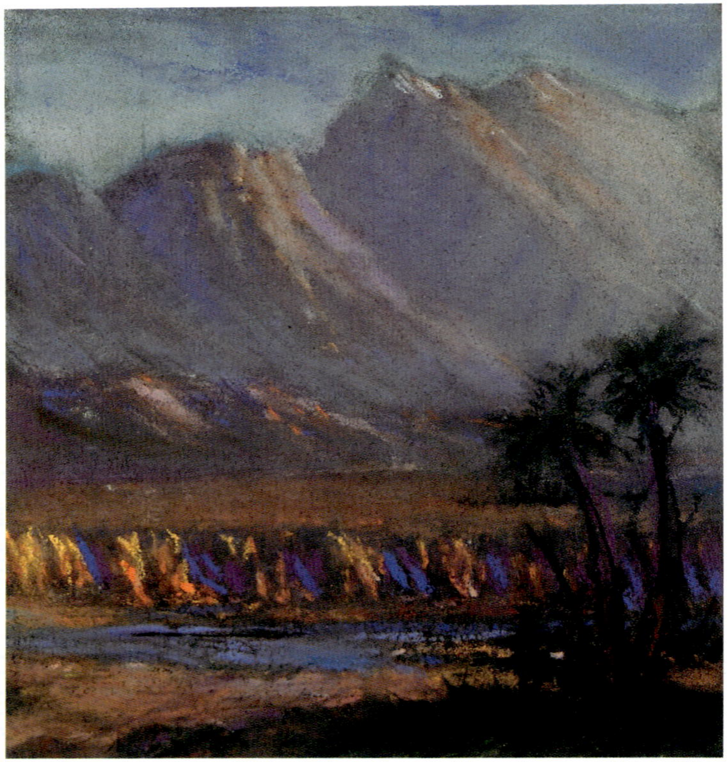

Algeria was an unusual feature of this winter of painting in the lands that border the western Mediterranean. It was not a regular stop for American painters, and of North African sites certainly Morocco and Egypt were more popular. Moreover, Burpee chose to venture inland to Biskra, an ancient spa at the eastern edge of the Sahara Atlas mountains on a river that runs to a dry lake at the edge of the desert, which is below sea level. The area was developed by the Romans because of the mild climate, and the warm spas they used to treat rheumatism, and because it had one of the few rivers that flowed all year. The Arabs and Berbers continued the development of the oasis as a garden of date palms, fruit trees, and vegetables for the country. It has been called everything an oasis should be. Burpee must have been well aware that he was about to turn 60. There is nothing to indicate that he ever craved a life of luxury. Yet his trip this winter of 1905 – 06 suggests that, in addition to seeking out new and picturesque subjects for painting, he was choosing a route of mild climates and warm spas.

It is almost certain that the Atlas Mountains are the subject of a series of small striking pastels, all executed on black paper, that show the landscape glowing. Likewise, Burpee's pastels showing dry landscape studded with date palms are probably from Biskra. It would be interesting to know why he selected Algeria at the outset of his trip and who suggested that he settle for part of the winter in this oasis. Burpee had complained when he first went to Europe in 1897 that travel tired him and that he was less inclined than other travelers to rush around. The evidence is that he had the luxury, this time, for at least a month at each site and that he viewed this trip as an opportunity for painting instead of sightseeing. It may be that when he departed Algiers he took the White Star Line to Marseilles, which was the line's next port of call, and continued to the French Alps. This itinerary would have provided the opportunity to do the studies for the pastel of Mont Blanc that he exhibited in 1910 (or that work could have been based on his hurried trip to Switzerland and the French Alps of 1898).

He returned to Boston with the fruits of this winter of painting in time to enter three works in the 74th exhibition of the Boston Art Club, which opened April 6: *View of the Bay Eastward, Ponta Delgada*; *Looking Down into the Valley of Furnas*; and *At the Fountain*, which was reviewed as "a vivid sketch, with fine color contrasts."[36]

Once he had come back to the Studio Building at 110 Tremont Street in Boston, he kept the same address until he departed Boston permanently, although he moved from studio to studio in the building. Similarly, he returned to living in the South End and remained on Warren Avenue, although he changed houses.

New York and Cape Ann

Burpee began to expand his studio work beyond Boston. In the winter of 1906 – 07 he began a period of spending the winter in New York with his family, probably with his niece, Winifred (Shaw) Fales, in Manhattan. This led to opportunities to create a series of pastels of the Palisades and battleships in the Hudson River that probably continued through the mid-1920s. It was noted that during the several winters that he spent in New York, he took the opportunity to paint the country outside the city.[37]

In addition to his studio in Boston and his winter months in New York, by 1907 Burpee also maintained a studio in East Gloucester. *The Cape Ann Shore* reported on July 4, 1908, "W. P. Burpee, the well-known Boston artist and an old comer at the Harbor View is here for another season and will occupy the Green Studio." The Harbor View in East Gloucester was a grand house and complex of buildings that took visitors and had, as additional space, two studios for rent. "The studio is big and cool with dark corners, and scattered about on easels, tables, and even on the floors are pictures and sketches from Venice, Spain, Algiers, and many other parts of the world...Studies of sea and shore, sunsets on the harbor, and bits of foreign landscape are found in his studio. Mr. Burpee is an enthusiastic pastellist, and makes many of his best pictures in this elusive material." There is a spate of Gloucester pictures in a soft Impressionist style that seem

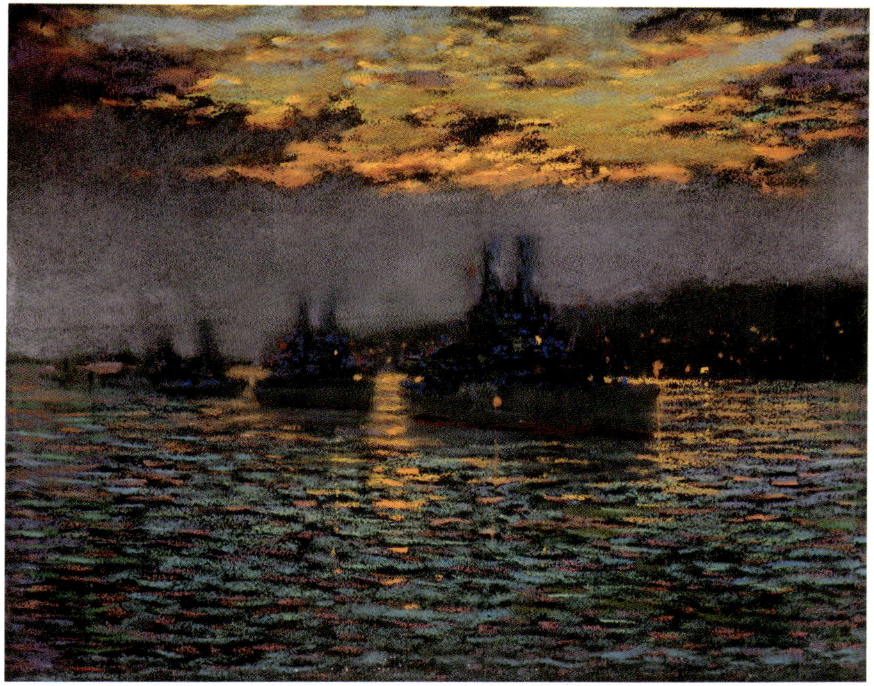

above

BATTLESHIPS IN THE HUDSON RIVER, 1910 – 25.

Pastel on black paper, 9 1/2 x 12 1/8 inches.
Beginning in 1906, Burpee spent winters in New York which resulted in a series of pastels of the lower Hudson River and the Palisades.

opposite

OASIS, ATLAS MOUNTAINS, 1906.

Pastel on black paper, 6 3/4 x 6 1/4 inches.
The Sahara Atlas mountains at the Biskra oasis in Algeria were the subject of a series of pastels on black paper.

to date from this time. It is clear that he was going to Gloucester and Cape Ann almost from the moment he returned to Boston, and that he had taken the studio in earlier years at the Harbor View; he would return to the same Green Studio for the summer of 1910.[38]

A Well-Known Painter

At age 60 he seemed to increase his exhibition schedule. At the Boston Art Club Autumn Exhibition in November 1906 he exhibited three paintings, and had three paintings in the January 1907 Boston Art Club show. In the latter exhibition he received the accolades of the critic for the *Boston Globe* who prefaced his remarks with, "The standard which the jury set is very high, and it shows the wonderful advances that have been made, especially in landscape painting, in this country during the past decade. The technical skill of the artists leaves nothing to be desired, and the manner in which this skill is applied shows that American artists have the quality of intellectual force which produces great pictures. *Looking Over the Dunes*, by William P. Burpee, is a brilliant bit of work in which the warm sand dunes with bluish shadows make a fine color note against the sea and sky."[39] In February Burpee exhibited in Washington his *Evening Light Over Gloucester Town* at the 1st Corcoran Exhibition of Oil Paintings by Contemporary Artists. In March he exhibited four works at the Boston Art Club watercolor exhibition and served on the jury; a critic noted,"*In a Palace Garden, Granada* is characteristic of this painter. It is a carefully considered study, true in drawing and values, and not dependent upon its beauty of subject for its attractiveness."[40] Burpee became one of the three members of the Boston jury of selection (with Ross Turner and Theodore Wendel) for the 19th Exhibition of Water-colors, Pastels, and Miniatures by American Artists at the Art Institute of Chicago in May. He submitted two works for that show. He also exhibited *Comber Coming Around Ledges* in the 1907 annual watercolor exhibition at the Pennsylvania Academy of the Fine Arts.

In 1908 Burpee again exhibited in both the oil and watercolor shows of the Boston Art Club, in the Boston Society of Watercolor Painters, and at the 20th exhibition at the Art Institute of Chicago. For 1909 his schedule included the January Boston Art Club exhibition, the 20th exhibition of the Boston Society of Watercolor Painters, the Brockton 4th Annual Exhibition, and an exhibition at the Art Institute of Chicago. In 1910 he continued the pace by showing at the 105th Annual Exhibition of the Pennsylvania Academy, which opened January 22 in Philadelphia; at the Brockton 5th Annual Exhibition January 29; at the Boston Society of Watercolor Painters, which opened February 28; at the special exhibition of the Boston Art Club, which opened March 30 to celebrate remodeling; and with the Boston Society of Watercolor Painters at Marshall Field & Co., Chicago, in December.

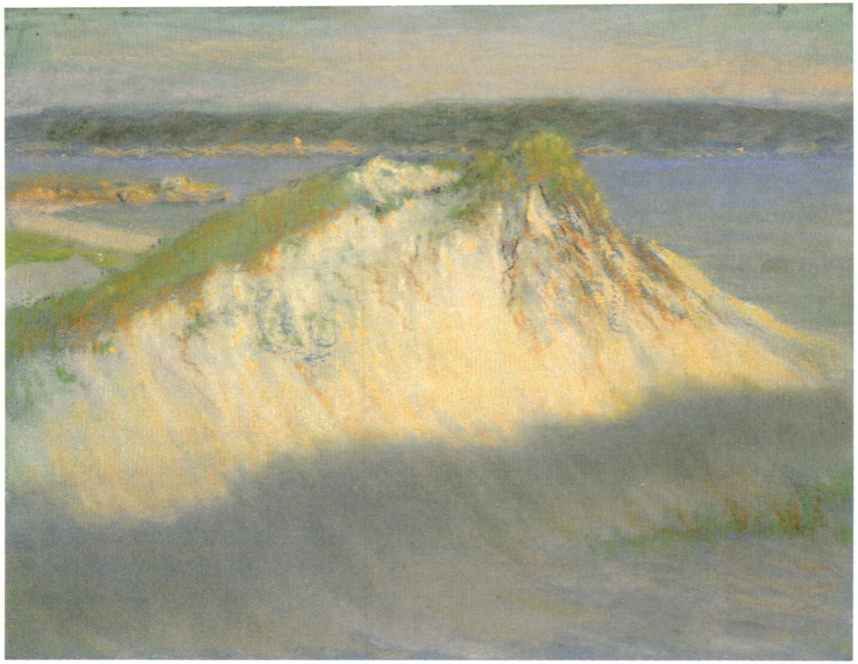

GLOUCESTER DUNES, c.1907.

Pastel on blue paper, 9 3/16 x 12 inches.

GLOUCESTER, c. 1907.

Oil on canvas, 12 1/8 x 14 7/8 inches.

ICEBOUND, c. 1910.

Pastel on black paper, 7 5/16 x 9 7/16 inches.

His pastels continued to fare well with the critics.

> There are several architectural things which we found interesting ... Mr. Burpee's interior of a jolly kitchen in the Azores [among several others]. Beyond these there are not many notable things.[41] William P. Burpee's group of eight works [at the Boston Society of Watercolor Painters, 1909] is composed wholly of pastels. One of his most novel compositions is a church interior in the Azores with a crowd of worshippers entitled *Day of Notre Dame Ponta Delgada, Azores*; although the drawing of his figures is not particularly convincing, he suggests a crowd very well and by the dramatic effect of his lighting he succeeds in giving considerable vitality to the impression. His landscapes, as usual, are original and interesting for their warm and pleasing color. The *Mists Rising from a River at Sunrise* is excellently observed, and the *Mountain Side and Valley* is an uncommonly interesting landscape.[42]

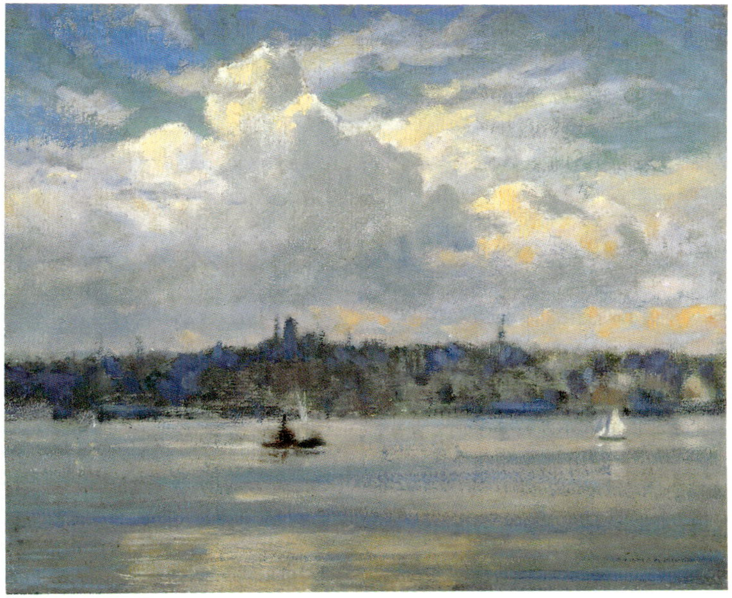

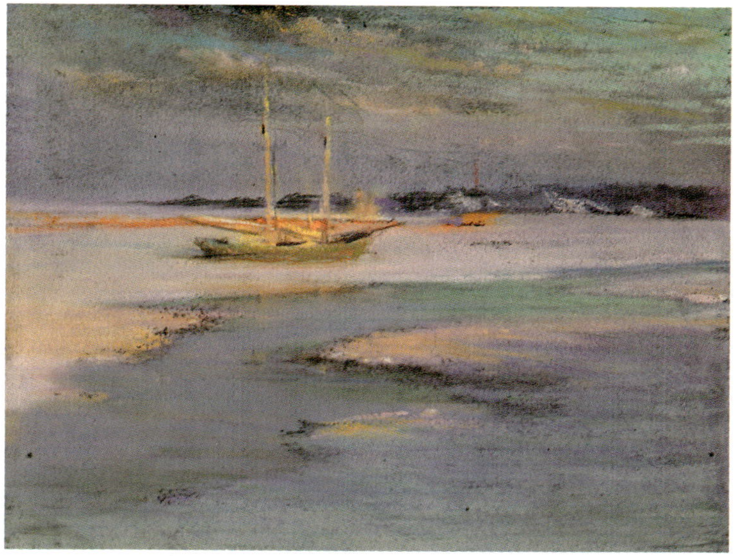

> Mr. Burpee has taken to painting pastel pictures of snow scenes, and all of his dozen contributions are of this nature. In the middle of this group [at the Boston Society of Watercolor Painters in 1910] is an ambitious mountain subject entitled *Gold and Rose on Mt. Blanc*, a view of the sunset glow creeping over the vast snow fields of the great peak and the Glacier des Bossons as seen from the West with the wooded foreground in shadow. Among his other winter scenes, we note one painting in the Public Garden of Boston, and a series of snow-framed streams and brooks in the country with the white surfaces depicted in various effects of light. On the whole, he makes a very interesting exhibit.[43]

> William P. Burpee's group of nine pastels [at the Boston Society of Watercolor Painters in 1911] has one of the best places in the large gallery. The best things in his group are the *Rose and Gold*, *Winter's Gray*, and *Sunset Through Raindrops*.[44]

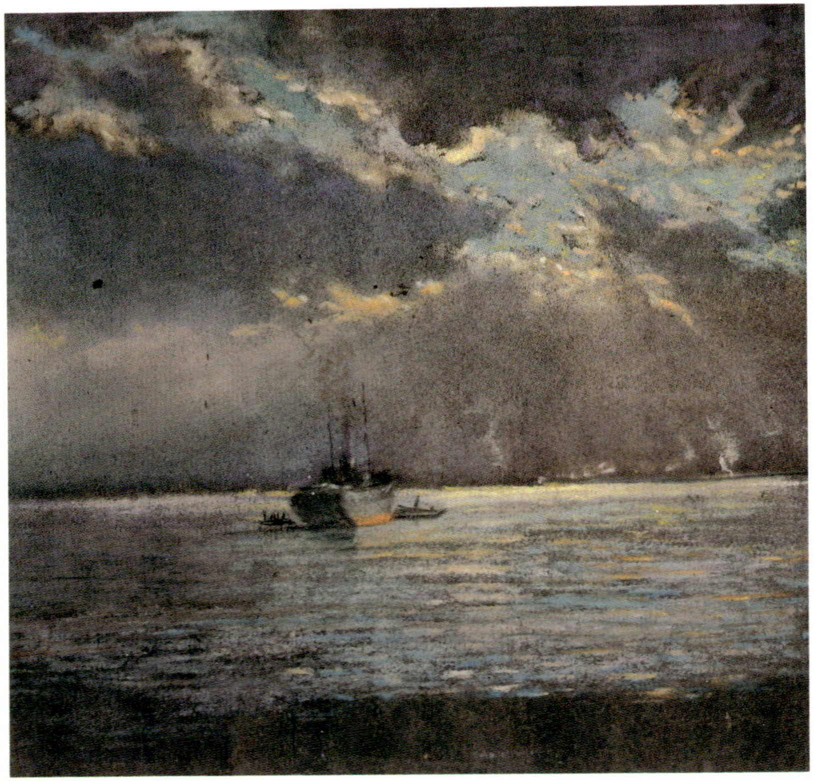

above

SKY EFFECT, c.1910.

Pastel on black paper, 10 1/4 x 10 3/4 inches.

opposite

SUNSET SAIL, c.1910.

Pastel on black paper, 7 1/16 x 8 1/2 inches.
Burpee developed, in his pastels at least, into fully Post-Impressionist and even Pointillist works.

On March 6, Burpee and three of his fellow artists in the Studio Building decided to open their studios to the public in a joint exhibition. Again the critics responded:

> An old custom is revived in the joint studio exhibition made by four of the artists having rooms in the Studio building, 110 Tremont Street, this week. The exhibitors are William P. Burpee, Felix A. Gendrot, J. K. Chambers and Henry Plympton Spaulding, whose rooms, Nos 85, 86, 87 and 92 are all quite close together . . . . Mr. Burpee is exhibiting a considerable number of his pastels, which include a few recent works of much interest. Five of these are hung on the east wall of the room, and make a very handsome group. In the center is a sunrise effect on the Merrimac River, with mist rising from the stream, and the sky and water slightly tinted with rosy light. At the right of this hangs an ideal landscape with a handsome lighting effect and dramatic feeling for oppositions, and at the left is a small picture of a Rockport granite sloop at sunset. At either side of the group are snowy winter landscapes with the sunlight falling on the fresh fallen snow and forming a strong contrast with the shadowed passages. One of these was painted in the Middlesex Fells and the other in New York State. Among the rest of Mr. Burpee's works we note a charming little marine piece from Katwyck and two well-drawn and interesting studies of the interior of Seville Cathedral.[45]

From 1904 onward, the critics singled out Burpee's work in pastel for praise and he seems to have become more confident about exhibiting; he showed pictures more often, in greater numbers, and more widely. It is suprising, therefore, that the 1911 Brockton Women's Club exhibition beginning March 20 seems to be the last time that Burpee exhibited publicly in the Boston area. This remarkable exhibition brought together paintings by artists from Boston, New York and Europe. Burpee's pictures hung for the last time with Monet's, whose *Prairie à Giverny* was included. We know little about his activities for 1912 and 1913 except that he listed himself in the *American Art Annual*, in addition to his other

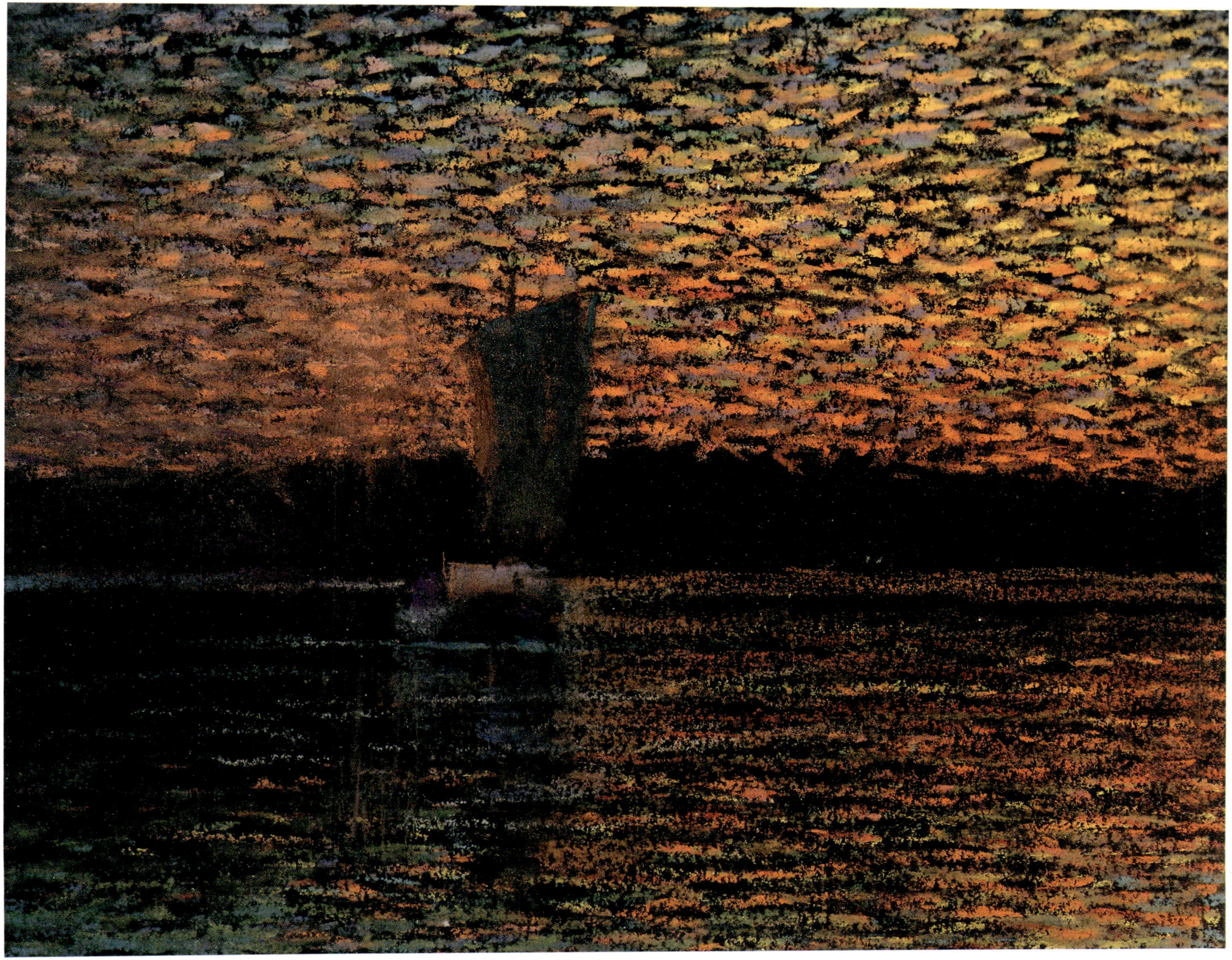

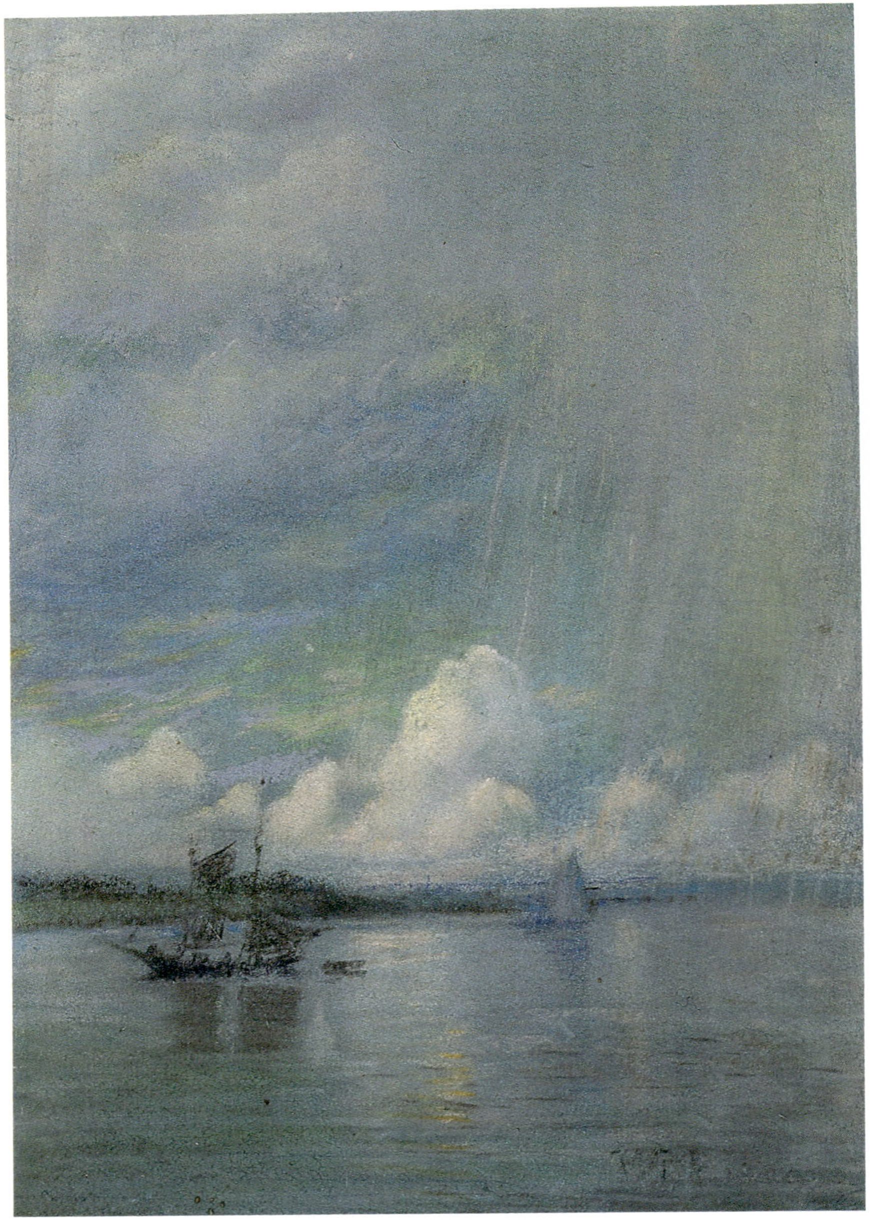

abilities, as "teacher." He had first designated himself as such in 1909 and nothing is known about where, how, or whom he might have taught.

Burpee is said to have wintered in Germany and to have maintained a studio there as he did in Spain in 1905 – 06.[46] The most likely time for this to have taken place was the winter of 1911 – 12 or 1912 –13. There is no prior exhibition record of the German pictures, suggesting that they had not yet been painted, nor are there any Boston exhibitions by Burpee from this point on in which to see the results of a winter in Germany. There are a significant number of German pictures that are noted in pencil as "Germany" or "Berlin" (some showing snow), and there may be other paintings that date from this period that have not yet been identified as German. He certainly would not have been in Germany after 1914.

Burpee was visiting or living in Rockland in early November 1913, for it was noted that he and Mr. and Mrs. James Wight (Burpee's sister Emma and her husband) were leaving shortly and would spend the winter in Ridgewood, New Jersey.[47] This signified the end of Burpee's Boston career and of his exhibiting in Boston. He resigned his membership in the Boston Art Club and embarked on a new chapter in his life as he returned to Maine and set himself new challenges in painting.

left

SUMMER SHOWER, c. 1910.

Pastel on blue paper, 13 3/8 x 9 7/16 inches.
Burpee sought drama in the subject he knew best through effects of both light and weather.

opposite

SPRING IN GERMANY, c. 1912.

Pastel on black paper, 10 1/8 x 9 7/8 inches.
Most of the German pastels, many of them nocturnes, are on black paper, and their striking colors and contrasts are more modern and less conventional than Burpee's watercolors of the same period.

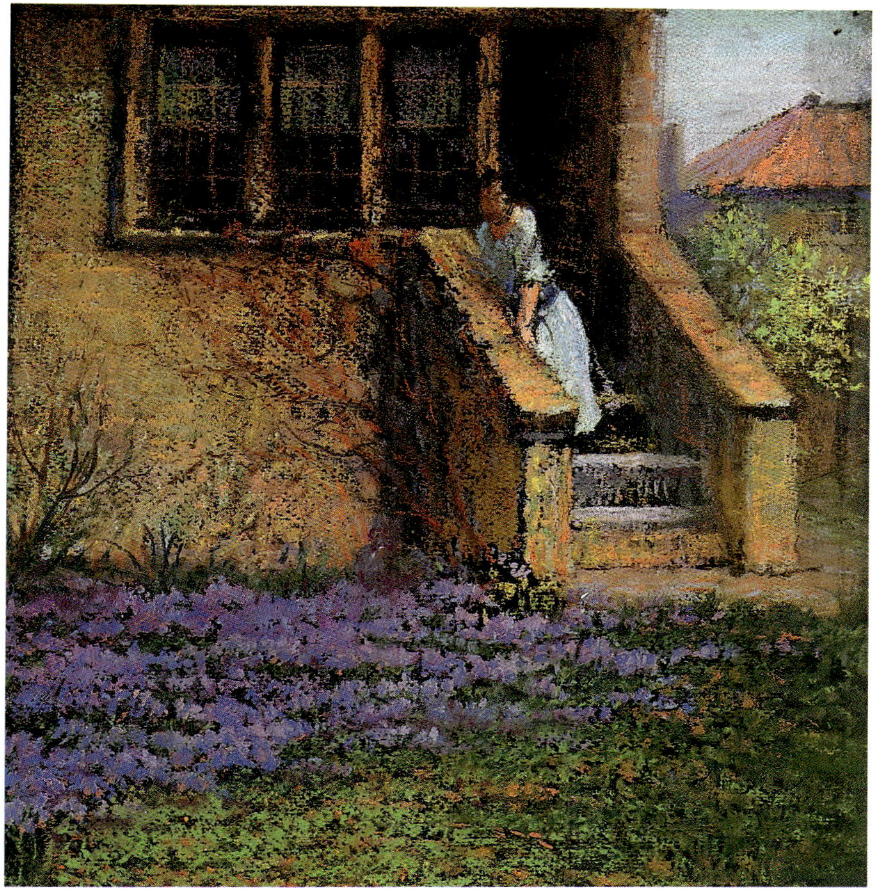

NOTES, Chapter Four

[1] William Howe Downes, "Art at St. Louis: A Preliminary Survey of the Field," in the *Boston Transcript*, Oct. 29, 1904, p. 21.
[2] *Boston Transcript*, Nov. 5, 1904, p. 14; ibid., Feb. 6, 1904.
[3] *Boston Herald*, Jan. 4, 1902, p. 3.
[4] *Boston Journal*, April 6, 1901, p. 4.
[5] *Boston Transcript*, April 6, 1901, p. 19.
[6] *Boston Herald*, Jan. 4, 1902, p. 3.
[7] *Boston Journal*, April 5, 1902, p. 5.
[8] *Rockland Courier Gazette*, Feb. 6, 1904, p. 3.
[9] Thomas Allen, "Massachusetts in the Department of Fine Arts: Louisiana Purchase Exposition, Saint Louis, 1904,"[1905]; typescript in the manuscript collection of the Missouri Historical Society, St. Louis.
[10] *Rockland Courier Gazette*, Feb. 6, 1904, p. 3; ibid., Aug. 2, 1904, p. 3.
[11] *Boston Transcript*, Feb. 3, 1904, p. 18.
[12] Thomas Allen, op. cit.
[13] *Boston Transcript*, Feb. 8, 1904, p. 12, col. 6.
[14] *Boston Advertiser*, Feb. 6, 1904.
[15] Alice Frost Lord, op. cit., and catalogue where Burpee had one priced at $300. Works on paper in the 1927 Portland show were $125.
[16] C.T.D. Fox letter to Halsey C. Ives, Jan. 9, 1905, concerning the Louisiana Purchase Exposition, Department of Art, Exhibitors' Bureau of Sales, manuscript collection, the Missouri Historical Society, St. Louis, Missouri.
[17] Thomas Allen, op. cit.
[18] C.T.D. Fox, op. cit.
[19] William Howe Downes, *Boston Transcript*, Oct. 19, 1904, p. 4., col. 4.
[20] *Boston Transcript*, Nov. 5, 1904, p. 14.
[21] *Rockland Courier Gazette*, Oct. 25, 1904, p. 3.
[22] *Boston Transcript*, Nov. 12, 1904, p. 5.
[23] *Rockland Courier Gazette*, Nov. 15, 1904, p. 3.
[24] *Boston Sunday Herald*, Nov. 13, 1904, section 1, p. 6.
[25] *Boston Herald*, Nov. 12, 1904, p. 5.
[26] "Whistler's Great Works," *The Boston Transcript*, Feb. 23, 1904, p. 2.
[27] Abbie B. Kirkpatrick, "The Whistler Exhibition," *Rockland Courier Gazette*, March 26, 1904, p. 2.
[28] Sharon Flescher in *From Realism to Symbolism: Whistler and His World*, Columbia University, New York1971.
[29] *Rockland Courier Gazette*, June 20, 1905.
[30] The William A. Farnsworth Library and Art Museum in Rockland owns several of Copeland's Criehaven watercolors.
[31] *Rockland Courier Gazette*, Oct 1905, clipping in the Burpee archives; White Star Line, "Proposed Sailings" broadside in the Peabody Museum of Salem, Massachusetts.
[32] *Boston Globe*, Nov. 18, 1905, p. 4; *Boston Herald*, Nov. 18, 1905, p. 6.
[33] *Boston Advertiser*, Jan. 6, 1906, p. 4; *Boston Herald*, Jan. 6, 1906, p. 2; and *Boston Saturday Evening Transcript*, Jan. 6, 1906, p. 6.
[34] Burpee letters AAA, Oct. 22, 1897 [with later additions through Nov. 1.], Gibraltar, to Mrs. N. A. Burpee.
[35] Burpee letters AAA, Nov. 30, 1897, Naples, to 'My Dear Friends'.
[36] *Boston Saturday Evening Globe*, April 7, 1906, p. 6.
[37] *Bangor Daily News*, Dec. 16/17, 1940.
[38] *Boston Evening Transcript*, Aug. 28, 1908, p.10, col. 4; Jean N. Oliver, "Where Artists Swarm," *Boston Evening Transcript*, Sept. 14, 1910, p.22, col. 5-6; Cape Ann Shore, July 9, 1910.
[39] *Boston Globe*, Jan. 5, 1907, Part 2, p. 8.
[40] *Boston Advertiser*, March 16, 1907, p. 5.
[41] *Boston Transcript*, March 27, 1908.
[42] *Boston Transcript*, March 1, 1909.
[43] *Boston Transcript*, Feb. 28, 1910.
[44] *Boston Transcript*, Jan. 17, 1911; also Edith Burnham, *Boston Traveller*, Jan. 20, 1911, p.11.
[45] *Boston Transcript*, March 6, 1911.
[46] Lord op. cit. : Lord says that Burpee spent one year each in Spain and Germany.
[47] *Rockland Courier Gazette*, Nov. 8, 1913, p. 7.

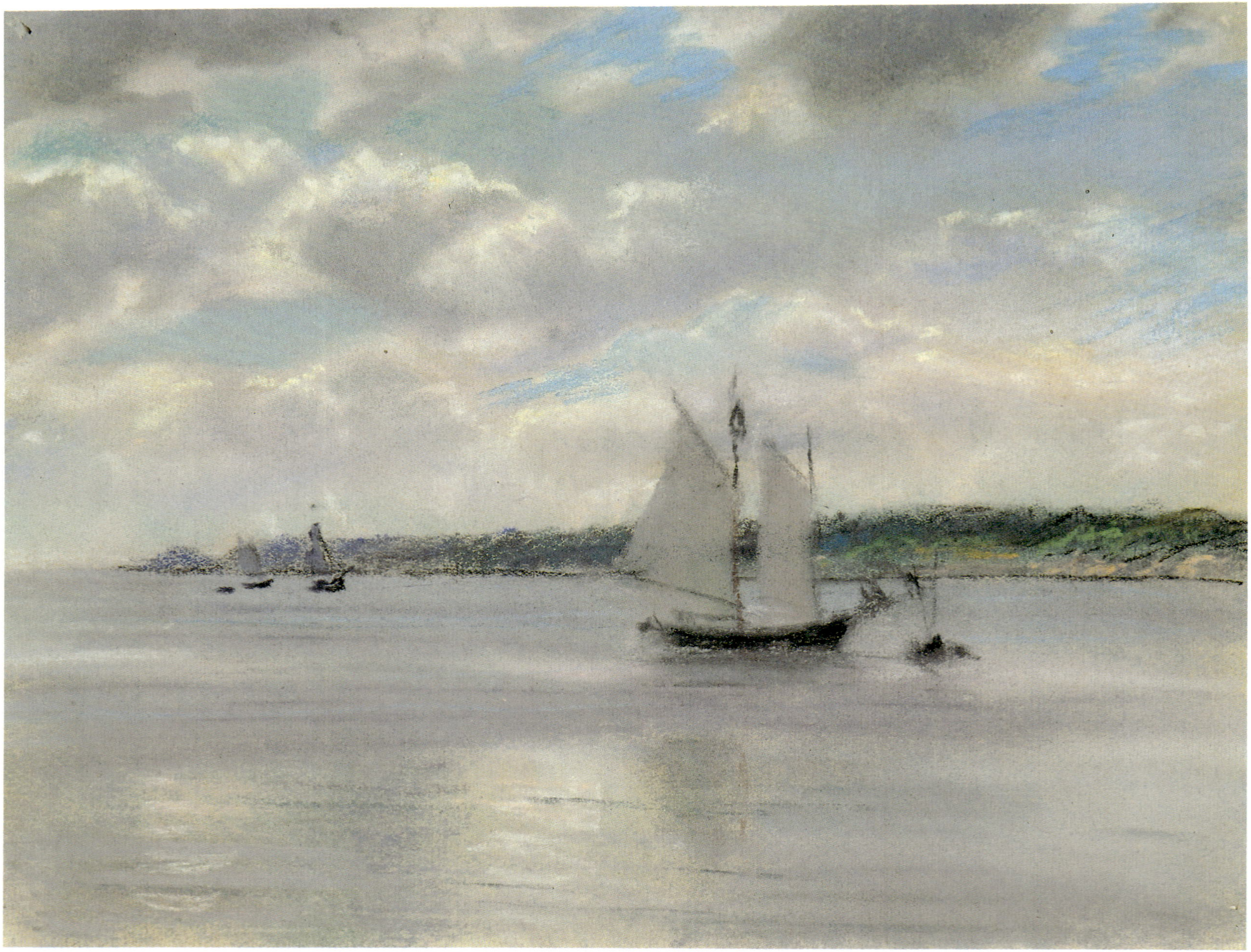

CHAPTER FIVE

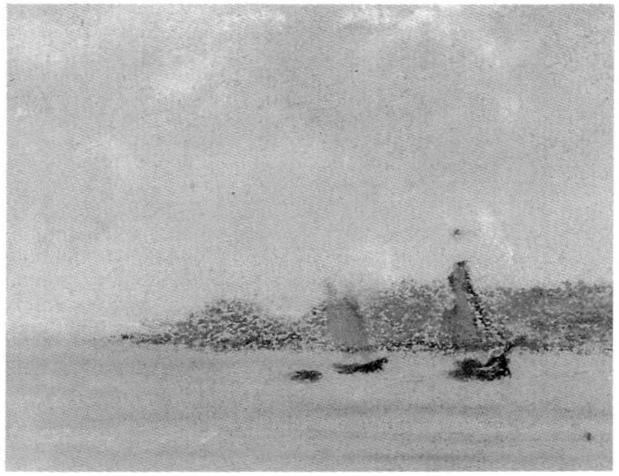

Return to Maine: *Evening On Penobscot Bay (1913 – 1940)*

Rockland had always been a retreat for Burpee, who had returned there regularly throughout his Boston years. His affectionate letters to his family show the comfort and security that they gave to him, although he may have been distant physically. He seems to have been close to both of his sisters, and the invitation by Mr. and Mrs. James Wight to spend the winter with them in Ridgewood, New Jersey, illustrates this point. His mother, having died in 1908, must have left a void in his circle in Rockland, but other family and friends remained. The Wights, Winnifred Fales, and Carrie Burpee Shaw returned to Rockland and to Cooper's beach summers and holidays, as did other Burpee family members. He was also a property holder and had business interests in the town. Perhaps no artist ever intends to "retire," but Burpee had planned his finances carefully and the availability of his family home at 43 Park Street would have had sentimental as well as practical appeal. He had amassed more than $25,000 in income-producing capital, as well as $6,000 worth of Rockland real estate.[1] He had always been careful with his spending; and his latter years in Rockland would not be lavish or luxurious, but they would be comfortable.

He is said to have begun spending time in the summer on Cooper's beach with his family as early as 1906. The Maine coast had had an appeal for him as an artist from his earliest days, and now he returned to paint it in earnest. Burpee had probably been visiting the islands off Maine since childhood, and had taken the opportunity to set up a studio and paint at Criehaven at Matinicus at least by 1905. Edwin H. Crie had become a close friend and now visits were possible more often. Just how early he began to visit Monhegan Island is unclear, but in 1922 he exhibited two paintings at the Portland Society of Art annual spring exhibition at the L.D.M. Sweat Museum (now the Portland Museum of Art). Although he appears to have worked his way around the island, he fixed on the most prominent feature, Blackhead. This dramatic headland juts into the Atlantic with waves crashing against its base. Its surface is scored by valleys and crags so that changing light reveals a variety of forms. Burpee painted it in oil and pastel, as studies and as finished exhibition pictures, at least three

SUMMER SKIES, c. 1913.

Pastel on cream paper, 8 x 10 1/2 inches.
Burpee's return to Rockland made no abrupt break in his work's subject matter or style.

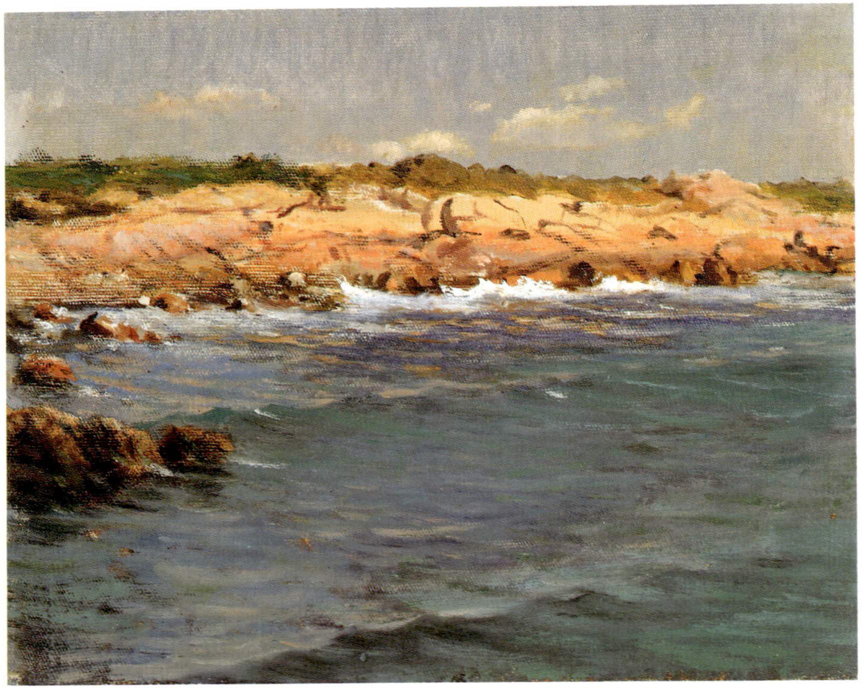

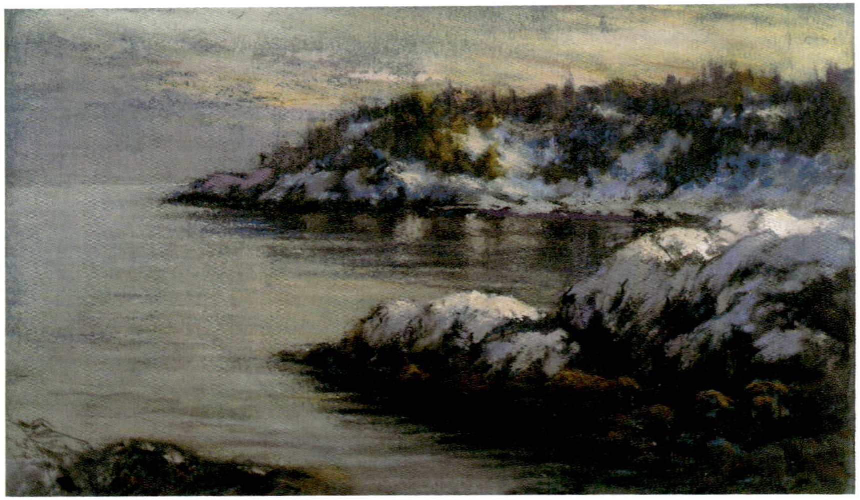

dozen times. He certainly was fascinated with its form, but he may have been consciously or subconsciously aware of the similarity of his own series of studies with Monet's headland pictures of the late 1890s of the cliffs at Pourville and the headland at Petit Ailly.

When he chose to present a painting to the high school in Rockland in 1928, it was one of his Monhegan pictures, although not Blackhead. According to the Rockland paper, it "depicts a harbor scene at Monhegan. Here and there on the water, which is a glowing blue, are small fishing boats, with a larger one in the foreground whose yellow sail and masts are reflected in the waters below. The background shows the picturesque old fish houses, the cottages and homes nestled in trees and foliage of soft browns, greens and yellows."[2]

He continued to exhibit in Portland, although irregularly. In 1925 he was in very distinguished company when he sent *Through Golden Mists* to an invitational show at the L.D.M. Sweat Museum under the sponsorship of the Portland Society of Art. It was for sale at $600. (By contrast, Frank W. Benson's *Elizabeth* was offered at $3500.) Each of 21 artists from four of the New England States were invited to send one painting to a summer exhibition with the theme "New England Artists Greet You at the Portland Art Museum," in honor of the Business and Professional Woman's Club annual meeting. The show also included work by Edmund Tarbell, George Noyes, Guy Wiggins, and Charles Woodbury, among others. It was a reunion of sorts, for Burpee had exhibited with most of them many times before in Boston, Philadelphia, Washington, or Chicago. In 1927, at 81, he entered his last pictures in a museum exhibition, the annual spring exhibition sponsored by the Portland Society of Art at the Sweat Museum. If *Sunlight and Shadow* or *Marsh and Mountain* were identifiable as Maine or New Jersey pictures, Burpee did not deign to assist in identifying the locations by the titles. This also proved to be a final opportunity to exhibit with some of his old Boston Art Club members and exhibitors, Henry H. Ahl, Charles Gruppe, and M. Bradish Titcomb and with some of the younger exhibitors there such as Sydney Burleigh and Gertrude Fiske.

His winters in New Jersey continued to provide the opportunity to explore the changing light on the Palisades in New Jersey above the Hudson River as he had since 1906. Burpee worked from the New York side

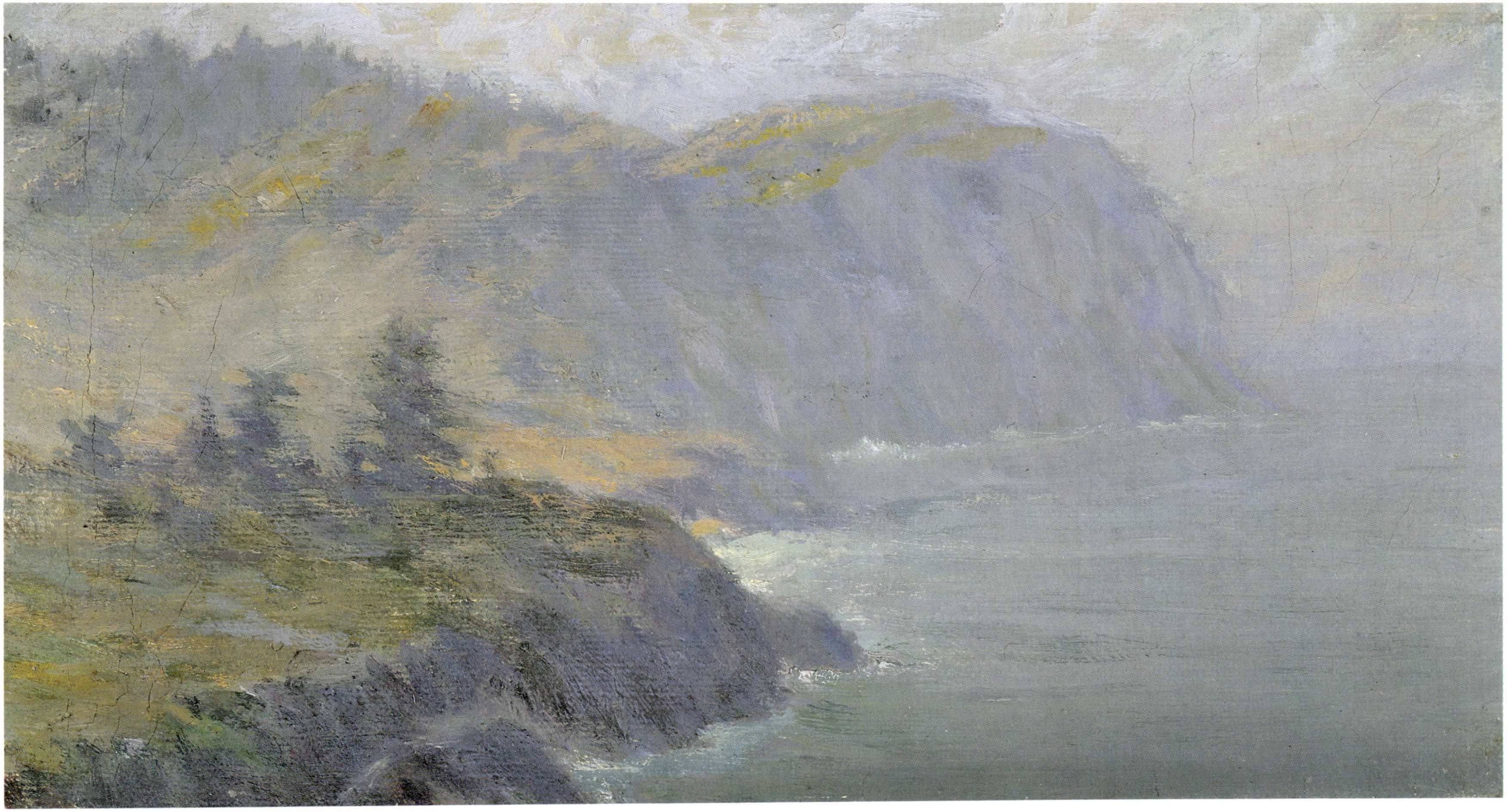

opposite, top

A ROCKY SHORE, 1910 – 15.

Oil on canvas, 12 1/8 x 15 inches.

opposite, bottom

MAINE COAST IN WINTER, c. 1915.

Pastel on black paper, 7 5/16 x 12 1/4 inches.

above

MISTY MORNING, BLACKHEAD, c. 1920.

Oil on canvas, 6 3/4 x 12 1/8 inches.
This is one of the most Tonalist or Whistlerian of Burpee's many paintings of Blackhead on Monhegan Island.

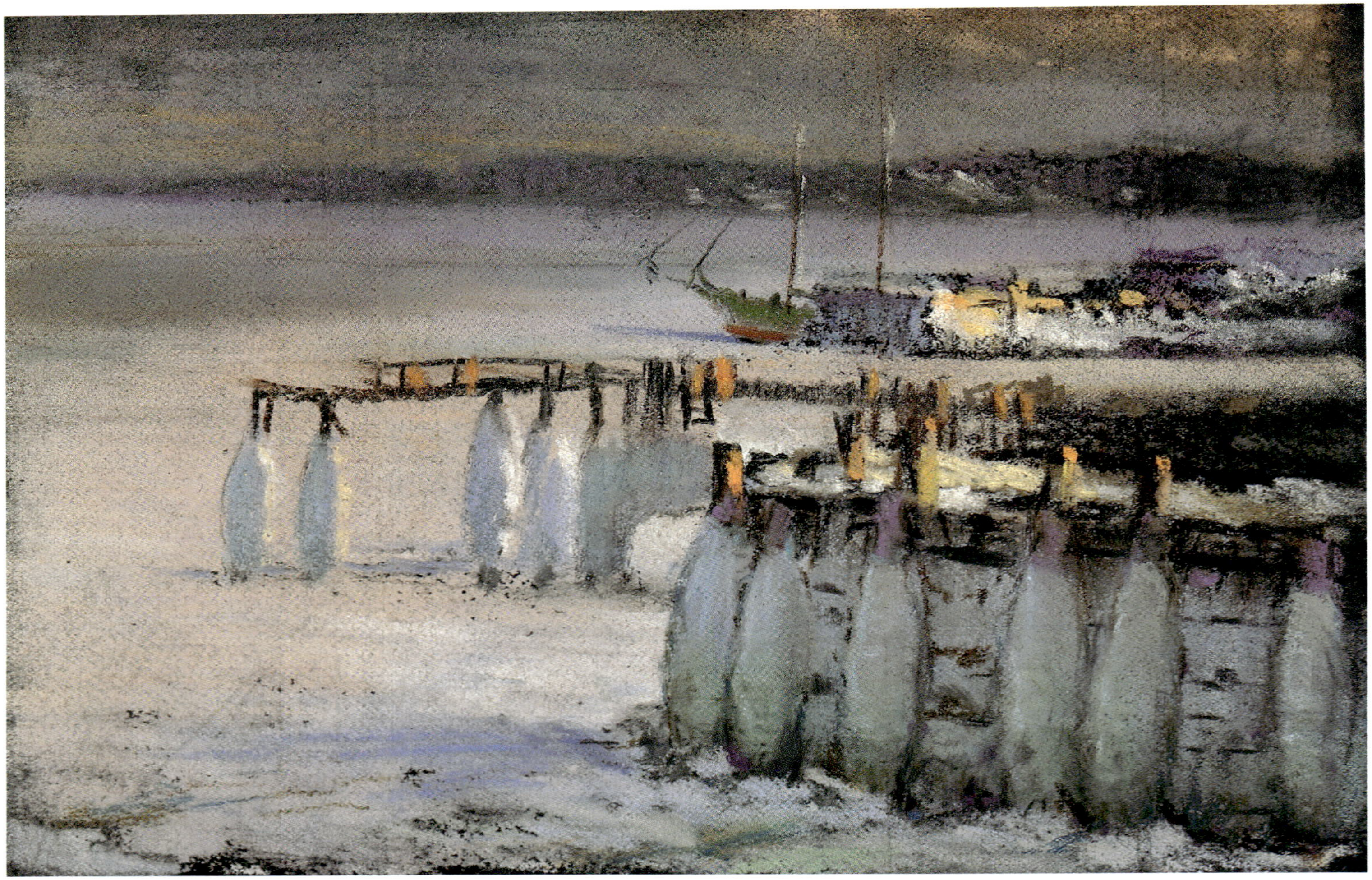

to create more than a dozen pastel compositions of various atmospheric effects and times of day. In addition he supplemented the series with pictures of battleships in the Hudson River, which sometimes show the Palisades in the background and sometimes do not. Burpee's lifetime interest in ships included the new battleships of the U.S. Navy, which he had painted in Boston Harbor about 1905 (p. 92) and continued to portray between 1910 – 25 in the Hudson River. He presumably continued his winter painting outside New York City.[3] When he moved from Ridgewood to East Orange, New Jersey, he had the countryside there, and at Branch Brook Park in nearby Newark, to provide rural landscape themes in winter and spring.

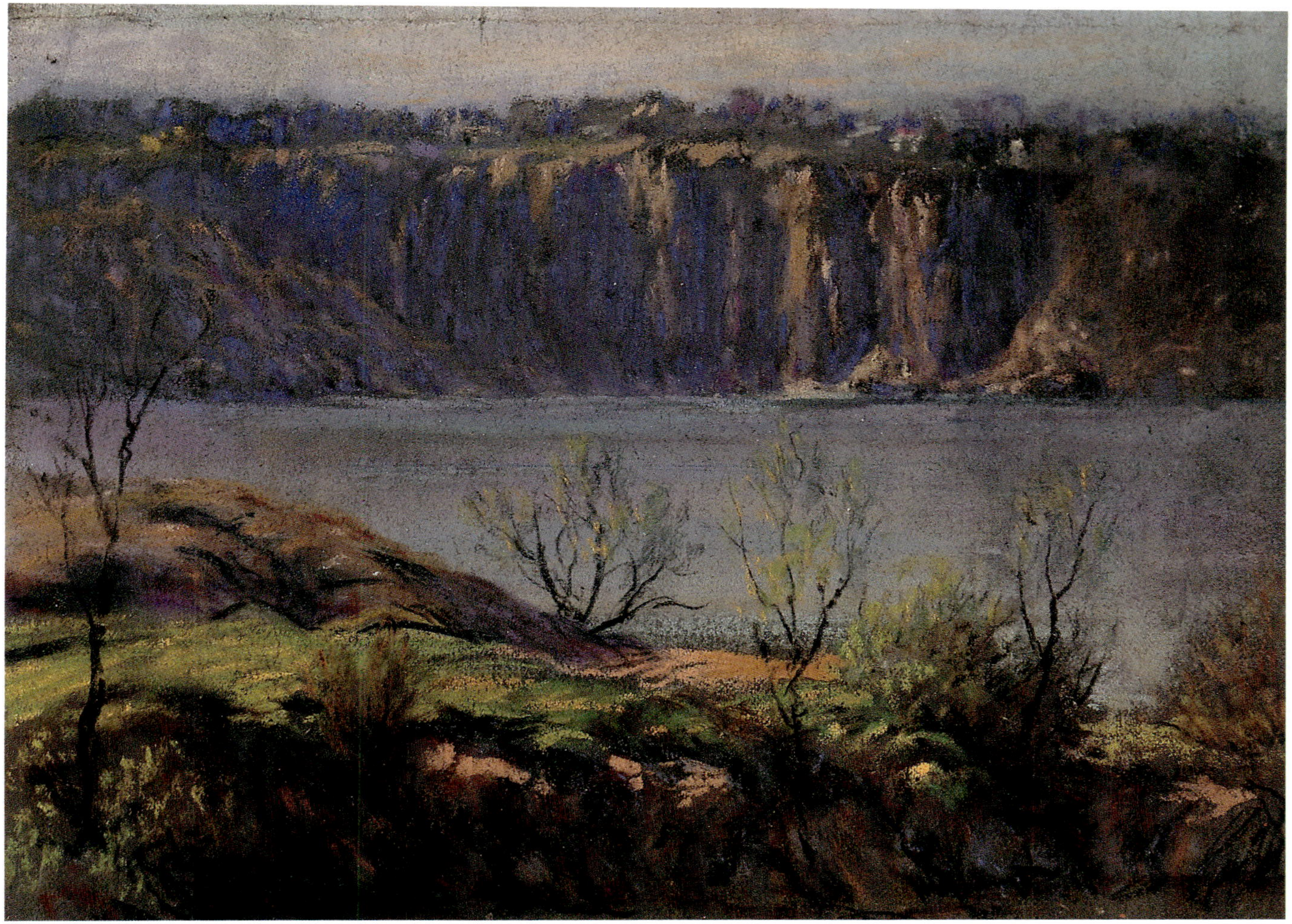

opposite

WINTER ICE, c. 1915.

Pastel on black paper, 6 3/4 x 9 15/16 inches.
Winter Ice shows the effect of the tide as well as light on a frozen harbor.

above

PALISADES IN SPRING, 1906 – 20.

Pastel on gray paper, 7 x 9 1/2 inches.
Part of a series of pastels of the Palisades done over nearly two decades.

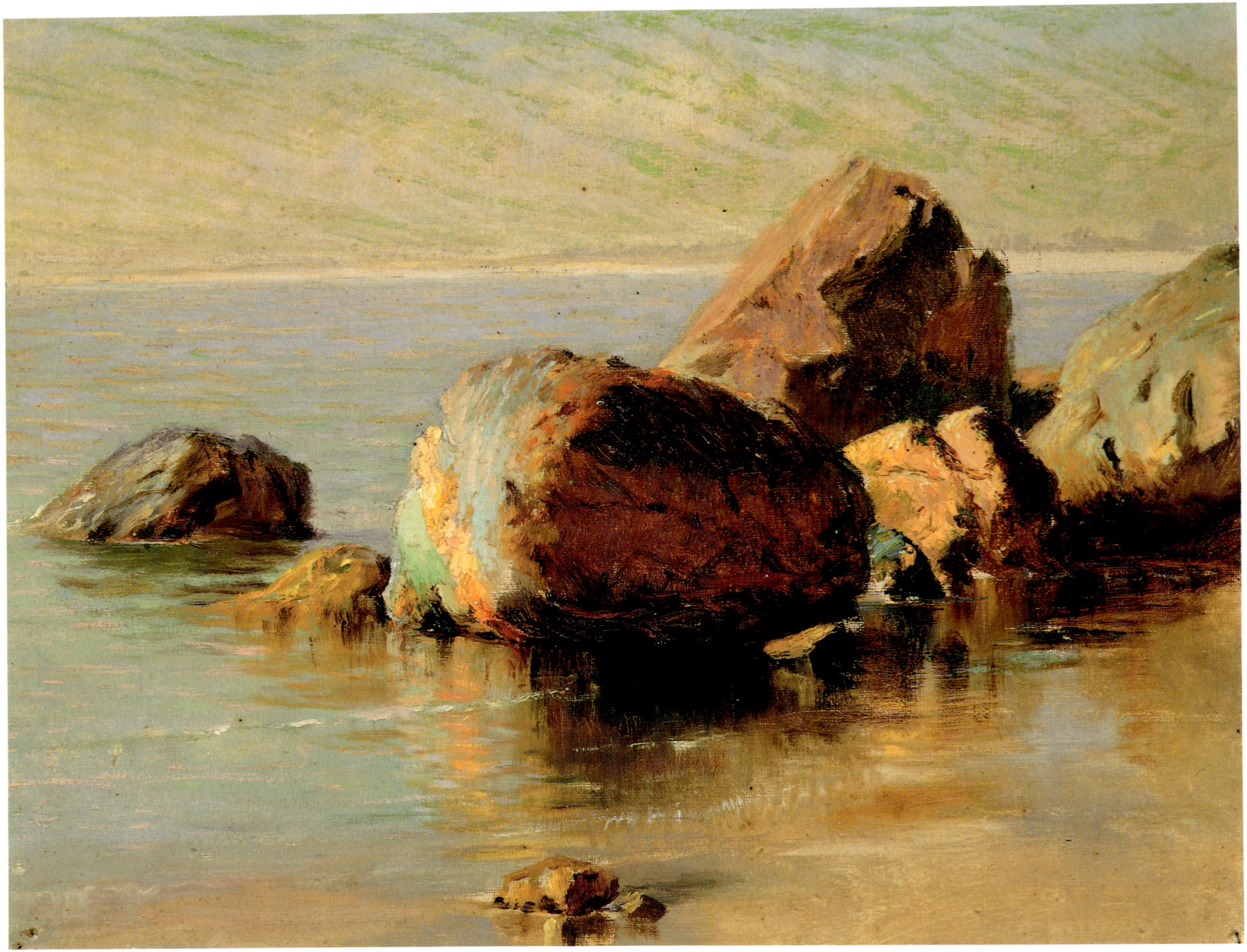

When Burpee returned to Rockland he became close friends with Edwin L. Brown. Brown, who was 23 years Burpee's junior, had been born in the neighboring town of Camden. He studied painting with Henry B. Snell and Anson K. Cross and taught at the Cross Summer Art School at Boothbay Harbor. He would have been a kindred spirit for discussing art and bringing artists together in the Rockland area.[4] Rockland may not have been an artists' colony, but it was the largest town on Penobscot Bay, which certainly could lay claim to being the summer home of myriad artists. Frank W. Benson and Bela Pratt (the sculptor Burpee had visited in Paris in 1898) both summered in North Haven, and Rockland was, as it is today, the logical point of departure for the island. Monhegan was visited by many artists in this period; some lived there and some visited for only a short while. In the period of 1914 –1930 Monhegan saw Henri, Bellows, Kroll, Hopper, Kent and the Impressionists Charles Ebert, Ernest Albert, and Wilson Ervine, as well as S. P. Rolt Triscott with whom Burpee had often exhibited in Boston. Perhaps Burpee associated with some of the younger artists who were going to Monhegan, for it was then, as it is today, a very small place. And Burpee's niece, Ada, was an artist in Rockland to whom he lent encouragement and advice. In any event, his art was not static.

Particularly in the Maine paintings Burpee continued to abstract and use higher key colors while maintaining his best-loved subject matter, the edge of the sea. In his late work he chose a collection of granite boulders in an ocean pool and explored them in a composition of color and light. In *Maine Rocks at Sunset* Burpee composed five boulders into an abstraction of soft light and color, applying much of the warm color of the rocks with the tip of his palette knife and drawing acid green sgrafitti across the sky with his brush. The total effect is a calm meditation on an exceptionally ordinary subject, but the technique is a century removed from *New England Village at Sunset* (p. 8). In neither case did the artist intend to shock his viewer or attract notoriety. His progress had been evolutionary, not revolutionary.

About six years before his death Burpee was struck by an automobile and as a result of his injuries was unable to continue to paint out of doors. At the age of 88 or 89 his career as an artist closed. In March of 1934 he made his last will and testament, probably as a result of this decline in his health.[5] He continued to live in the modest family house at 43 Park

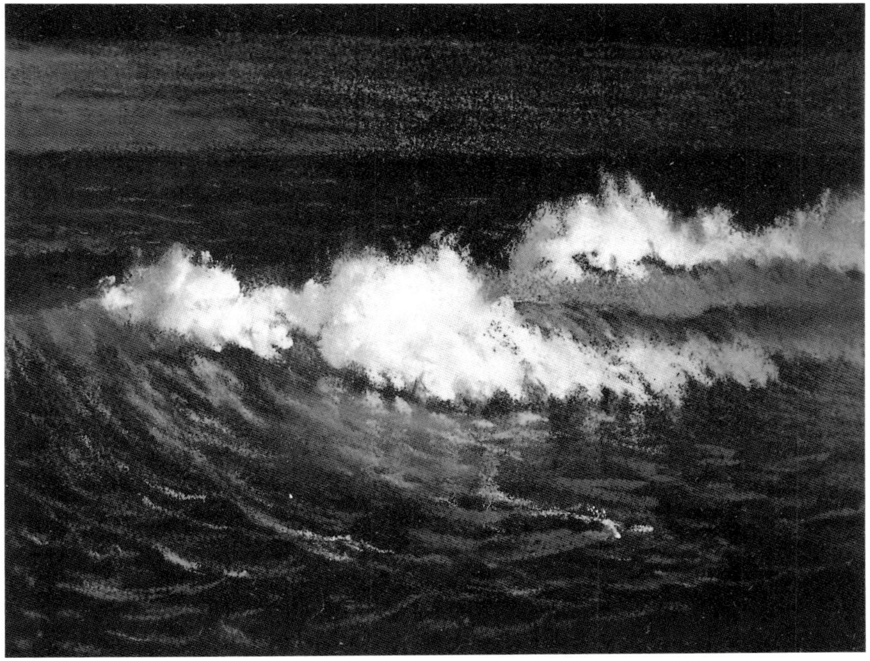

above

ELECTRIC WAVE, c. 1915.

Pastel on black paper, 9 7/16 x 12 1/16 inches.
The colors of this dramatic wave study suggest that the subject was observed at night by electric light.

opposite

MAINE ROCKS AT SUNSET, c. 1925.

Oil on paper mounted on panel, 10 3/4 x 13 5/16 inches.
This painting is a century removed in style and composition from Burpee's first works.

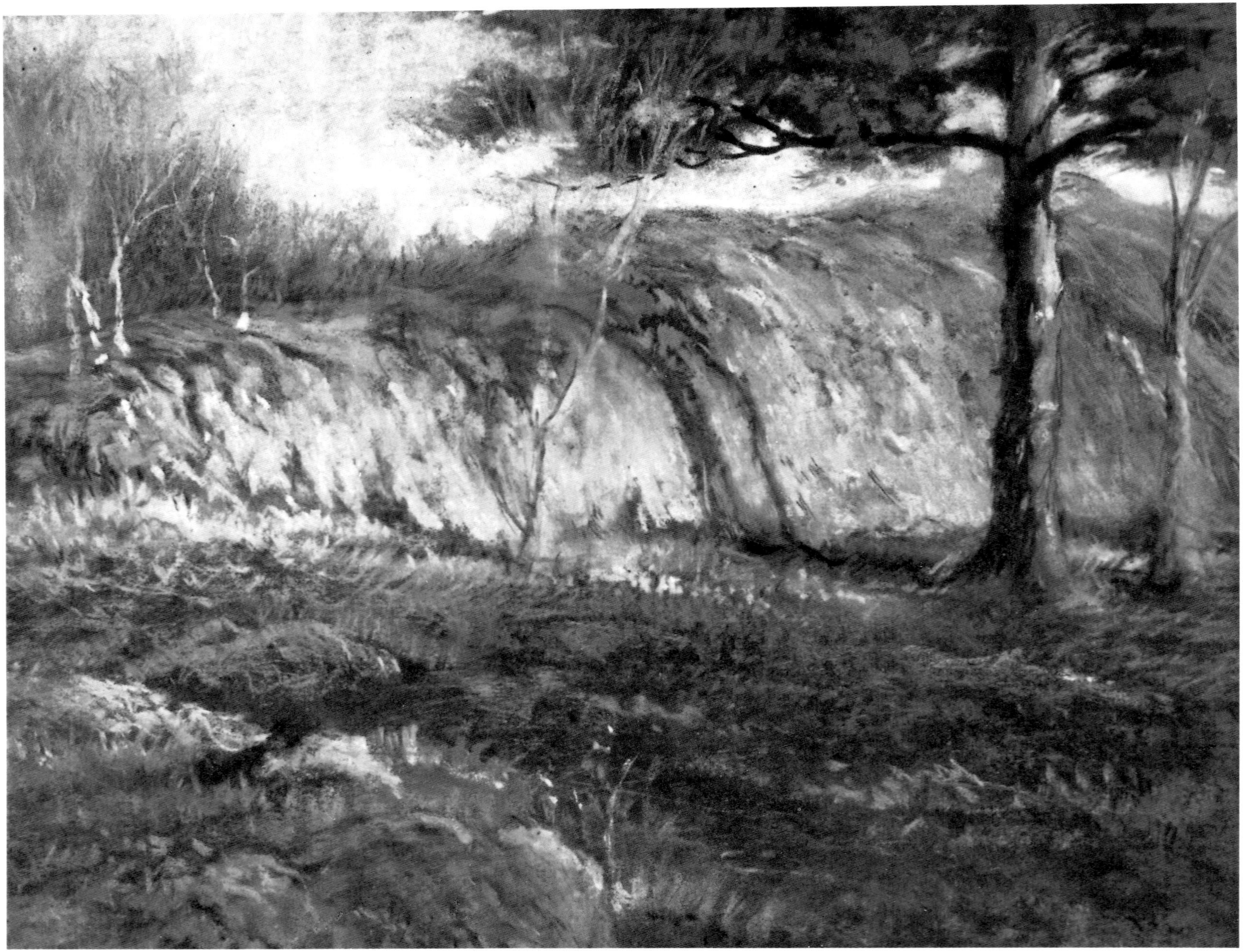

opposite

AUTUMN'S GLOW, c. 1925.

Pastel on paper, 11 7/16 x 13 9/16 inches.

right

TIDAL POOL, c. 1930.

Pastel on paper, 10 1/2 x 12 1/16 inches.

below

Burpee's house and studio at 43 Park Street, Rockland, Maine.

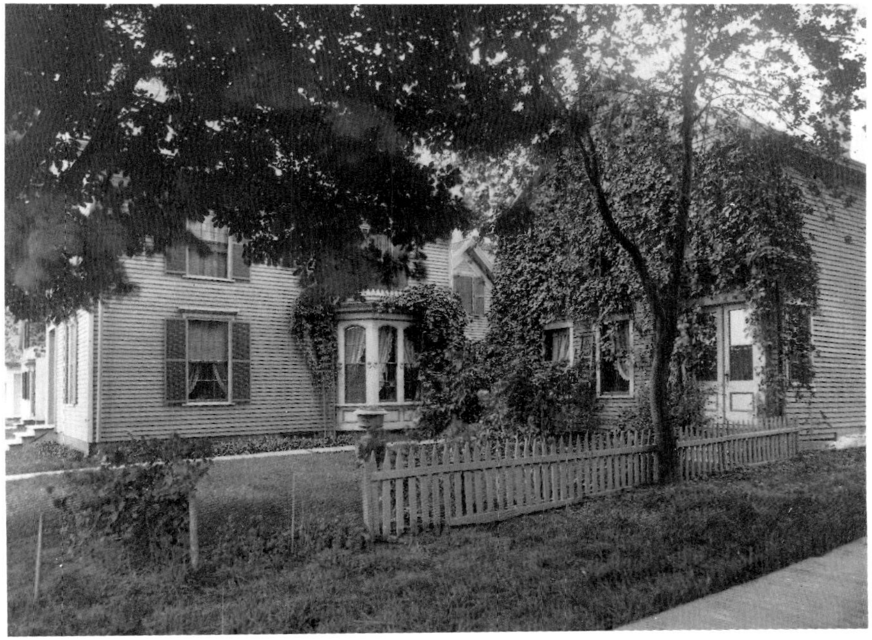

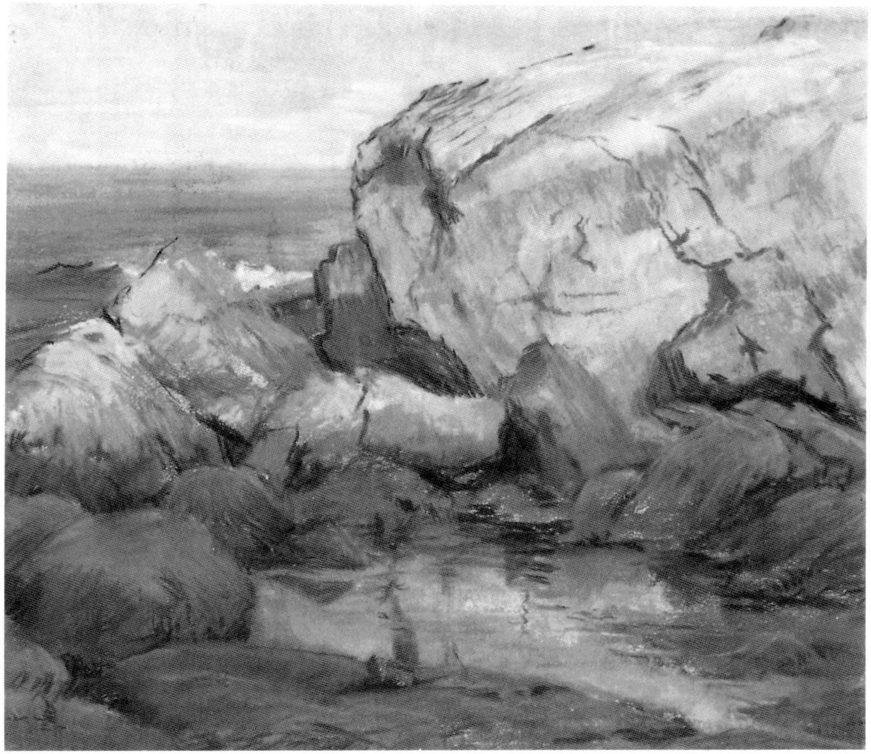

Street, where he died, after a nine day bout with influenza, on December 15, 1940. Winnifred Fales, the writer, notified the doctor of his death. Appropriately, the funeral was handled by the Burpee Funeral Home, which his father had founded; the services were at the First Baptist Church, where his painting *The River Jordan* hung at the baptistery; his friends Edwin L. Brown and Edwin H. Crie served as pall bearers; and he was buried in the family plot at the Sea View Cemetery.

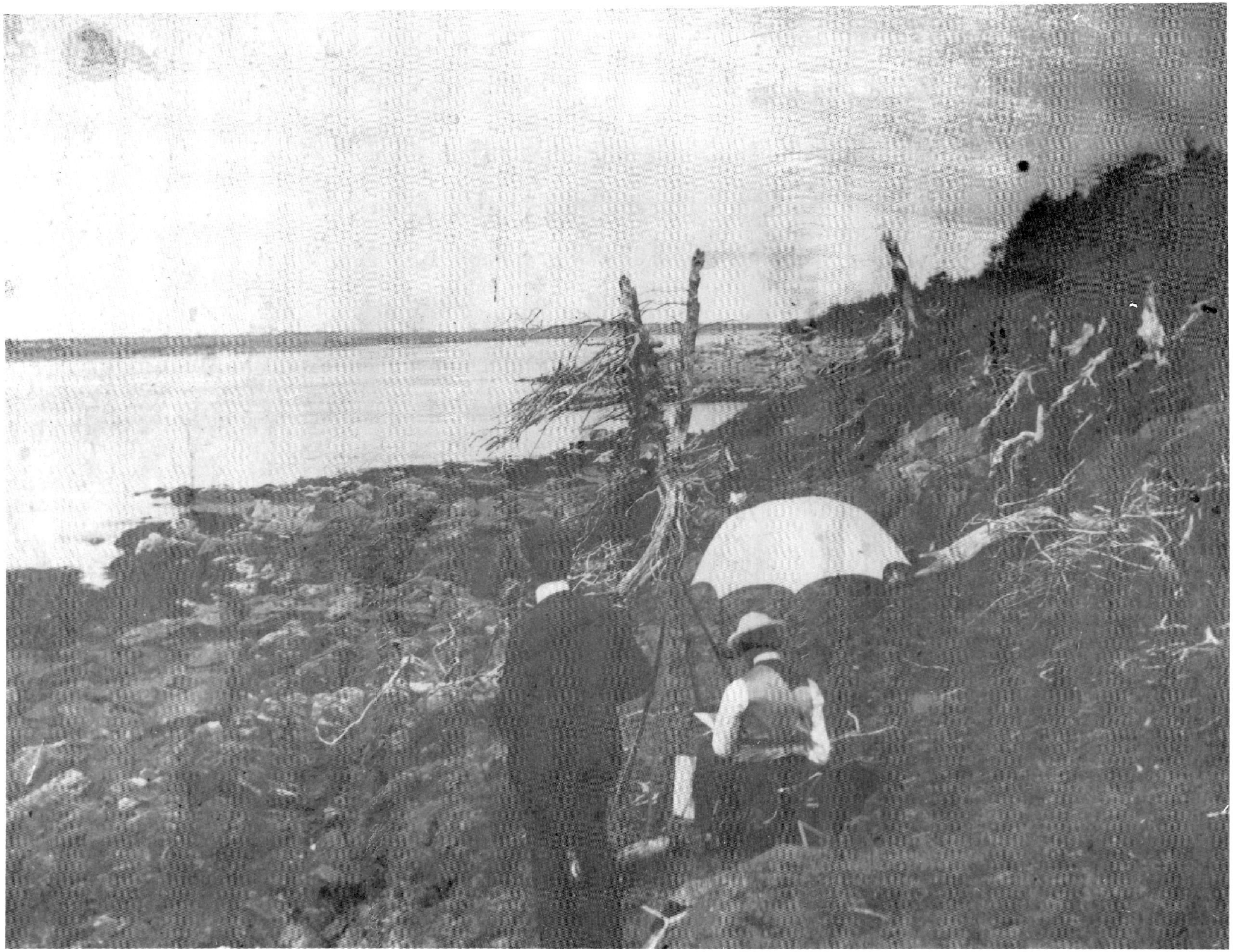

Edwin Brown noted at the time of Burpee's death:

> Mr. Burpee was especially successful in depicting the sea in all its moods; his rough sea pictures have won widespread praise for their boldness and exquisite color. The passing of Mr. Burpee removes from the art world a man of great skill; a gentleman, modest and unassuming to a marked degree; a kind and loving character; a man who loved his work and like the true artist was ever striving for perfection. His painting speaks far more eloquently than words can describe it and has a certain appeal to the poetic and artistic imagination. Mr. Burpee's impressionism conformed to the principles of truth and beauty and he was one of the best of those painters who used broken color to produce the effect of vibrating light.[6]

From his birth in Rockland, at the edge of the sea, to his perfection of the art of coastal painting on both sides of the Atlantic, William Partridge Burpee returned to be buried within the sound of his much-loved sea.

BURPEE'S PALETTE WITH BLACKHEAD, MONHEGAN ISLAND, mid 1920s.

Oil on paper and board, 7 1/8 x 12 inches.

opposite

Burpee painting at Criehaven, Maine with Edwin L. Brown, c. 1905.

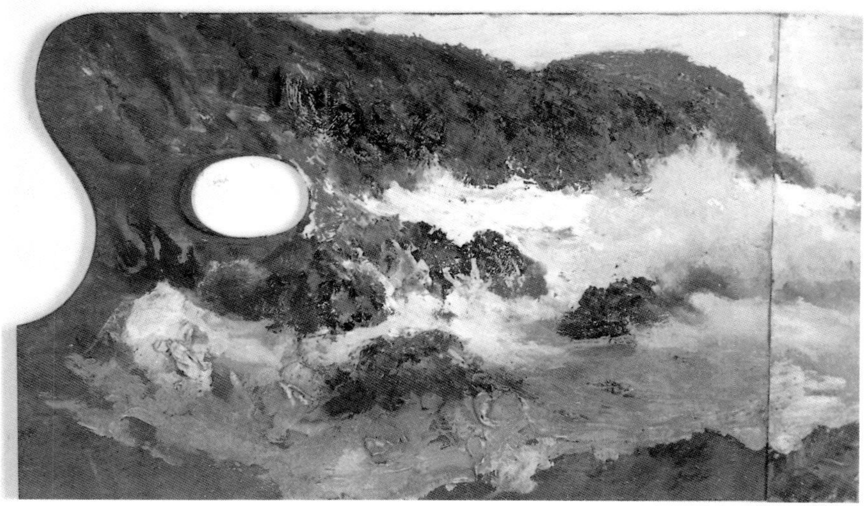

NOTES, Chapter Five

[1] "Inventory of Real — Personal — Estate, William Partridge Burpee," Probate Court, Knox County, Maine, by Homer E. Robinson, filed February 18, 1941; Burpee's inventory shows that he invested conservatively in bonds issued by Bell Telephone, New England Telephone, 8 railroads, municipal water companies, first mortgages, and a drug company as well as U.S. Treasury bonds; in addition, he held stock shares in the Pennsylvania Railroad, American Type Founders, American Car and Foundry, Eastman Kodak, Reynolds Tobacco, and the Camden and Rockland Water Company; at the time of his death he had a one-quarter interest in 43 Park Street and in the Burpee Block, as well as full ownership of three State Street buildings; of even greater interest, the appraiser valued Burpee's entire collection of "Paintings, pictures and studies" at $250.

[2] *Rockland Courier Gazette*, Oct. 23, 1928, p. 2.

[3] *Bangor Daily News*, Dec. 16/17, 1940.

[4] Edwin L. Brown was a pall bearer at Burpee's funeral and wrote his obituary. He was with him at Criehaven, as evidenced in the photograph at the Archives of American Art.

[5] "William P. Burpee's Will," filed at the Knox County Courthouse, Rockland, Maine; Abstract of Will, Knox County Courthouse, recorded book 260, page 132; Burpee made his niece, Winnifred Fales, executrice, and left her one-half of his estate and the other half-in trust to his sister Carrie for her life, the residue to go to Winnifred Fales on Carrie Shaw's death.

[6] Edwin L. Brown, "William P. Burpee — His Death removes a Prominent Personality From the World of Art," *Rockland Courier Gazette*, Dec. 19, 1940.

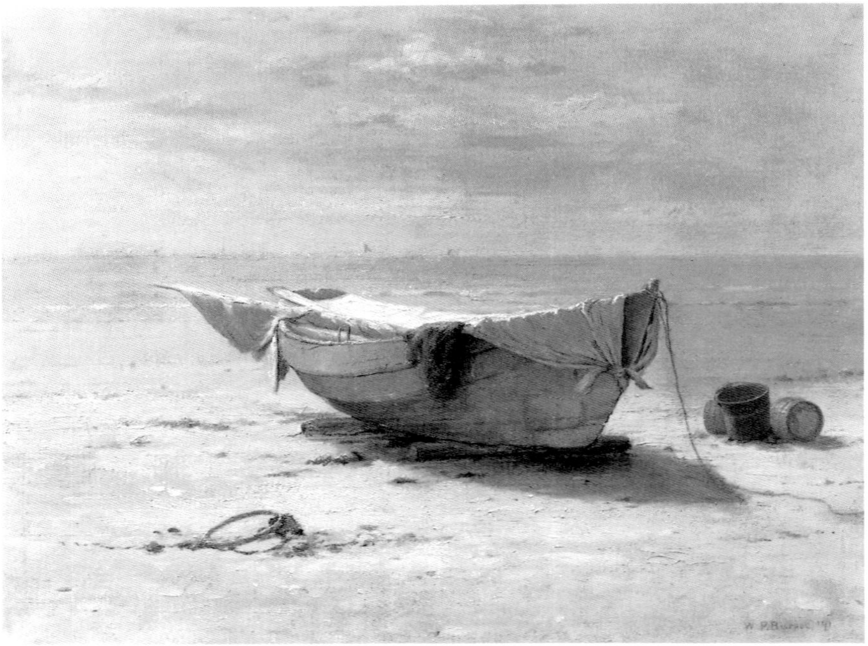

SWAMPSCOTT DORY, 1891.

Oil on canvas, 18 x 24 inches.
This may be the painting exhibited by Burpee at the Boston Art Club in January, 1892.
From a private collection courtesy of Alfred J. Walker, Fine Art.

CHRONOLOGY

1846	• April 13, born in Rockland, Maine.
	• Went to public schools, and then to Kents Hill Academy.
1868	• Earliest signed and dated oil paintings.
1873	• Sister (Carrie M. Burpee) marries (at Rockland) the Rev. E.M. Shaw of the Baptist Church, Antrim, N.H.
1882	• Listed in the Rockland City Directory as "artist, 22 Park, boards do."
	• Listed in the Boston City Directory (BCD) as "William P., 48 State, bds. 747 Tremont."
1883	• Listed in BCD as "William P., 48 State, bds. 154 West Concord."
1884	• Listed in BCD as "William P., 23 Court, rooms 150 Warren."
1885	• Listed in BCD as "William P., 23 Court, r. 29, rooms 150 Warren."
	• September 1, paints *Lynn Beach, Egg Rock in Distance.*
1886	• Listed in BCD as "William P., rms. 150 Warren av."
	• Paints series of oil figure studies at Boston Art Club.
1887	• Listed in BCD as "William P., rms. 150 Warren av."
	• December 11, father, Hon. N.A. Burpee, dies at Rockland.
1888	• Listed in BCD as "William P., artist, 150 Warren av."
1889	• Listed in BCD as "William P., artist, 26 Pierce bldg. rms. 34 Dartmouth"; also listed under "Painters: Portrait and Landscape."
1890	• Listed in BCD as "William P., artist, 135 Huntington av. rms. 566 Columbus av."
	• January 18 – February 15, exhibited at the Boston Art Club (BAC) 41st exhibition (oils), #177 *On the Beach at Swampscott.*
1891	• Listed in BCD as "William P., artist, 135 Huntington av. rms. 566 Columbus av."
	• January 9 – December 23, regularly attended the every other Friday life classes at the BAC.
1892	• Listed in BCD as "William P., artist, 135 Huntington av. rms. do."
	• Continues life classes.
	• January 6 – February 13, exhibited at BAC (45th)-1892 (oils), #84 *Swampscott Dory*, #139 *On the Saugus Marshes.*
	• April 8 – 23, exhibited at BAC (46th), (watercolor), #5 *Moonrise by the Sea*, #216 *A Sunset Study (Wind against Waves).*
1893	• Listed in BCD as "William P., artist, 18 Harcourt bldg. rms. do." Harcourt Building is the same as 23 Irvington St.
	• January 2 – February 17, exhibited at BAC (47th) (oils), #122 *Bright Morning.*

- April 8 – 29, exhibited at BAC (48th) (watercolors), #154 *Sunny Morning in Marblehead*, #208 *Where White Waves Foam*.

1894 • Listed in BCD same as 1893.
- January 20 – February 17, exhibited at BAC (49th) (oils), #73 *Golden Sunset at Brookline*, #88 *In Glowing Sunset Light—Swampscott*
- April 7 – 28, exhibited at BAC (50th) (watercolor), #3 *A Smiling Sun — at Marblehead*, #178 *By Sunset Shore, Across*.
- Becomes an artist-member of the Boston Art Club.

1895 • Listed in BCD as "William P., artist, 14 Harcourt bldg. rms. do."
- January 19 – February 16, exhibited at BAC (51st) (oils), #97 *The Rising Tide*.
- April 6 – 27, exhibited at BAC (52nd) (watercolors), #186 *A Dewy Morning*.

1896 • Listed in Brookline CD as "William P. bookkeeper, Country Club, Clyde, h.12 Kent sq." (With George C. Burpee).
- April 11 – May 2, exhibited at BAC (54th) (watercolors), #98 *Sunset — Brookline*.

1897 • Listed in Brookline CD same as 1896.
- April 3 – 24, exhibited at BAC (56th) (watercolors), #218 *February Sunset*.
- October 23 sails on *Werra* for Gibraltar.

1898 • Travels in Italy, France and Switzerland.

1899 • Travels in Italy, France, Germany, Holland and England.
- August 1, returns to Boston on *Winifredian*.

1900 • Probably spends the summer in Katwijk, Holland.

1901 • Listed in BCD as "William P, artist, 27 Harcourt bldg."
- April 6 – 27, exhibited at BAC (64th) (watercolors), #61 *Old Church on the Sands — Katwyk*, #67 *Near St. George of the Seaweed — Venice*, #92 *By Sunset Shone Across*.

1902 • Listed in BCD same as 1901.
- January 4 – February 1, exhibited at BAC (65th) (oils), #5 *Pergola at Capri*, #37 *Early Morning — Capri — Ischia*, #95 *Sunrise — Point Shirley [Revere]*.
- January 20 – March 1, exhibited at the Pennsylvania Academy of the Fine Arts (PAFA) (71st), #535 *Speeding Home*.
- April 5 – 26, exhibited at BAC (66th) (watercolors), #88 *The Onrushing Wave*, #100 *Early Summer — Capri*, #183 *Nocturne Mt. Etna*. Burpee was on the jury of admissions.
- November 14 – December 16, exhibited at the Copley Society Annual Exhibition (2nd) at Copley Hall, #36 *Speeding Homeward* (oil).

1903 • Listed in BCD same as 1901.
- First listed in the *American Art Annual*.
- January 3 – 31, exhibited at BAC (67th) (oils), #77 *Island of Capri — Sunrise*, #79 *Beacons of the Night*, #96 *At Swampscott*.
- January 19 – February 26, exhibited at PAFA (72nd), #575 *Near the Close of a Winter's Day*.
- April 4 – 25, exhibited at BAC (68th) (watercolors), #77 *Surf on the North Shore*, #88 *Sunny Harbor*, #95 *Afternoon Light on Surf*. Burpee was on the jury of admissions.
- November 27 – December 12, exhibited at BAC Exhibition of Sketches. Burpee - Group #3, 1. *Springtime;* 2. *Sunset Light on Rocks and Surf;* 3. *Surf and Seaweed*; 4. *Thatcher's Island East Gloucester*; 5. *Autumn on the River at Readville*; 6. *November*.

1904 • Listed in BCD same as 1901; became a member of the Boston Society of Watercolor Painters.
- January 1 – 30, exhibited at BAC (69th) (oils), #114 *Sunset in Holland*, #92 *Fishing Station — Coast of Maine*.
- February 3 – 13, exhibited at Walter Kimball and Co., Boston, *Snow Covered Rocks at Sunset* (oil), *Winter Sunset* (pastel) at the Massachusetts exhibit of Paintings for the Louisiana Purchase exposition..
- February 6 – 20, exhibited at Boston Society of Watercolor Painters (BSWCP) (16th) at BAC, #18 *Mountains of Sicily*, #19 *Tumbling Waters of a 'Comber' — Sunset*, #20 *A Sungleam off Shore*, # 21 *Pines at Sunset*, #22 *In Wooded Depths*, #24 *Willows Bordering a Stream*, #25 *And Having Done All, to Stand*, #26 *Winter Evening*, #27 *Moonrise*.
- Spring – Winter, exhibited at the Louisiana Purchase Exposition, St. Louis, *Snow Covered Rocks at Sunset* (oil), *Winter Sunset* (pastel).
- June 2 through August, exhibited at Williams & Everett Company Summer Exhibition of Paintings by Boston Artists.
- July, exhibited at (10th) Annual Exhibition of Paintings at the Poland Spring Art Gallery, #36 *Sunrise at Capri*, #96 *Sunset*, #100 *Mountains of Sicily*.
- November 5 – 19, exhibited at BAC Semi-Centennial Exhibition of oil paintings, #11 *Almond Blossoms*, #57 *The Pier*, #100 *Clear, Breezy and Sunny*.
- November 11, 23 Irvington St (Harcourt Studios) fire.
- Wins bronze medal, for pastel *Winter Sunset* at Louisiana Purchase Exposition, St. Louis.

1905 • Listed in BCD 110 Tremont St, rm 52. Listed in *American Art Annual*: Burpee, William Partridge, 110 Tremont St. Boston Mass. (P.).
- January 6 – February 4, exhibited at BAC (71st) (oils), #96 *The Harbor Evening*, #147 *A Winding River Valley*, on the jury of admissions. The Boston Art Club purchased *The Harbor Evening*

for its collection.

- February 11 – 25, exhibited at BSWCP (17th) at BAC, #78 *A Quiet Heaven*, #79 *'Primavera' in Sicily*, #80 *Rainfall at Sunset* [sold], #81 *A Turn in the River* [sold], #82 *Where Fisher-Folk Dwell*, #83 *Moonrise*, #84 *After a Heavy Easterly Storm.*
- April 7 – 29, exhibited at BAC (72nd) (watercolor), #13 *Willow Brook — Springtime*, #189 *Thunder Shower at Sea*, #223 *Moonlight.*
- June, exhibited at the Copley Society at Copley Hall, #77 *Clear, Breezy and Sunny.*
- February 20 – March 4, exhibited at Charles E. Cobb's Gallery, Boston, exhibition of *Oil Paintings by Leading Boston Artists.*
- March 6 – 20, exhibited at Cobb's Gallery, Boston, exhibition of 24 Boston watercolorists. Exhibited 4 pastel landscapes including #8 *A Woodland Path*, #9 *Sand Dunes at Annesquam, Evening.*
- October 28 on the *Romanic* left for Azores, Spain, Algeria for winter.
- November 17 – December 2, exhibited Boston Art Club Autumn Exhibition, #47 *Edge of the Woods*, #66 *Last Vacation Days*, #80 *Sand Dunes at Sunset.*

1906
- Not listed in the BCD.
- January 6 – February 3, exhibited at BAC (73rd) (oils), #111 *Sunshine and Shadow.*
- Late March returned from Europe to Boston, to 110 Tremont Street (the Studio Building, #49).
- April 7 – 28, exhibited at BAC (74th) (watercolors), #140 *View of the Bay Eastward, Ponta Delgada*, #103 *Looking Down into the Valley of Furnas*, #35 *At the Fountain.*
- Burpee family began summering at Cooper's Beach near Rockland, Maine.
- November 16 – December 1, exhibited at BAC Autumn Exhibition, #25 *A Hillside Village, Azores*, #26 *A Sunny Gleam*, #27 *In a Palace Garden, Granada.*

1907
- Listed in BCD, 110 Tremont rm 52, bds 177 Warren av. listed in *American Art Annual*, 110 Tremont St. Boston, Mass. and East Gloucester Mass. (P.).
- January 5 – February 2, exhibited at BAC (75th) (oils), #2 *Looking over the Dunes*, #86 *Under Gray-Green Willow*, #162 *Morning Sunbeams.*
- February 6 – March 9, exhibited 1st Corcoran Exhibition of Oil Paintings by Contemporary American Artists (Biennial), #254 *Evening Light Over Gloucester Town.*
- March 15 – April 6, exhibited BAC (76th) (watercolors), #43 *A Palace Garden Granada*, #94 *The Foaming Wave*, #96 *Bridges on the Darro, Granada*, #136 *Roman Gateway, Toledo*, on the jury of admissions.
- May 7 – June 16, exhibited 19th Exhibition of Water-colors, Pastels, and Miniatures by American Artists at the Art Institute of Chicago, #43 *A Sunny Morning in Granada*, #44 *Evening Katwyk*, on the jury of admissions.
- Summered at the *Green Studio* at the Harbor View in East Gloucester.
- December 2 – 28, exhibited 5th annual Philadelphia watercolor exhibition at the Pennsylvania Academy of the Fine Arts, #432 *Comber Coming Around Ledges.*

1908
- Listed in BCD 110 Tremont (Studio Building)
- January 3 – February 1, exhibited at BAC (77th) (oils), #100 *Evening Light over Gloucester.*
- February 8 – 22, exhibited at BSWCP (19th) at BAC, #1 *Visitors to the Palace —Tangier*, #2 *In the Time of Blossoms*, #111 *Sunlit Valley of Rhonda — Spain*, #112 *Court and Fountain — Ponta Delgada*, #113 *Springtime*, #114 *Algerian Women*, #115 *A Sunken Garden in Ponta Delgada*, #116 *Evening — Katwyk*, #117 *On the Shore at Katwyk*, #118 *A Field of Daisies*, #119 *Garden House in Biskra..*
- March 25 – April 18, exhibited BAC (78th) (watercolors), #3 *Azorean Kitchen*, On hanging committee.
- April 28 – June 7, exhibited in the 20th Exhibition of Water-colors, Pastels, and Miniatures by American Artists at the Art Institute of Chicago: Boston, Mass. #32. *Early Morning Mists, Merrimac River* (pastel).
- Summers at the *Green Studio* at the Harbor View in East Gloucester.

1909
- Listed in BCD 110 Tremont rm 52, bds 193 Warren av. and in the *American Art Annual* as "Also Teacher."
- February 2 – 27, exhibited BAC (79th) (oils), #57 *A Dream Day in May.*
- February 27 – March 13, exhibited BSWCP (20th) in the gallery of Charles E. Cobb, 346 Boylston St., #9. *Day of Notre Dame, Ponta Delgada, Azores*, #10. *Mists Rising From a River at Sunrise*, #11. *A Mountain Side and Valley*, #12. *Coming Through the Moors After a Rain*, #13 *Harbor Scene, Boston*, #14 *Two Faithful Servators*, #15 *Sunset, Ponta Delgada*, #16 *A Woman at a Fountain, Azores.*
- March 17 – 20, exhibited at the Brockton Woman's Club Annual Art Exhibition (4th), *The Faithful Servants*, *A Spring Morning* (pastels).
- May 11 – June 13, exhibited in the 21st Exhibition of Water-colors, Pastels, and Miniatures by American Artists at the Art Institute of Chicago, #48 *Two Faithful Servants* (pastel), #49 *Sunset at a Boston wharf* (pastel).

1910 • Listed in BCD 110 Tremont rm 52, bds 193 Warren av.
• January 23 – March 20, exhibited at the PAFA (105th), #217 *Barriers of the Sea.*
• January 24 – 29, exhibited at the Brockton Woman's Club Annual Exhibit (5th), *Surging Waves, Harbor View, Sunrise.*
• Exhibited at Annual PAFA.
• February 28 – March 12, exhibited at BSWCP (21st) in the gallery of Charles Cobb, at least eight pastels including #10 *Gold and Rose on Mt. Blanc*, #17 *[Winter-Public Garden, Boston].*
• March 30, exhibited at the BAC Members' Exhibition, #5 *Early Morning Effect — Gloucester Harbor.*
• Summered at the *Green Studio.*
• December, exhibited at the BSWCP at Marshall Field and Co. Chicago.
• December 17 – January 7, 1911, exhibited BAC Informal Exhibition by Artist Members of the Club. #39 *Sunrise*, #45 *Winter Sunshine.*

1911 • Listed in the BCD 110 Tremont rm 92, bds 193 Warren av.
• January 14 – 28, exhibited at BSWCP at BAC, #15 *Foaming Billows*, #16 *Tempestuous Seas*, #17 *Morning Song*, #18 *Rose and Gold*, #19 *Winter's Gray*, #20 *Windbent Trees*, #21 *Barnacled Rocks at Sunset*, #22 *Early Autumnal Evening*, #23 *Sunset Through Raindrops.*
• March 6 – 11, exhibited in open studio exhibition in rm 92 of the Studio Building.
• March 20 – 25, exhibited at the Brockton Woman's Club Annual Art Exhibit (6th), *When the Bees are Humming, Morning Song*, (oils) and *A Golden Sunset* (watercolor).

1912 • Not in BCD.
• Made a trip to Germany and maintained a studio in Berlin.

1913 • Listed in the *American Art Annual* 110 Tremont, rm 92, and East Gloucester "Also Teacher".
• Resigned from Boston Art Club.
• Summer/fall, moved to 43 Park Street, Rockland, Maine.
• November 8, began winter season with Mr. and Mrs. James Wight in Ridgewood, N. J.

1914 • Listed in RCD boards 43 Park Street, Rockland Maine.

1915 • April 4, donates *A Vision of the Jordan* to the First Baptist Church, Rockland.

1922 • Living in Rockland.
• April 18 – May 20, exhibited with the Portland Society of Art at the L.D.M. Sweat Museum, Portland, Maine, *Low Tide Rocks, Monhegan, Maine*; *Bright Morning, Monhegan, Maine.*

1923-24 • Listed in *American Art Annual*, 43 Park Street Rockland, Maine.

1924-25 • Listed in *Who's Who in American Art*, 43 Park Street, Rockland.

1925 • July 1 – September 15, exhibited in Portland Society of Art *Summer Exhibition 1925 — Representative New England Artists* at the L.D.M. Sweat Museum, Portland, Maine, #3, *Through Golden Mists.*

1927 • Listed in *American Art Annual*, 365 William St, East Orange, N. J.; and 43 Park St., Rockland, Maine.
• April 15 – May 15, exhibited at Portland Society of Art *Annual Spring Exhibition* at the L.D.M. Sweat Museum, Portland, Maine, #18 *Sunlight and Shadow*, #19 *Marsh and Mountain.*

1929 • Listed in *American Art Annual*, 356 William St, East Orange, N. J.; and 43 Park St., Rockland, Maine.

1930-31 • Listed in *Who's Who in American Art*, Summer --- Rockland, Maine, Winter --- 356 William St., East Orange, N.J.

1931 • Listed in *American Art Annual*, as above.

1933 • Listed in *American Art Annual*, as above.

1934 • Injured as a pedestrian by an automobile, makes last will and testament March 18, 1934.

1936-37 • Listed in *Who's Who in American Art*: 356 William St., East Orange NJ; and 43 Park St., Rockland, Maine.

1940 • December 15, died, Rockland, Maine.

1947-48 • December 8 – January 17, *Oil Paintings and Pastels by William Partridge Burpee*, exhibited at the Papermill Playhouse, Millburn N.J. (29 works)

1976 • July 16 – September 5, *William Partridge Burpee* at The William A. Farnsworth Library and Art Museum, Rockland, Maine.

1985 • May 12 – October 27, exhibition of *Meditation* in *Young America* at Hertitage Plantation Museum, Sandwich, Mass.
• Exhibition of 150 *Works by William Partridge Burpee* at the Bloomfield Public Library, N.J.

1988 • March 6 – April 3, *The American Seascape from John Smibert to John Marin*, at The Mansfield Art Center, Mansfield, Ohio.

1989 • September 17 – November 18, *William Partridge Burpee and His Time*, at Childs Gallery, Boston, Mass.
• December 9 – January 6, 1991, *At the Water's Edge: 19th and 20th Century American Beach Scenes*, organized by the Tampa Museum of Art, Tampa, Florida, *Doryman at the End of the Day.*

1990 • May 13 – October 14, *Romancing the Shore: Views of Coastal New England*, at Heritage Plantation Museum, Sandwich Mass., #16 *Beach with Clouds and Rain*, #17 *Boy on Beach*, #18 *Coastal Scene With Ships*, #19 *Fisherman With Wheelbarrow and Dory on Beach.*

1991 • January 13 – March 31, travelling retrospective of Burpee's works begins its tour at the Anglo-American Art Museum, Baton Rouge, Lousiana.

BIBLIOGRAPHY

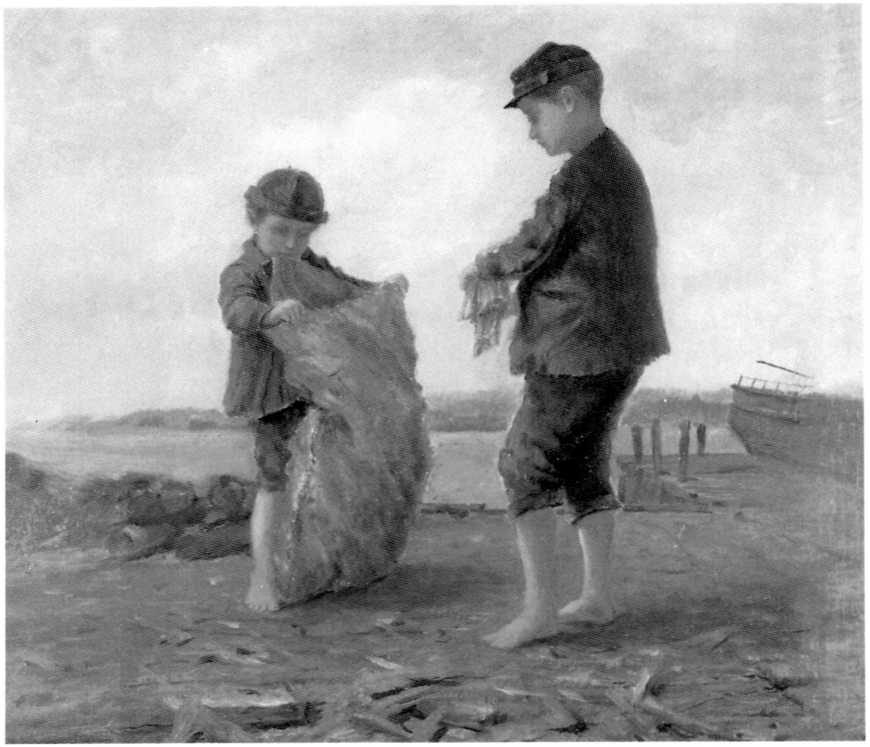

BOYS GATHERING CHIPS, c. 1875.

Oil on academy board, 10 1/4 x 11 1/2 inches.
The Post–Civil War date of the painting is indicated by the Union soldier caps worn by the barefoot boys.

American Painters of the Impressionist Period Rediscovered, exhibition catalogue. Waterville, Me.: Colby College, 1975.

At the Water's Edge — 19th and 20th Century American Beach Scenes, exhibition catalogue. Tampa, Fla.: The Tampa Museum of Art, 1989.

William Partridge Burpee, exhibition catalogue. Rockland, Me.: The William A. Farnsworth Library and Art Museum, 1976.

Burpee, William Partridge. "With Burpee in Europe." 8 articles published in the Rockland Courier Gazette, 1898 on March 1, May 7, May 17, June 4, June 14, June 25, July 12, and July 30.

Butts, Daniel H. III. *The American Seascape from John Smibert to John Marin*, exhibition catalogue. Mansfield, Ohio: The Mansfield Art Center, 1988.

Corn, Wanda M. *The Color of Mood, American Tonalism 1880 – 1910*, exhibition catalogue. San Francisco: M.H. de Young Museum, 1972.

Cullity, Brian. *Romancing the Shore: Views of Coastal New England*, exhibition catalogue. Sandwich, Mass.: Heritage Plantation of Sandwich, 1990.

Curry, David Park. *James McNeill Whistler at the Freer Gallery of Art*. New York and London: Smithsonian Institution in association with W.W. Norton & Co., 1984.

Czestochowski, Joseph S. *The American Landscape Tradition*. New York, E. P. Dutton, 1982.

Downes, William Howe. "Boston Art and Artists." In *Essays on Art and Artists* by F. Hopkinson Smith, Alfred Trumble, Frank Fowler, et al. Chicago: American Art League, 1896, pp. 265-80.

Fairbrother, Trevor J., et al. *The Bostonians: Painters of an Elegant Age, 1870 – 1930*, exhibition catalogue. Boston: Museum of Fine Arts, Boston, 1986.

Ferber, Linda S., and William H. Gerdts. *The New Path: Ruskin and the American Pre-Raphaelites*, exhibition catalogue. New York: The Brooklyn Museum, 1985.

Gerdts, William H. *American Impressionism*. New York: Abbeville, 1984.

__________. *American Impressionism*, exhibition catalogue. Seattle, University of Washington: Henry Art Gallery, 1980.

Gerdts, William H., Diana Dimodica Sweet, and Robert R. Preato. *Tonalism: An American Experience*, exhibition catalogue. Phoenix: Phoenix Art Museum, 1982.

Huntington, David C. *The Landscapes of Frederic Edwin Church — Vision of an American Era*. New York: George Brazillier, 1966.

Kelly, Franklin et al. *Frederic Edwin Church*, Washington, D. C.: National Gallery of Art and Smithsonian Institution Press, 1989.

Landscape in Maine 1820 – 1970: A Sesquicentennial Exhibition, exhibition catalogue. Waterville, Brunswick, and Orono, Me.: Colby College, Bowdoin College, and University of Maine, 1970.

Loria, Joan and Warren A. Seamans. *Earth, Sea and Sky — Charles H. Woodbury — Artist and Teacher, 1864 – 1940*, exhibition catalogue. Cambridge, Mass.: The MIT Museum, 1988.

Maine Library Bulletin, July – Oct. 1927, vol. 3, #1 and 2.

Moffatt, Frederick C. *Arthur Wesley Dow (1857 – 1922)*. Washington, D.C.: Smithsonian Institution Press, 1977.

Post-Impressionism — Cross-Currents in European and American Painting 1880 – 1906. Washington, D.C.: National Gallery of Art, 1980.

Ressmeyer, Richard H., Lynette Long, and Thomas J. Long. *Young America — Children and Art*, exhibition catalogue. Sandwich, Mass.: Heritage Plantation of Sandwich, 1985.

Rewald, John and Frances Weitzenhoffer. *Aspects of Monet*. New York: Harry N. Abrams, 1984.

Sellin, David. *Americans in Brittany and Normandy 1860 – 1910*. Phoenix, Arizona: Phoenix Art Museum, 1982.

Sharf, Frederic A. and John H. Wright. *Paintings by Essex County Artists, 1865 – 1910*, exhibition catalogue. Essex, Mass.: Essex Institute, 1971.

__________. *C.E.L. Green: Shore and Landscape Painter of Lynn and Newlyn*, exhibition catalogue. Essex, Mass.: Essex Institute, 1980.

Soissons, S.C. de. *Boston Artists — A Parisian Critic's Notes*. Boston: n.p., 1894.

Spassky, Natalie. *American Paintings in the Metropolitan Museum of Art: Volume II*. New York: The Metropolitan Museum of Art, 1985.

Staley, Alan, and Theodore Reff. *From Realism to Symbolism: Whistler and His World*, exhibition catalogue. New York: Wildenstein and Co., 1971.

Stebbins, Theodore E., Jr., Carol Troyen and Trevor J. Fairbrother. *A New World: Masterpieces of American Painting 1760 – 1910*. Boston: Museum of Fine Arts, Boston, 1983.

Tucker, Paul. *Monet in the '90s*. Boston: Museum of Fine Arts, Boston, 1989.

Wilmerding, John. *A History of American Marine Painting*. Salem, Mass.: Peabody Museum of Salem, 1968.

__________. *William Bradford 1823 – 1892*. Lincoln and New Bedford, Mass.: De Cordova Museum and Whaling Museum of New Bedford, 1969.

__________. *Fitz Hugh Lane*. New York, Washington, London: Praeger, 1971.

__________. *American Light — The Luminist Movement — 1850 – 1875*, Washington, D. C.: National Gallery of Art, 1980.

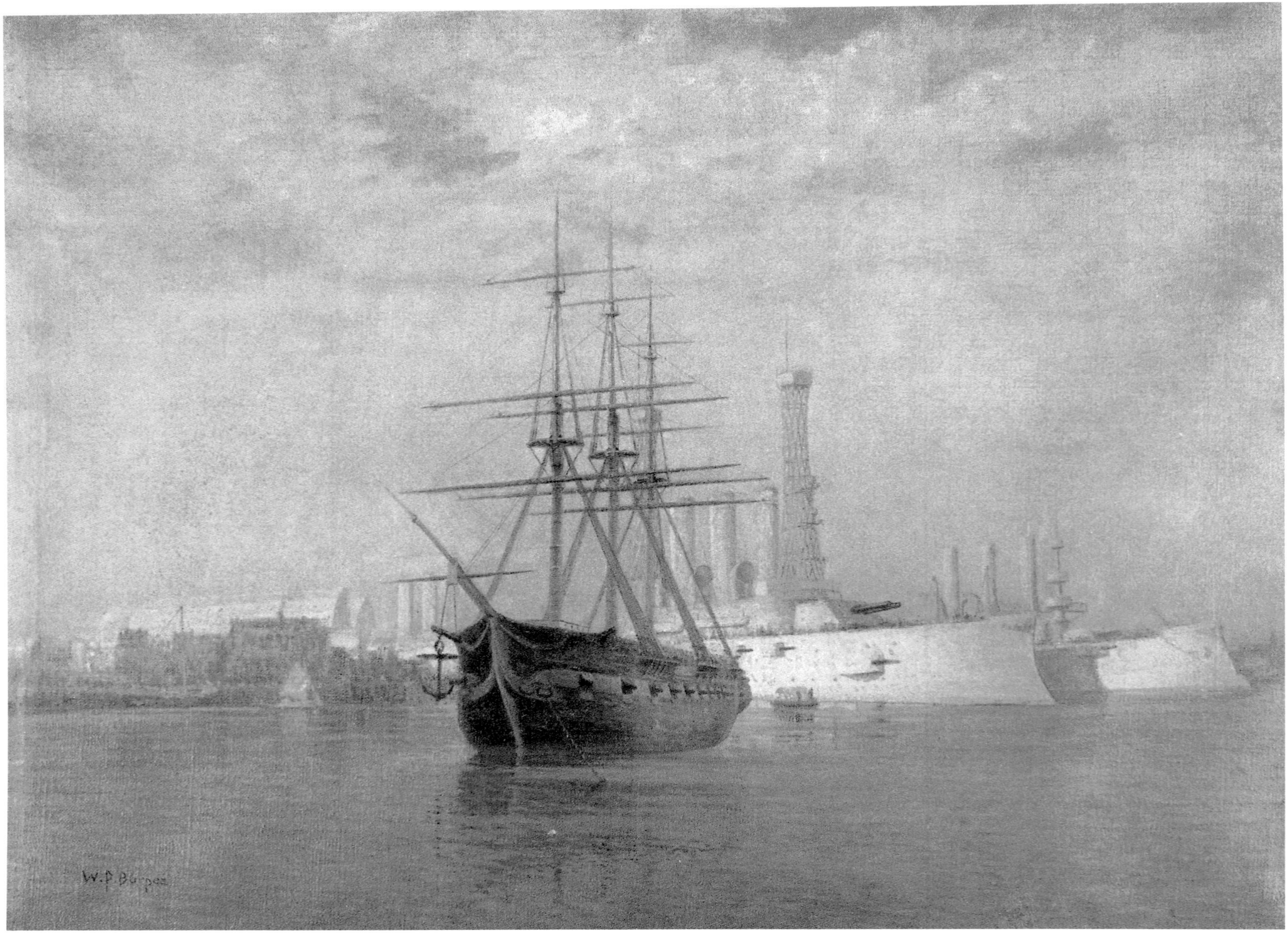
W. P. Burpee

INDEX

BOSTON NAVY YARD, c. 1905

Oil on canvas, 37 x 49 1/2 inches. Photo Courtesy of the William A. Farnsworth Library and Art Museum, Rockland, Maine.

PHOTO CREDITS:

All photographs courtesy of Carl Andrews except as noted:

Archives of American Art, p. 83.
Margaret Bezucha, p. 23 (*Two Figure Studies*, left).
The Boston Globe, p. 60.
The Boston Public Library, p. 22.
Christie's Auction House, p. 13.
D. Roger Howlett, p. 3.
Alfred J. Walker, Fine Art, p. 91.
The William A. Farnsworth Library and Art Museum, p. 92.

In 1932 Stanley Morison designed the typeface Times New Roman for the Monotype Corporation, Ltd. for use in the London Times newspaper. It was crafted to be compact, highly legible, and classically handsome. Morison was so successful that the English Linotype Company issued it simultaneously, a rare event in type founding. Later phototypesetting systems, and then CRT systems, adapted Morison's font. This book has been set "in house" at Childs Gallery by means of a personal computer using Aldus PageMaker software in their version of Morison's masterpiece, in this system called Times Roman.

Color separations, printing, and binding are by the South China Printing Company (1988) Ltd. of Hong Kong.

This book was designed by Richard C. Bartlett and Cynthia Baule.

endpapers

DUTCH CHILDREN ON THE BEACH, KATWIJK, 1900.

Watercolor on paper, (each) 4 1/2 x 8 inches.

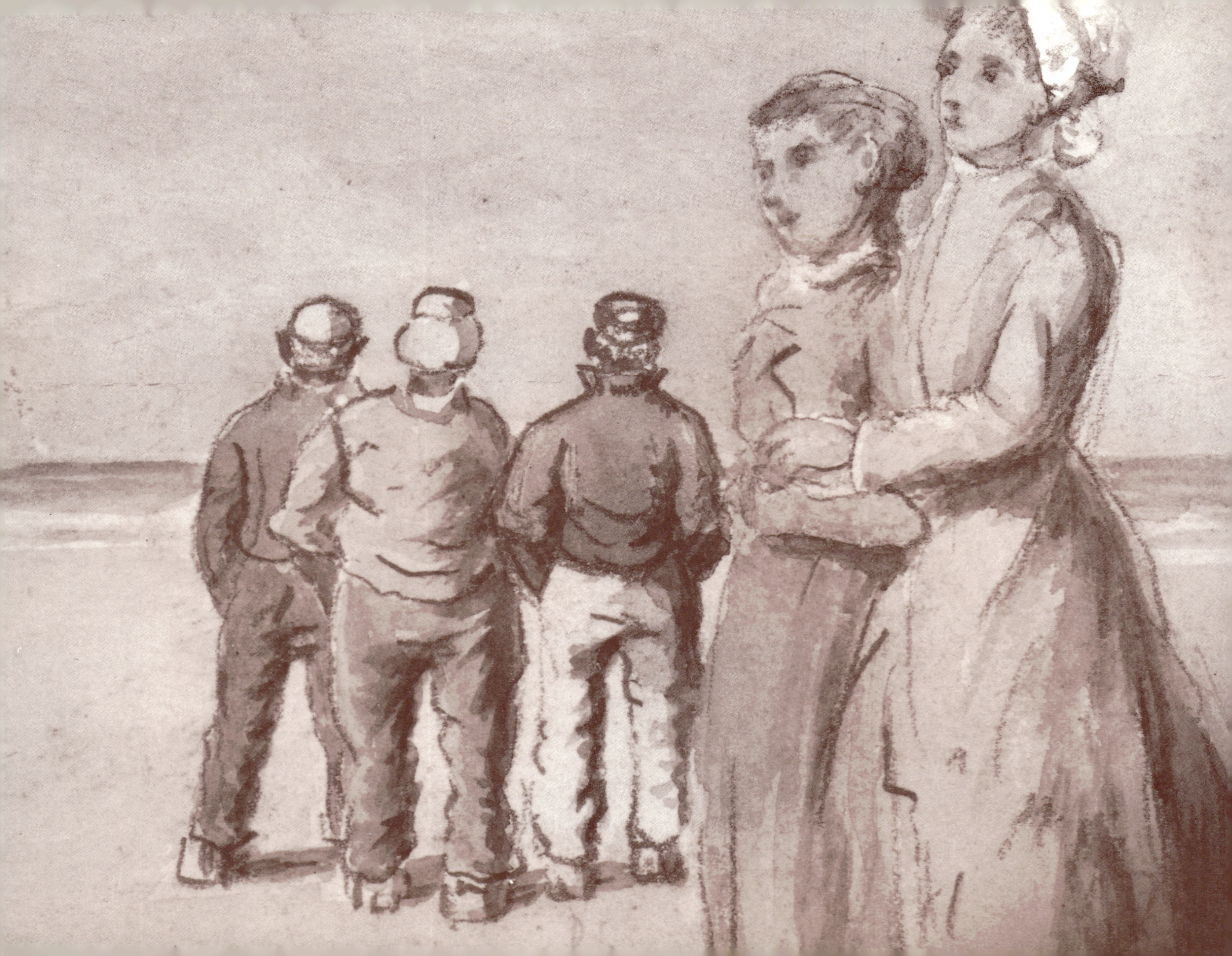